THE HYPOMANIC EDGE

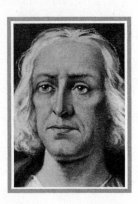  

SIMON & SCHUSTER   New York   London   Toronto   Sydney

The Link Between (a Little) Craziness

and (a Lot of) Success in America

John D. Gartner

SIMON & SCHUSTER
Rockefeller Center
1230 Avenue of the Americas
New York, NY 10020

Illustration credits appear on page 355.

SIMON & SCHUSTER and colophon are registered trademarks
of Simon & Schuster, Inc.

For information about special discounts for bulk purchases,
please contact Simon & Schuster Special Sales at
1-800-456-6798 or business@simonandschuster.com

Designed by Jeanette Olender
Manufactured in the United States of America

10 9 8 7 6 5 4 3 2 1

Library of Congress Cataloging-in-Publication Data
Gartner, John D.
The hypomanic edge: the bipolar disorder that made America
the most successful nation in the world / John D. Gartner.
p.   cm.
Includes bibliographical references and index.
1. Hypomania—United States—History.
2. Hypomania—Patients—United States—Biography.   I. Title.
RC516.G376   2005
62.196'895'00922—dc23   2004062624

ISBN 0-7432-4344-7

FOR DAD

Contents

Introduction

The Hypomanic American

THE HYPOMANIC ENTREPRENEUR

The 1990s will be remembered as the age of Internet mania, a time when entrepreneurs making grandiose claims for their high-tech companies swept up millions of Americans with their irrational exuberance, inflating the biggest speculative bubble in history. The idea that some entrepreneurs may be a little manic is hardly new. A Google search for "manic" and "businessman" yields more than a million hits. Entrepreneurs, as well as the markets they energized, were commonly described in the media as "manic." Yet, until now, there has never been a serious suggestion that the talent for being an entrepreneur and mania, the genetically based psychiatric disorder, are actually linked. Perhaps because I am a clinical psychologist, it was clear to me that "manic" was more than a figure of speech in this case.

I called several reporters who had written profiles of these "manic" entrepreneurs and asked them, "Do you think he really was manic?" None said yes. "Not *really* manic; not clinically," was a typical response. They resisted applying the psychiatric diagnosis because the entrepreneurs they had interviewed were boastful, hyperenergized, and zany, but they "weren't crazy." And the journal-

1

ists were right. Their subjects were not manic. They were *hypo-manic.* Hypomania is a mild form of mania, often found in the relatives of manic depressives. Hypomanics are brimming with infectious energy, irrational confidence, and really big ideas. They think, talk, move, and make decisions quickly. Anyone who slows them down with questions "just doesn't get it." Hypomanics are not crazy, but "normal" is not the first word that comes to mind when describing them. Hypomanics live on the edge, betweeen normal and abnormal.

For example, Jim Clark, cofounder of Netscape, was described in *Business Week* by Netscape's other cofounder, Jim Barksdale, as "a maniac who has his mania only partly under control."[1] In *The New New Thing,* Michael Lewis profiled Clark as a perpetual motion machine with a short attention span, forever hurtling at unsafe speeds in helicopters, planes, boats, and cars. When his forward motion is impeded, Clark becomes irritable and bored. In his search for the stimulation of the "new new thing," he quickly loses interest in the companies he founds and tosses them into the laps of his bewildered employees. His Netscape IPO is credited with starting the Internet gold rush. After that it seemed he could do no wrong. When he pitched a new company, Healtheon, a medical Web site, his only business plan was a diagram with five words. His "magic diamond" put Healtheon at the center of four vertices labeled "doctors, consumers, providers, and payers." That was it. His magic diamond, he claimed, was going to "fix the U.S. health care system."[2] It was going to be "bigger than Microsoft, AOL, Netscape and Yahoo!" As Lewis wrote, "Any other human being would have been thrown into an asylum for thinking such grandiose thoughts."[3] Those who followed Clark had faith in his messianic mission. "There was a feeling that we *were* about to change the world," said one of Healtheon's chief engineers.[4]

Successful entrepreneurs are not just braggarts. They are highly creative people who quickly generate a tremendous number of ideas—some clever, others ridiculous. Their "flight of ideas," jumping from topic to topic in a rapid energized way, is a sign of hypomania. Consider Bill Gross, CEO of Idealab. Bill Gross's job was not to build or run companies, but just to think of ideas for them. Idealab was an "Internet incubator." On *Fortune*'s cover, next to a picture of a cheerful Bill Gross, was the caption "I Lost $800 Million in Eight Months. Why Am I Still Smiling?" The author, Joseph Nocera, *Fortune*'s managing editor, begins his article with an unusual mea culpa. He apologizes to his readers for his previous *Fortune* article that hyped Gross and Idealab just before the Nasdaq crash. He confesses that Gross converted him into a believer:

> I believed him because I was dazzled by him. A small, wiry man, Gross had an infectious boyish enthusiasm that was charming and irresistible. He spoke so rapidly—jumping from topic to topic as if he were hyperlinking—that it was hard to keep up with him, and had so much energy he seemed constantly on the verge of jumping out of his skin. He bubbled over with irrepressible optimism.
>
> And his brain! That's what really set him apart. You could practically see the ideas bursting out of it, one after another, each more offbeat, more original, more promising than the last. The sheer profusion of ideas—and the way he got excited as he described them—was a large part of his charisma.[5]

The reason Bill Gross was still smiling was that his *newest* new idea was "going to be unbelievably huge" and "revolutionize the Internet." Eight hundred million. Eight hundred *shmillion*. Nothing could dim Gross's enthusiastic confidence.*

---

* I have never met Mr. Lewis or Mr. Gross and am not suggesting that either man has a mental illness. As shall be explained further on, hypomania must alternate with depression for a person to meet the criteria for a bipolar *disorder,* and there is no reason to believe that either man has suffered from depression. I cannot even say for certain that either man meets full criteria for hypomania. Rather, I am using these men as examples to illustrate some of the traits of hypomania found among successful entrepreneurs.

During the 1990s, I was paying attention to such behavior because I was planning to write a book about religious movements started by manic prophets. But I began to be distracted by messianic movements happening around me in real time, particularly because, as an avid technology investor, I was a member of one— the believers in the new economy. I was even a millionaire on paper for one exhilarating day in March 2000 at the peak of the market, before my portfolio lost 90 percent of its value. I began to suspect I was writing the wrong book.

My new hypothesis became that American entrepreneurs are largely hypomanic. I decided to undertake what social scientists call a pilot study: a small-scale, inexpensive, informal investigation meant to test the waters. I placed announcements on several Web sites devoted to the technology business, expressing my interest in studying entrepreneurs and requesting volunteers. I interviewed a small sample of ten Internet CEOs. After I read them each a list of hypomanic traits that I had synthesized from the psychiatric literature, I asked them if they agreed that these traits are typical of an entrepreneur:

* He is filled with energy.
* He is flooded with ideas.
* He is driven, restless, and unable to keep still.
* He channels his energy into the achievement of wildly grand ambitions.
* He often works on little sleep.
* He feels brilliant, special, chosen, perhaps even destined to change the world.
* He can be euphoric.
* He becomes easily irritated by minor obstacles.
* He is a risk taker.
* He overspends in both his business and personal life.
* He acts out sexually.

* He sometimes acts impulsively, with poor judgment, in ways that can have painful consequences.
* He is fast-talking.
* He is witty and gregarious.
* His confidence can make him charismatic and persuasive.
* He is also prone to making enemies and feels he is persecuted by those who do not accept his vision and mission.

I feared they might find the questions insulting. I needn't have worried. *All* of the entrepreneurs agreed that the overall description was accurate, and they endorsed all the hypomanic traits, with the exceptions of "paranoia" and "sexual acting out" (these traits in particular are viewed as very negative and thus may be more difficult to admit to). Most expressed their agreement with excitement: "Wow, that's right on target!" When I asked them to rate their level of agreement for each trait on a standard 5-point scale, many gave ratings that were literally off the chart: 5+s, 6s. One subject repeatedly begged me to let him give a 7. I was startled by the respondents' enthusiasm, though perhaps I shouldn't have been. As a psychotherapist, I am familiar with the way people become energized when they feel understood, especially when it helps them understand themselves better.

Having learned in our conversation that they were hypomanic, the CEOs wanted to talk about it. One now understood better why he regularly rented palatial office space he could not afford and why his wife hid the checkbook. Another could finally explain what drove him to impulsively send broadcast e-mails at 3 A.M. to all his employees, radically revising the company's mission. It was as if merely by asking these questions I had held up a mirror in which these men could see themselves. After talking to them for just fifteen minutes, it seemed as if I was the first person to truly understand them.

One respondent seemed to be in an intense hypomanic state

when I interviewed him. He responded to my Web site solicitation by e-mailing me in huge blue block letters: "CALL ME IMMEDI-ATELY." When I did, he talked rapidly and loudly and laughed quite often. At the same time he was charming, witty, and engaging. The interview was a bit chaotic because he was driving and carrying on another phone call at the same time. He was a serial entrepreneur. After founding one successful company, he had felt he needed to quit his own corporation because he couldn't "make things happen fast enough," leaving him frustrated and bored. Now he was on to a new venture. He was very enthusiastic about my research and volunteered to send me the phone numbers and e-mail addresses of half a dozen well-known high-tech entrepreneurs (which I never received), who he claimed were his "very close friends."

This was a small pilot study, but nonetheless, I was overwhelmed. I had never seen data like this. Because humans are so complex, most effects in psychology are modest and nearly drowned out by the great variability that exists naturally between people. Not in this case. One hundred percent of the entrepreneurs I interviewed were hypomanic! This couldn't be chance. The odds of flipping a coin ten times and getting ten heads in a row is less than one in a thousand. It felt as if I had tested the waters with my little pilot study and been hit with a tidal wave. It was then that I knew I had stumbled onto something big that had been hiding in plain sight.

MANIA AND HYPOMANIA

A colleague of mine once told me about a manic inpatient he had treated for many years at an Ivy League–affiliated psychiatric teaching hospital. The patient's father was the CEO of a Fortune 500 company. Each time he visited his son on the unit, he would behave in a dramatically hypomanic fashion. For example, he would make numerous business phone calls around the world on the patients' pay phone, while frantically yelling "Back off!" at patients or staff who tried to interrupt him. Clearly, Dad was not normal, but he had made his hypomania work for him. He was a very rich man.

This family's story illustrates the concrete relationship between mania and hypomania. Manics and hypomanics are often blood relatives. Both conditions run together in families at much higher rates than we would predict by chance.[6] We know that their genes overlap, though we don't know how.

This family's story also illustrates the most radical *difference* between mania and hypomania. Mania is a severe illness. The son was disabled—a long-term inpatient at a psychiatric hospital. Manic episodes almost always end in hospitalization. People who are highly energized, and also in most cases psychotic, do bizarre things that are dangerous, frightening, and disruptive. They urgently require external control for everyone's safety, especially their own. Most people who have experienced a manic episode remember it as a nightmare.

By contrast, hypomania is not, in and of itself, an illness. It is a temperament characterized by an elevated mood state that feels "highly intoxicating, powerful, productive and desirable" to the hypomanic, according to Frederick K. Goodwin and Kay Redfield Jamison, authors of the definitive nine-hundred-page *Manic-Depressive Illness.*[7] Most hypomanics describe it as their happiest and healthiest state; they feel creative, energetic, and alive. A hypomanic only has a *bipolar disorder* if hypomania alternates, at some point in life, with *major depression*. This pattern, first identified only in 1976, is called bipolar disorder type II to distinguish it from bipolar disorder type I, the classic manic-depressive illness, which has been well known since the time of the ancient Greeks. If a hypomanic seeks outpatient treatment it is usually for depression, and he will define recovery as a return to his old energetic self. Not all hypomanics cycle down into depression. What goes up can stay up. Thus, we cannot conclude that someone has a psychiatric disorder just because he may be hypomanic. The most we can say is that hypomanics are at much greater risk for depression than the average population. The things most likely to make them depressed are failure, loss, or anything that prevents them from continuing at their preferred breakneck pace.

Given how radically different mania and hypomania are, it is perhaps surprising that the diagnostic criteria for these two conditions are identical according to the *Diagnostic and Statistical Manual of Mental Disorders* of the American Psychiatric Association (usually referred to simply as *DSM-IV*):

A. A distinct period of abnormally and persistently elevated, expansive, or irritable mood, lasting at least one week.
B. And at least three of the following:
   1. Inflated self-esteem or grandiosity
   2. Decreased need for sleep (e.g., feels rested after only three hours of sleep)
   3. More talkative than usual or pressure to keep talking
   4. Flight of ideas or subjective experience that thoughts are racing
   5. Distractibility (i.e., attention too easily drawn to unimportant or irrelevant external stimuli)
   6. Increase in goal-directed activity (either socially, at work or school, or sexually) or psychomotor agitation
   7. Excessive involvement in pleasurable activities that have a high potential for painful consequences (e.g., engaging in unrestrained buying sprees, sexual indiscretions, or foolish business investments) [8]

The only guideline offered to mental health professionals in distinguishing between mania and hypomania is "degree of severity." Hypomania is "not sufficiently severe to cause marked impairment in social or occupational functioning or to require hospitalization." But *DSM-IV* tells us little else, when there is so much more that could be said.[9]

This relative neglect of hypomania by psychiatry is striking when we consider that it affects many more people than does mania. We know from numerous large-scale studies, replicated both nationally and internationally, that classic manic depression exists in slightly less than 1 percent of the general population.[10] A notably smaller but growing amount of literature on hypomania suggests that 5 to 10 percent of the population is hypomanic.[11] Whatever the exact percentage, psychiatry's most recent discovery is not a rare expression of bipolar genes, but its most common form.*

That hypomania is so much more common than mania may give us a crucial clue to its genetic function and evolutionary importance. Mania, according to one school of thought, is a disease like sickle-cell anemia.[12] Sickle-cell anemia is a blood disease that primarily affects people of African origin. To contract the disease, you must inherit the recessive sickle gene from *both* your mother and your father. Far more often, people inherit only a single sickle gene from one parent; epidemiologists call these people "carriers" because they carry the gene without manifesting the illness. As it turns out, they are much more than that. They are the reason the gene exists. A single sickle gene greatly enhances resistance to

---

* The few large-scale NIMH-funded epidemiological studies that have included measures of hypomania have measured it in a way that grossly underestimated its frequency (some studies have found hypomania in only .1 percent of the population). The first question they ask is "Have you been in an unusually good mood, so good that you were a little high or out of control?" If the answer to this "stem question" is no, the interviewer discontinues asking about symptoms of hypomania. The problem with this approach, according to Jules Angst of Zurich University, is that hypomanics don't feel they are high or out of control when they are hypomanic. So of course they say no. Angst and his colleagues found that if their stem question was "Have you had a period of greatly increased energy?", the rates of hypomania came closer to the 5 to 10 percent range.

malaria, a deadly disease prevalent in Africa. This gene has been favored by natural selection, even though it causes a deadly disease, because it saves more people than it kills.

We have not isolated one singular manic gene. Investigators at the Department of Psychiatry at Johns Hopkins University Medical School, where I teach, and at other institutions around the world, have homed in on half a dozen genes associated with mania.[13] Though the numbers may be more complex, the same principles may apply: a less probable combination of genes produces the undesirable disease of mania, while a more frequent combination produces the advantageous outcome of hypomania. It could be that quantitatively *more* hypomanic genes are required to produce mania. Call this the slot machine model. Three cherries produces a moderate payout: hypomania. But once in a great while you get five cherries, and you're flooded with coins: mania. Alternatively, there may be a *specific* gene that needs to be combined with hypomanic genes to produce mania. Raymond DePaulo, James Potash, and their colleagues at Johns Hopkins have found a gene that mania and schizophrenia share in common—a possible "psychoticism gene." Mania might be the result when one is unlucky enough to inherit *both* hypomanic genes and the psychotic gene.[14]

The story of the CEO father and his hospitalized son helps us understand why hypomanic genes exist. Relatives of manic patients, who have high rates of hypomania, have consistently been found to be far above average in income, occupational achievement, and creativity.[15] Hypomania gives them an *edge* over the competition.

If there is any one trait that distinguishes highly successful people, it is that they are, by temperament, highly motivated. From our studies of the brain we now know that mood is an intrinsic part of the apparatus that controls motivation. Mood is meant either to facilitate or inhibit action. When someone is depressed, he has no motivation to act. What's the point? Nothing seems worth doing, he has no energy to do it, and it probably won't work anyway. Hypomania is the polar opposite. The drives that motivate behavior surge to a screaming pitch, making the urgency of action irresistible. There isn't a minute to waste—this is going to be huge—just do it!

This pressure to act creates overachievers, but it also leads to impulsive behavior (ready, shoot, aim) and confident leaders who glibly take their followers over a cliff. Depending on how you look at it, the Internet phenomenon was either an exciting breakthrough of human ingenuity or a colossal error in judgment that forces us to ask: What were we thinking? In truth, it was both. The paradox of the hypomanic edge is that it is a double-edged sword.

A HYPOMANIC NATION?

Energy, drive, cockeyed optimism, entrepreneurial and religious zeal, Yankee ingenuity, messianism, and arrogance—these traits have long been attributed to an "American character." But given how closely they overlap with the hypomanic profile, they might be better understood as expressions of an *American temperament,* shaped in large part by our rich concentration of hypomanic genes.

If a scientist wanted to design a giant petri dish with all the right nutrients to make hypomanic genius flourish, he would be hard-pressed to imagine a better natural experiment than America. A "nation of immigrants" represents a highly skewed and unusual "self-selected" population. Do men and women who risk everything to leap into a new world differ temperamentally from those who stay home? It would be surprising if they didn't. "Immigrants are unusual people," wrote James Jaspers in *Restless Nation.* Only one out of a hundred people emigrate, and they tend to be imbued "with special drive, ambition and talent." [16]

A small empirical literature suggests that there are elevated rates of manic-depressive disorder among immigrants, regardless of what country they are moving from or to. [17] America, a nation of immigrants, has higher rates of mania than every other country studied (with the possible exception of New Zealand, which topped the United States in one study). In fact, the top three countries with the most manics—America, New Zealand, and Canada—are *all* nations of immigrants. Asian countries such as Taiwan and South Korea, which have absorbed very few immigrants, have the lowest rates of bipolar disorder. Europe is in the middle, in both its rate of immigrant absorption and its rate of mania.[18] As expected, the percentage of immigrants in a population correlates with the percentage of manics in their gene pool.

While we have no cross-cultural studies of hypomania, we can infer that we would find increased levels of hypomania among immigrant-rich nations like America, since mania and hypomania run together in the same families. Hypomanics are ideally suited by temperament to become immigrants. If you are an impulsive, optimistic, high-energy risk taker, you are more likely to undertake a project that requires a lot of energy, entails a lot of risk, and might seem daunting if you thought about it too much. America has drawn hypomanics like a magnet. This wide-open land with seemingly infinite horizons has been a giant Rorschach on which they could project their oversized fantasies of success, an irresistible attraction for restless, ambitious people feeling hemmed in by native lands with comparatively fewer opportunities.

*   *   *

Alexis de Tocqueville, a Frenchman who traveled throughout America in the 1830s, was among the first to define the American character. He found us to be "restless in the midst of abundance," and the proof was that we were always moving. Tocqueville was astonished to meet people moving from east to west and west to east. That so many people would surrender the comfort and safety of their home in pursuit of an "ideal" struck him as odd. And we are still the most voluntarily mobile people on Earth. The average American changes residences every five years—more often than the inhabitants of any other nation. We change jobs more frequently, too.[19] Tocqueville "found an entire people racing full speed ahead, and we've kept on racing for more than three hundred years," wrote Michael Ledeen in *Tocqueville on American Character*.[20]

One outlet for this restless energy has been business. "Americans are constantly driven to engage in commerce and industry. . . . This is the characteristic that most distinguishes the American people from all others," wrote Tocqueville in *Democracy in America*.[21] He sensed that the American motivation to get rich was more about the *excitement* of making money than it was about wealth itself. "The desire for prosperity has become an ardent passion . . . which they pursue for the emotions it excites as much as for the gain it procures."[22] And these people never stopped working. "Everybody works," wrote Tocqueville. The aristocratic European ideal was to become so wealthy that one did not need to labor. In America, "work opens a way to everything; this has changed the point of honor quite around." To Americans it was a disgrace not to work.

Americans work more hours than any other people in the world.[23] We've changed little in that regard since Tocqueville's day. We tend to attribute this habit to cultural influences, without even considering biological causes. America's workaholism is typically attributed to its Puritanical "Protestant work ethic." But is it reasonable to ascribe such enormous influence to a defunct seventeenth-century English Protestant sect on the contemporary day-to-day behavior of hundreds of millions of diverse Americans? The average American recalls only the barest outline of who the Puritans were. When you talk to these strivers, they tell you that their drive comes from *within* and that they have been strongly "self-motivated" since they were children. They hit the ground running and couldn't tell you why. I would attribute the number of hours Americans work to what I call the "immigrant work drive," an internal biological compulsion passed from parent to child through their hypomanic genes.

Tocqueville noticed that Americans were entrepreneurial risk takers: "Boldness of enterprise is the foremost cause of [America's] rapid progress, its strength and its greatness." Though some individuals failed, the collective efforts of entrepreneurs drove the nation forward. Americans believed so deeply in the "virtue" of "commercial temerity" that they had all but removed the stigma surrounding financial failure:

> Commercial business is there like a vast lottery, by which a small number of men continually lose, but the state is always the gainer. . . . Hence arises the strange indulgence that is shown to bankrupts in the United States; their honor does not suffer by such an accident.[24]

At that time, a European who went bankrupt might end up in debtor's prison, so Tocqueville was surprised that there was little shame in bankruptcy here. The stereotypic American success story is of an entrepreneur who fails numerous times before achieving his big success. Such "serial entrepreneurs" will tell you that they shake off failure like a dog shakes off water and are soon raring to go again with a new idea.

That America rewards and celebrates such people is culturally unique. When asked, "Do you think that starting a new business is a respected occupation in your community?" 91 percent of Americans said yes, as compared to 28 percent of British and 8 percent of Japanese respondents.[25] In Japan there is still deep disgrace attached to business failure. Men who lose their jobs often hide it from their families and pretend to go to work each day. Some economists have argued that Japan has been slow to bounce back from its decade-long recession because the population has lost all taste for risk after the fallout of the stock and real estate bubbles of the early 1990s. Most Japanese save a substantial portion of their money in secure savings accounts that yield zero interest, tying up capital that could either be invested in businesses or stimulate the economy through consumption. Americans, by contrast, bounce back from failures, scandals, and bubbles with infinitely renewable confidence. After the stock market and the World Trade Center came crashing down in succession, one might have expected a pessimistic mood to take hold in America. But a subsequent poll taken in 2002 found that 59 percent of American college students believed that they were on their way to becoming millionaires.[26] Our immigrant genes predispose us to optimism. "You had to be an optimist to move. Pessimists didn't bother," wrote Yale historian George Pierson.[27] Because this optimism comes from within, it is not easily discouraged by external events. And optimism, like pessimism, often becomes a self-fulfilling prophecy.

Immigrants are often described as a highly entrepreneurial group. "There is more than a grain of truth to this perception," according to a 1997 report by the International Migration Policy Program at the Carnegie Endowment for International Peace. In every census from 1880 to 1990, as long as they have been keeping records, immigrants were significantly more likely to be self-employed than natives.[28] The single exception to this 110-year-long trend was the roaring 1990s. In that decade, when every American college student wanted to found the next Yahoo!, native-born Americans increased their level of self-employment to match the immigrants': *both* immigrants and native-born Americans were self-employed at a very high rate, just above 11 percent. Temperament may not be the only factor. An immigrant who doesn't speak the language of his new country might find economic opportunities limited outside ethnic niche industries, such as Korean grocery stores, where fellow countrymen can help him start his own business. But even this speaks to the psychology of the immigrant: if he had stayed in Korea, no one would be extending him credit to open a store.

Thus, it follows that nations that absorb more immigrants should have more entrepreneurial activity, and that is indeed the case. In the past decade, America, Canada, and Israel were the top three countries in new company creation, according to a 1999 cross-national survey of ten industrial nations conducted by the Global Entrepreneurship Monitor, a joint project of the London Business School and Babson College.[29] "What's unique about the top countries is that all three have been created by people moving into them," Paul Reynolds, one author of the report, told *Business Week*.[30] Moreover, the magnitude of these differences is large. The average American is four times more likely to be the founder of a company than a Frenchman, for example.

As Tocqueville predicted, there is a solid statistical relationship between entrepreneurial activity and the wealth of a nation. Gross domestic product growth and employment rates both correlate with new business creation. Because they are "constantly driven to participate in commerce and industry," Americans, who make up only 5 percent of the world's population, account for 31 percent of its economic activity.[31]

Because of its origins, America has an abundance of people with hypomanic temperaments. And it has made good use of them by giving them freer rein, more opportunity, and greater respect than they have received elsewhere. As British economic historian Edward Chancellor noted in his history of financial speculation, *Devil Take the Hindmost,* the result is a society of people both culturally and genetically predisposed to economic risk:

> The American is equipped with more than just a hopeful vision of the future and a drive for self-improvement. He is prepared to take enormous risks to attain his ends. To emigrate to America was itself a great risk. This appetite for risk—so great one might say it was imprinted in American genes—has not diminished with time but remains a continuing source of the nation's vitality.[32]

The next gold rush, the next boom, the next market mania is coming. Hold on to your seat. America has been a ship riding the waves of irrational exuberance for hundreds of years, and she's not likely to change course any time soon. It's in our blood.

CAPTAINS OUTRAGEOUS

America has been good to hypomanics—a land of opportunity that has liberated their energies and lifted their spirits. In return, hypomanic Americans have been good to America, powering a wilderness colony ahead of every other nation on the planet in just a few hundred years. They may be our greatest natural resource. An untold number of hypomanics helped make America the richest nation on Earth. This book tells the stories of just a few.

It was not easy choosing the people to focus on, nor was it a scientific selection process. There were so many candidates to choose from. To show America's development through a kind of time-lapse photography, I searched for people from each century of our five-hundred-year history who played a leading role in America's growth, especially her economic growth. Christopher Columbus discovered America; prophets such as John Winthrop, Roger Williams, and William Penn populated it; Alexander Hamilton was one of a handful of men who conceived its national future and economic potential; Andrew Carnegie sparked an industrial revolution that led to mass production; the Selznick and Mayer families helped create Hollywood, usher in the age of mass media, and portray a national self-image; and Craig Venter cracked our genetic code, the implications of which are only beginning to be fathomed.

Each chapter of this book is a small biography. Written by a psychologist, they are also clinical case histories that illustrate hypomania in action. These men were outrageous—arrogant, provocative, unconventional, and unpredictable. They were not "well adjusted" by ordinary standards but instead forced the world to adjust to them. Their stories are inspiring, comical, and sometimes tragic, as the hubris that fueled their improbable rise often led to their fall as well. Yet without their irrational confidence, ambitious vision, and unstoppable zeal, these outrageous captains would never have sailed into unknown waters, never discovered new worlds, never changed the course of our history.

I Christopher Columbus

Messianic Entrepreneur

Christopher Columbus is the archetype of the American entrepreneur. Like the Internet CEOs of the 1990s, he boasted that he would change the world and get rich doing it. In that respect, you couldn't have picked a better person to find America. Columbus was always a "messianic character," but his special sense of destiny evolved into a grandiose delusional system.[1] Unlike most of the characters in this book, Columbus may have crossed the line into mania.

THE VISION

Columbus claimed it was a divine revelation that launched him on his voyage of discovery. "With a hand that could be felt, the Lord opened my mind to the fact that it would be possible to sail from here to the Indies, and he opened my will to desire to accomplish the project."[2] From that moment, the drive to sail west in search of the Far East became "a fire that burned within me." "Continually, without a moment's hesitation, the Scriptures urge me to press forward with great haste."[3]

Columbus claimed he heard celestial voices.[4] And on one occasion, he wrote that the Holy Spirit had spoken to him, announcing, "God will cause your name to be wonderfully proclaimed throughout the world . . . and give you the keys of the gates to the ocean, which are closed with strong chains."[5]

Thirty-nine percent of manic patients report religious revelations similar to those described by Columbus.[6] These patients experience intense feelings of well-being and closeness to God, along with the sense that some great secret truth has been revealed to them. The revelation feels hyperreal—that is, more real than normal reality. These experiences are remarkably "analogous to the beatific and mystical experiences of saints and other religious leaders," wrote Goodwin and Jamison.[7] They are usually accompanied by the conviction that one has been chosen for a unique mission of cosmic importance. The urgent "sense of moral imperative" to accomplish the mission is intense.[8] Hypomanics also can have revelatory experiences, but unlike the manics, theirs are not accompanied by hallucinations or bizarre grandiose beliefs.

According to Columbus, God assigned him a much greater role in history than just discovering the westward passage to the East. God had predestined Columbus to play a heroic role in the recapture of the Holy Land as well. Columbus proclaimed that he would find large quantities of gold in the Indies, and he urged King Ferdinand and Queen Isabella of Spain to use these funds to recapture Jerusalem.

In the log of his first voyage, he would write to the sovereigns, reminding them of his plan:

> I urged your Highness to spend all the profit of this, my enterprise, on the conquest of Jerusalem. And your Highness laughed. And said it would please you and even without that profit you would desire it.[9]

From the very beginning, Columbus clearly had an idea of launching a crusade.

In 1493, he gave himself a new name and began signing documents "Christoferens." This idiosyncratically Latinized version of his name means "Christ-bearer." As if that weren't peculiar enough, "on virtually every thing he signed from 1493 until his death in 1506," he used not a name at all but the mysterious symbol: [10]

.S.

.S.A.S

XMY

Xpo FERENS

It has never been deciphered.

In 1500, after returning from his third voyage, Columbus wrote to a member of the Spanish court:

> God made me the messenger of the new heaven and the new earth of which he spoke in the Apocalypse of St. John, after having spoken of it through the mouth of Isaiah; and he showed me the spot where to find it." [11]

The "spot" Columbus was referring to was the entrance to the Garden of Eden, which he claimed to have found in August 1498 off the coast of Venezuela. According to some religious writings, the righteous would once again inhabit this earthly paradise. Thus, Columbus's discovery of Eden satisfied a requirement necessary to prepare the way for the Kingdom of God.

In 1502, during his fourth voyage, he wrote to the king and queen that he had discovered the gold mines of Solomon in modern-day Panama. Solomon had built his Temple in Jerusalem with gold from these mines. Ferdinand and Isabella, Columbus informed them, had been chosen by God to restore the Temple with gold from these same mines.

That year, Columbus assembled *The Book of Prophecies*—eighty-four pages of biblical and other religious prophecies that he claimed God had chosen to fulfill through him. By now, Columbus's ideas had crystallized into an elaborate messianic delusional system. Regaining the Holy Land, Columbus's original quest, now became part of an even larger, more ambitious scheme to usher in the Apocalypse—bringing all of human history to its climactic end. Historian Delno West summarized the logic of *The Book of Prophecies:*

> Secular history would end in 150 years. But before that awesome event three prophesied milestones had to occur: (1) the discovery of the Indies, (2) the conversion of all people, and (3) the recapture and rebuilding of the Holy Temple in Jerusalem. Columbus believed that he was the instrument of Divine Providence who had been chosen for these events.[12]

Columbus's illness clearly progressed, as his thinking became more grandiose. "Although Columbus did regard himself before and after 1492 as a man with a providential mission ... in 1501–1502 Columbus linked the crusading tradition to an apocalyptic vision with himself cast in the role of the Messiah."[13] *The Book of Prophecies* was evidence that Columbus "drifted away from reality" and "turned to mad ravings," according to biographer Gianni Granzotto.

One might think that being God's instrument to redeem human history would be sufficient reward in itself. But Columbus had to get rich off the deal as well, and that was nonnegotiable.

THE PITCH

In the 1990s, entrepreneurs seeking financial backing were advised to prepare an "elevator pitch," a fifteen-second sales talk they could deliver to a venture capitalist if they had his ear only for a moment. Billion-dollar deals were made with such speed. Columbus had to make a fifteen-*year* sales pitch to launch his voyage of discovery. He spent the first eight years trying to get his project off the ground in Portugal. King John's expert advisers correctly informed him that Columbus's calculations were grossly inaccurate. Columbus was, in fact, wrong in many of his basic assumptions. For example, he greatly underestimated the size of the earth and overestimated the size of Asia's eastward extension. Both these miscalculations conveniently made his proposed journey seem much more achievable than it was.

When finally given the opportunity to present his plan to King John, Columbus flattered the king, comparing him to Alexander the Great, Nero, and other great leaders who had commissioned legendary explorations. And he talked excitedly about the gold he would bring back. John's impression of Columbus was that he was "more fanciful and imaginatively inspired than accurate in what he said," according to João de Barros, a faithful chronicler of Portuguese events at the time.[14] In the play *El Nuevo Mundo* by Lope de Vega, first performed a hundred years later, the king dismisses Columbus, saying "Go get a cure for your insanity!"[15] Columbus was "judged a madman," according to Granzotto.[16]

In hindsight, John's failure to back Columbus appears wildly shortsighted, like passing up a chance to buy Manhattan for $24. But John's assessment of Columbus was not inaccurate. Columbus *was* driven by "fanciful imagination." Not trusting him was a rational decision.

What was irrational was Columbus's faith in himself. The "certainty of Columbus" has itself been the subject of some scholarly curiosity.[17] "He was a stranger to doubt," wrote Granzotto. Columbus was mystified that others could be so skeptical of his plan to find the Indies by sailing west.[18] Ironically, he didn't find them, though to his dying day he claimed that he had. Had Columbus not been so grandiose, he might have given up on his divine mission.

Instead, Columbus went to Spain. One of his first stops was the Franciscan monastery in La Rabida. The Franciscans had an intense interest in cosmology. One of their most famous friars, Duns Scotus, had been among the first to assert that the world was round. Scotus had dared to disagree with Augustine, who claimed that the world to the east was an uninhabitable void. These Franciscans wanted to prove Duns Scotus right, and Columbus quickly convinced them he was the man to do it. He sketched out his grand vision to Father Antonio de Marchena, a cosmologist well-known at court, and Father Juan Pérez, one of the queen's confessors. They often spoke late into the night, and Columbus converted these priests into true believers. With their support he won the right to make his pitch to the two most powerful monarchs in Europe.

A Night in Córdoba

Columbus had an audience with King Ferdinand and Queen Isabella in May 1486 at their residence in Córdoba. The king is said to have tired quickly and gone to bed, leaving Columbus alone with the queen. Legend has it that a sexual attraction emerged between Isabella and Christopher. They were both thirty-five years old and quite attractive. According to her secretary, Isabella "was blond, with blue-green eyes, a gracious mien, and a lovely, merry face; most dignified in her movements."[19] Columbus was "tall in stature, with an aquiline nose, and hair prematurely white," according to his son Ferdinand, who wrote a biography of his father.[20] Pedro de Las Casas, a contemporary of Columbus who also wrote a biography, stated that he had a "singular grace" that "induced others to see him easily with love."[21] Hypomanics are often charming, persuasive, and attractive.

Beyond any possible sexual attraction, Columbus and Isabella shared a religious passion. Isabella is often described in history books as "devout," but that seems an understatement. Like Columbus, she saw herself playing a global role in the growing ascendancy of Christianity. Isabella launched the Inquisition. She expelled the Jews from Spain, ending hundreds of years of peaceful and mutually profitable coexistence. And she became the first Spanish ruler to drive the Moslems from the Iberian Peninsula in seven hundred years. She was a true Christian crusader.

On this night she met a handsome, exciting, and charming stranger who spoke with inspired confidence about the new lands he would claim for Spain. In one breath, he predicted she could liberate Jerusalem with the gold he would bring her, and in the next he promised to convert the heathen of the new world. They talked deep into the night on that spring evening. Las Casas wrote that "his passionate eloquence when he spoke of the mission God had bid him fulfill, moved the Queen to confidence and sympathy."[22] She allowed the interview to go quite late. "Columbus kept talking. It seemed he would never stop," wrote Granzotto.[23] Hypomanic speech often seems unstoppable. This night, with God's help, Columbus believed his words had worked their magic. He would later write to her, "Everyone made mock of my project. . . . Your Majesty alone gave proof of faith and loyalty, inspired, surely, by the light of the Holy Spirit."[24]

Unfortunately, Columbus's request came at a time when Ferdinand and Isabella were preoccupied with a holy war of their own, against the Moslems. It would have been like "trying to interest Lincoln in a polar expedition when he was in the middle of the Battle of Gettysburg," wrote biographer Samuel Eliot Morison.[25]

"Their majesties took note of his request, received it with gracious countenance, and decided to submit the matter to a committee of learned men," wrote Las Casas.[26] This committee of learned men would become a living purgatory for Christopher Columbus for the next six years, which he would call "years of great anguish."[27]

The Trial of Salamanca

The committee, headed by Father Hernando de Talavera, was made up of some of the most respected theological and scientific scholars of the day. Compared to his inquisitors, Columbus had to admit that he appeared unschooled. "They say that I am not learned in letters, that I am an ignorant sailor, a mundane man."[28] Columbus was not only intellectually outgunned, but, from the perspective of these medieval academics, his case was hopelessly flawed.

On theological grounds, what he proposed flew in the face of accepted dogma. Saint Augustine had said that the region of the world where Columbus proposed to sail was uninhabitable, empty, and so hot that it would incinerate any creature foolish enough to go there. On what authority did Columbus dare contradict Augustine? On scientific grounds, Columbus's calculation of the earth's size was still a gross underestimate, even according to the limited knowledge of the day. Likewise, his assertion that the earth was predominantly covered by land was also wrong and contradicted by existing data. As in the court of King John, Columbus's fuzzy math did little to inspire confidence. Columbus tried to bolster his argument by pointing out that he had been specially chosen by God for this mission, but, as one might expect, this did little to strengthen his case.

In the final weeks of 1490, the committee issued its verdict: "We can find no justification for Their Highnesses' supporting a project that rests on extremely weak foundations and appears impossible to translate into reality to any person with any knowledge, however modest, of these questions."[29] They called his hypotheses "mad" and his errors "colossal."[30]

Despite this damning report, Isabella had not entirely lost faith in Columbus. She left him with a thread of hope. The project would be reconsidered "at a more convenient time," she wrote.[31] That time, Columbus understood, would be when Spain had won her war against the Moslems. But the war dragged on and on, and Columbus's chances seemed to dwindle. In the play by Lope de Vega, Columbus cries out to heaven in frustration, "I am like someone who has wings on his hands and a stone around his ankle."[32]

THE DEAL

In 1492, Ferdinand and Isabella won their interminable war, to-tally defeating a Moorish kingdom that had occupied the Iberian Peninsula since 711. The Spanish court was ecstatic. Now it too was in an expansive mood and ready to consider a speculative venture. The queen sent Columbus an invitation to court, along with a purse of coins "so he could dress himself decently, buy a horse and pre-sent himself to her Highness."[33] After fifteen years of agony, Columbus's moment had arrived.

The court had moved its military headquarters to Santa Fe, just outside of Granada, where the terms of surrender were being nego-tiated. Columbus arrived in time to participate in the monarchs' tri-umphant procession into Granada on January 2, 1492. Columbus saw the royal banners and the Cross raised over the impenetrable towers of the Alhambra, the Moorish mountain fortress. The Moorish king came through the gates and kissed Ferdinand's hand as a supplicant.

Isabella hastily called together a second commission of experts to consider Columbus's plan. They were split in their opinion. But Isabella decided for herself. Her answer was finally . . . yes!

But instead of being grateful and relieved, Columbus began to dictate "outrageous" terms in a most "arrogant" manner, according to Granzotto. He was a penniless foreigner facing two monarchs at the zenith of their power and glory, yet somehow he seemed to be-lieve that "now it was his turn to call the shots . . . because they needed him."[34] His hypomanic grandiosity was breathtaking.

First, Columbus demanded a host of noble titles: "He was to be knighted; he was to be a don, he was to be grand admiral; he was to be Viceroy," and "these titles were to remain in the family in perpetuity."[35] How outrageous were these demands? Such conces-sions were both unprecedented and probably illegal, according to historian Helen Nader: "The granting of hereditary offices, especially to foreigners, went against royal policy; Castilian law prohibited the monarchy from permanently giving away or selling any portions of the royal domain or any royal office." [36] To put Columbus's requests into perspective, only King Ferdinand's uncle held the perpetual offices of admiral and viceroy. [37] Thus, Columbus was explicitly elevating himself to the level of the royal family. "Knowing the great message I bore, I felt myself equal to both crowns," he would later write in his journal. [38] Furthermore, as viceroy governor, Columbus would have had full legal and political control of all the lands he discovered, subject only to the authority of the sovereigns, and his descendants would inherit this power. Columbus was anointing himself prince of the new world.

And finally, Columbus demanded money—and a lot of it. He insisted on 10 percent ownership of everything he found. Ten percent of the value of all gold, spices, and anything else exported from the lands he discovered would automatically belong to him and his heirs. Columbus was willing to sail into the new world only as the monarchs' full partner.

It was hard to know which was more shocking, the outrageousness of Columbus's demands or the arrogance with which he made them. Historians describe these demands with such words as absurd, mad, inconceivable, and ludicrous. "Moreover," Granzotto wrote, "he flew into a rage at any suggestion that he modify his claims." [39] He refused to even negotiate.

His demands were summarily denied, leaving Columbus nothing to do but leave town. On the verge of achieving it all, he now had only "the night and the day," as the Spanish say of someone who has lost everything. [40] It appeared that his grandiose entitlement had destroyed his fifteen years of work. Columbus had not given up, however. He now had plans to try to sell his idea to the king of France.

Columbus might have slipped into obscurity, were it not for a man who himself has been virtually forgotten by history. Don Luis

Santangel changed the sovereigns' minds. "History does not dwell upon him, but without him history would have nothing to say about the discoverer," wrote biographer John Stewart Collis. Santangel was a rich Jewish businessman and Spain's much-respected minister of finance. He argued that Spain was in a race with the other European powers for coveted undiscovered western routes to the East. He acknowledged that Columbus's unprecedented demands were offensive but argued that they were not a bad deal for the king and queen. The sovereigns could gain 90 percent of something very valuable, which was worth more than 100 percent of nothing. Furthermore, since Columbus would get nothing if he found nothing, he would have a strong incentive to discover great riches. The potential upside was enormous, and to eliminate the downside Santangel offered to lend the money for the expedition himself (the popular myth that Isabella offered her jewels as collateral is untrue). Finally, Santangel recommended keeping the deal a secret, so that the monarchs wouldn't be embarrassed if the venture failed. If, on the other hand, Columbus returned a hero, they could afford to lavish titles galore upon him. The king and queen ultimately agreed to Columbus's terms, as documented in the resulting contract, appropriately entitled "The Capitulations of Santa Fe."

The queen summoned a fast rider to overtake Columbus on the road. He found Columbus on a bridge heading toward Córdoba and gave him this message: he was to appear before the queen "at once." "Her Highness is ready to conclude the affair." [41]

The sovereigns kept their word, at first. Columbus was made viceroy over the new world. However, he was such a disaster as an administrator that they were later forced to remove him. Columbus also realized some money in the deal, but not as much as he expected, since he did not find the piles of gold he had promised. It was untenable in the long run that one man and his family could own 10 percent of the Spanish colonies. That was a contract made to be broken. Nonetheless, Columbus kept ample documentation, and his family did not settle its claims against the Spanish monarch until the eighteenth century.

Columbus fell short of his divine ambitions. He did not bring down the curtain on human history by ushering in the Apocalypse and establishing God's kingdom on Earth. But he did raise a curtain, one that even he could never have imagined, on the beginning of American history. Had he not been so utterly convinced of his messianic mission, that honor would have gone to someone else.

II Winthrop, Williams, and Penn

Prophets Prosper in the Land of Promised Lands

America was settled by Protestant prophets. Escaping persecution in England, they aimed to build utopia with their zealous followers. America would become a magnet for religious fanatics, and it's not hard to see why. In Europe, people had murdered one another over religion for centuries—a bloody trail of inquisitions, crusades, reformations, and counterreformations. By sharp contrast, prophets have been tolerated here, and that's one reason we have so many of them.

The origin of our tolerance has much to do with geography. The silent hero of early American history is the land herself. On a giant, sparsely populated continent it wasn't necessary to execute or imprison troublemakers. Religious dissidents like Roger Williams, who was banished from Massachusetts, could forge ever deeper into the endless wilderness to find their own promised lands (as the Mormons would do two hundred years later in their own "Great Migration" to Utah).

But prophets are not ordinary people, and they did not build an ordinary country. The new Moseses who settled America were bipolars with messianic missions of cosmic importance. And America has been teeming with messianic characters ever since.

JOHN WINTHROP AND THE CITY ON A HILL

The Bipolar Religious Experience

In *The Varieties of Religious Experience,* William James studied the spiritual memoirs of figures such as Saint Augustine, Ignatius Loyola, Martin Luther, George Fox, John Bunyan, and Jonathan Edwards. He found a consistent pattern: The protagonist of each salvation narrative began in a state of severe *depression,* which was relieved by an exhilarating revelatory illumination, achieving heights of *ecstasy* "equal in amplitude" to their previous depths of depression.[1] James likened these religiously transformed individuals to cases of "circular insanity," an antiquated term for manic depression.[2] For James, this did not invalidate religious experience. Instead, it elevated mood disorders into a potentially beneficial experience. Whereas modern psychiatrists describe depression as an illness that *distorts* perception, James argued the opposite. Depression, he felt, forced one to face the deepest existential truths of sin, suffering, evil, and death, which the more superficial "healthy minded" are able to deny. Depression can transform people into seekers of ultimate truth. The influence of James's insights has been unrivaled. Written in 1902, this classic book is still the most frequently cited work in the psychology of religion.

John Winthrop's spiritual narrative, found in the diary he kept as a young man, clearly fit the pattern described by James. Winthrop recorded his "highs and lows in his relations with the Holy Spirit," according to his biographer Lee Schweninger.[3] At times Winthrop would have ecstatic religious experiences: "I was so ravished with his [Christ's] love for me, far exceeding the affection of the kindest husband . . . I was forced to immeasurable weeping for a great while."[4] At other times, Winthrop felt profoundly worthless and guilty: "What am I but dust! A worm, a rebel wallowing in the blood and filth of my sins."[5] At these moments, the psychic pain was so intolerable that Winthrop sometimes "longed for the freedom death would bring," according to Schweninger. Psychiatrists call this *passive suicidal ideation:* you wish you were dead, even though you have no active plan to kill yourself. But suicidal despair was transformed into "joy unspeakable" when Winthrop had a definitely life-changing religious experience.[6] Soon thereafter, he would discover his messianic calling.

Winthrop's spiritual memoir was "like hundreds of others" written by fellow Puritans and follows a familiar "formula," according to Schweninger.[7] This formulaic sequence is the one outlined by James: despair, followed by joyful illumination and dedication to a mission from God. In fact, such a mood-swing-based conversion narrative was actually required to become a member of the churches of Massachusetts (and being a church member was a requirement to vote in civil elections). Does the appreciation of this cultural context imply that Winthrop's mood swings were within "normal limits"? No, it suggests that the Puritan population was made up of people with bipolar temperaments. Self-selected converts to an extreme religious movement are hardly a random sample of humanity. Winthrop was one fanatic among many, and in fact was hardly the most extreme of his fellow extremists. His comparatively sober judgment was often needed to keep his fellow saints in balance.

John Winthrop organized the Great Migration in 1629, when he became convinced that England's sins had provoked God beyond his breaking point. He wrote to his wife, "I am verily persuaded that God will bring some heavy affliction upon this land, and that speedily." Winthrop was not alone in these beliefs. The clergy who would constitute the religious oligarchy of Massachusetts became convinced that the end was near for Britain. John Cotton counseled that "a wise man who forseeth a plague should hide himself from it."[8] Thomas Hooker told his congregation before he departed to New England, "God told me yesterday night that he should destroy England and lay it waste. . . . New England shall be his refuge for his Noahs and his Lots."[9] Thomas Shepard wrote in his autobiography that God was about to bring "heavy plagues" upon England for its "national sins" that would include "sore afflictions of famine, war, blood, mortality and deaths."[10] You have to be at least a little manic to be certain you *know* that the Apocalypse is *now*.

The *Arabella* would sail less than a year after Winthrop had his revelatory insight. The rapidity with which he organized the expedition that founded New England can be attributed to his hypomanic pace and the intensity of his millennial urgency. In his recruitment letter, Winthrop warned his fellow Puritans to emigrate to safety. "God hath provided this place to be a refuge for many he means to save out of the general calamity . . . the Church has no place left to fly but into the wilderness." [11]

Even among the religious extremists, derisively called Puritans by their more conventional opponents, the settlers of New England represented a lunatic fringe whose paranoia was matched only by their grandiosity. They were not just fleeing Egypt one step ahead of the plagues. They were founding the New Jerusalem. They had been selected by God to be his new chosen people, his "New Israel," sent on "an errand in the wilderness." The Great Migration was motivated by messianism.

At the same time, the Great Migration reflected an entrepreneurial spirit. The zealous pursuit of God was reinforced by an equal zeal for mammon, most particularly in the form of land. "The search for land in America stood behind many migration decisions, even of the most religious emigrants," wrote Allan Kulikoff in *From British Peasants to Colonial American Farmers*.[12] In his recruitment letter, Winthrop stressed the availability of land: "Why then should we stand striving for a place of habitation and in the meantime suffer a whole continent as fruitful and convenient for the use of man to lie waste without improvement? The whole earth is the Lord's garden and he has given it to the sons of men with a commission: increase and multiply." [13] That England was in the beginning of an economic depression made Winthrop's call to develop this real estate, which he framed as a religious duty, all the more compelling.

The settlers were venture capitalists of a sort, but instead of risking their money they were risking their lives. "Human capital" was the only thing of value many had to risk or borrow against. Those who couldn't afford the ship's passage rented themselves into "indentured servitude," a time-limited contract under which, after a certain number of years working the land, they could pay off their debt and eventually become landowners themselves. Two thirds of the indentured servants did eventually become land-owners.[14] "Land was the principal capital of seventeenth-century America," and these early American start-up farmers were entre-preneurs.[15]

And there were Puritan investors, looking for an economic re-turn in exchange for funding the city of God. Puritan merchants who remained in England pooled their capital in a relatively new thing called a *joint stock company*. Companies such as Winthrop's Massachusetts Bay Company, the Plymouth Company, and the Virginia Company launched the ships that took settlers to Amer-ica. And their stockholders received huge swaths of prime real es-tate for their investment in nation building.

Religious zeal and entrepreneurial zeal may have different ob-jects but they require the same type of personality. It takes a special kind of person to obsessively pursue a vision, which is what zealots do. German sociologist Max Weber thought the seeds of modern capitalism could be found among seventeenth-century Protestant groups such as the Puritans and Quakers. The kind of fanatics who were attracted to such extreme sects were, much like Luther him-self, "a distinct species of men," Weber wrote in *The Protestant Ethic and the Spirit of Capitalism* in 1904.[16]* In the medieval Catholic Church, only the priests had a special relationship with God. But in Luther's "priesthood of all believers," every man had a *"calling"*—a "task set by God"—which transformed his secular labor into a holy

---

* To understand the psychology that animates Luther-like behavior it is important to know that Luther himself was manic depressive. Erik Erickson diagnosed him as suffering from a "severe manic depressive state," in his famous psychobiography, *Young Man Luther* (New York: Norton, 1958, p. 243). And, according to Goodwin and Jamison in *Manic-Depressive Illness* (New York: Oxford University Press, 1990, p. 262), Luther experienced periods of "deep, psy-chotic, occasionally suicidal melancholy" alternating with periods of "indefatigability and ex-altation." Not everyone concurs. John Wilkinson in his recent book, *The Medical History of the Reformers* (Edinburgh, Scotland: Handsel Press, 2001, pp. 18–19), flatly refuses to accept the manic-depressive diagnosis, taking it as an article of faith that "no mental disorder could have produced the historical movement called the Reformation." I would argue that it is precisely people of such temperament who produce historical movements like the Reformation.

quest. When this fanatical species of men applied themselves to commerce with their missionary intensity, new levels of industry and efficiency were achieved and, as a result, these men accumulated capital. Because these religious sects were ascetic, as well as zealous, they frowned upon the conspicuous consumption of their own wealth. Instead, they reinvested it in their businesses, creating commercial empires.

An Errand in the Wilderness

The first sighting of land was exhilarating to those aboard the *Arabella*. After two months of freezing rain, starvation, and "every manner of privation," Winthrop's followers could see the coast. "There came a smell off the shore like the smell of a garden," wrote Winthrop in his diary.

Just as Moses addressed the Jews before they crossed the Jordan River to take possession of the Promised Land, Winthrop spoke to the assembled faithful on the deck of the *Arabella,* delivering what has been called the most influential sermon in American history. Winthrop claimed that God had made a covenant with them, his new chosen people, and it contained the same warnings and promises Moses spoke of. If they were unfaithful to God, Winthrop warned, the American experiment would become a "shipwreck." But if they were faithful, God would "dwell among us as his people" and "command a blessing upon us in all our ways." National security ("Ten of us shall be able to resist a thousand of our enemies") and material wealth would automatically ensue. Winthrop defined America as a "city on a hill." America could become a beacon calling all the peoples of the world to God. "All eyes will be upon you," he prophesied. They were "on a mission of cosmic significance," nothing less than "the redemption of the world," wrote Loren Baritz in *City on a Hill*.[17]

When the Puritans aboard the *Arabella* reached the shore, they felt they had been saved. They shouldn't have. They were about to descend into the ice of a New England winter unlike anything they had ever experienced before. A thousand Puritans sailed with Winthrop: two hundred died that first winter, and almost that many took the first boat home. Yet, Winthrop's spirits were buoyant during this time of tribulation. He sailed in an "exuberant mood" and never lost it. He was relentlessly optimistic and wrote home that he had never felt better, despite the fact that the first casualty was his own son Henry, who drowned the day they arrived. They were building their theocracy, and he was excited. In the end, the numbers would justify his optimism. A few hundred souls were lost that first winter, but twenty thousand English colonists came to Boston Harbor over the next ten years. Winthrop would build his city of God, and it would thrive just as he had predicted.

The image of the city on the hill has become an eternal American archetype, emblazoned on our collective national unconscious. In his final address before leaving the presidency, Ronald Reagan spoke of the City on the Hill as the central guiding image of his life:

> I've spoken of the shining city all my political life . . . a tall proud city built on rocks stronger than oceans, windswept, God-blessed, and teeming with people of all kinds . . . a city of free ports that hummed with commerce and creativity. . . .
>
> And she's still a beacon, still a magnet for all who must have freedom, for all the pilgrims from all the lost places who are hurtling through the darkness towards home.[18]

The idea that America was chosen by God for a special role in his divine plan was as real for Reagan as it was for Winthrop. And it continues to be real for American leaders such as President George W. Bush, who has spoken openly about his feeling that God has called the United States to be the instrument of his divine will, and is waging a war in pursuit of that aim. Our indignant European allies would surely agree with Edmund Morgan, who wrote that our Puritan heritage has imbued us with "a sense of mission" and "divine favor" that has "added an ingredient of self-righteousness to every enterprise Americans undertook as a people." [19]

By any measure, Americans are still the most religiously fervent people in the developed world. Ninety percent of Americans believe in God, and 58 percent say their faith is important to them, as compared to 12 percent of the French and 19 percent of the British. Many Americans still have conversion experiences like those described by James. One out of five Americans, including President George W. Bush, claim to have experienced a religious conversion. [20]

This virgin continent was seeded by Protestant prophets, and you could say that since that moment of inception, America has been, and perhaps always will be, a messianic nation. At the very least, "the land is overrun with messiahs," as nineteenth-century observer Charles Ferguson noted. [21] America will never suffer a shortage of people with plans to change the world.

ROGER WILLIAMS: TROUBLER OF ISRAEL

Amid the suffering of that first winter, a ship from England arrived one cold February morning with much-needed supplies. John Winthrop recorded in his journal that it also brought a "godly minister," Roger Williams. [22] Winthrop instantly liked Williams, who radiated an unmistakable aura of holiness. He was a "palpable saint" in "a society that set a high value on sainthood," wrote Edmund Morgan. The magistrates of Boston quickly offered Williams their most exalted ecclesiastical position, the pastorate of the Boston church. As if by providential design, the man in the Boston pulpit at that time was going back to England on the very same ship. Williams appeared to be a godsend. Soon after he touched land, the cold weather broke.

But Williams, the Puritans' Puritan, didn't find Winthrop's City of God to be pure enough. The first hint of trouble, according to Winthrop's diaries, occurred when Williams insisted that the congregation in Boston "make a public declaration of their repentance for having communion with the churches of England while they lived there."[23] When they refused, he refused the pastorate. "I durst not officiate to an unseparated people," Williams proclaimed.[24] Moreover, he felt morally obliged to separate from the unseparated people of Boston. He "could follow a belief to its conclusion with a passionate literalness that bordered on the ridiculous," according to Morgan.[25] And he only became more radical and strident over time. This "anti-establishment eccentric" was a man of "wild and volatile opinions," Paul Johnson wrote in *A History of the American People*.[26]

The problem was that Williams was "divinely mad," according to Richard Hubbard, who wrote a history of New England in 1680.[27] Williams's racing thoughts, a clear sign of hypomania, flew from one idea to another. John Cotton, the most popular preacher in Massachusetts, compared Williams's mind to a windmill whirling so fast that it set itself on fire.[28] Even otherwise appreciative modern scholars become exasperated when commenting on his windmill-like writing style. Though brilliant, his work is described as hurriedly written, endlessly verbose, and chaotically punctuated.

Williams moved on to the church in Salem, where he was offered a teaching position despite the controversy in Boston. Winthrop intervened, however, pressuring the Salemites to rescind their offer. As a result, Williams left Salem in 1631 for Plymouth, the explicitly separatist community founded by the Pilgrims. As in Boston and Salem, the people there were initially impressed with Williams's fervor. Plymouth's founding governor, William Bradford, admired the "truth" of even his "sharpest admonitions and reproofs." But gradually Bradford began to recognize that Williams was "a man godly and zealous, having many precious parts, but very unsettled in judgment."[29] In 1633, he noticed that Williams "began to fall into strange opinions, and from opinion to practice; which caused some controversy between the church and him."[30] The combination of extreme zeal, odd ideas, and poor judgment is the classic presentation of the hypomanic. Such individuals stir up controversy in any organization as they aggressively seek converts to their idiosyncratic way of thinking. They try, often in dramatic fashion, to take charge of the group and change its mission.

Williams would leave Plymouth disillusioned. Even the separatists of Plymouth were not, in his view, true separatists. He was shocked to discover that a few weak souls attended Church of England services when visiting their relatives back home. When the Plymouth church did nothing to discipline these backsliders, Williams felt compelled to separate from them too. He tried to impose "his own singular opinions" about "rigid separation" on the congregation and chose to leave when he failed to get their support, according to a book published in 1699 by Plymouth congregant Nathaniel Morton.[31]

Williams went back to Salem, where they took him in as a teacher—unofficially, to avoid conflict with Boston. There he built a following among a group in the throes of a separatist revival. This adulation probably only fanned the firebrand's hypomania. In his state of heightened grandiosity he felt ready to take on the king. He sent an outrageous letter to Winthrop and Bradford, addressed to King Charles. The patent the king had granted the Massachusetts Bay Colony was based on a "solemn public lie," Williams proclaimed. The land had never been the king's to grant in the first place; it belonged to the Indians. He also charged the king with "blasphemy" for referring to Europe as "Christendom." And he "did personally apply to our present King, three very unflattering passages from Revelations," wrote Winthrop.[32]

The Massachusetts magistrates immediately summoned Williams to court in December 1633. Winthrop persuaded Williams to promise not to publicly repeat his allegations against the king, and the matter was deemed resolved. But Williams was soon found preaching against the king's patent again, only now he was proclaiming that it should be returned to the king. He drafted a letter to Charles I, asking the king to acknowledge the "evil" of the patent, along with a request that he rewrite it without his former lies.[33] When the court met again in March 1635, it was "ready to deal with this madman," according to Morgan.[34] But John Cotton, who ironically would later become Williams's greatest enemy, intervened on Williams's behalf and resolved the matter by convincing Williams to drop his recklessly provocative letter. In typical hypomanic fashion, Williams seemed oblivious of the potentially dire consequences his letter could produce both for himself and the colony. The Massachusetts Bay Company held their charter at the king's pleasure, and it could be easily revoked. In 1635, America was hardly strong enough to declare independence from Britain.

Rather than calming down, Williams seemed to escalate his pace of dissent. "His separatism now began to spin faster," wrote Morgan.[35] The standard hypomanic response to opposition is to speed up, escalate, crank up the volume. Only a few months later, Williams was again called before the court for preaching against a law that required all male inhabitants over the age of sixteen to swear an oath of allegiance to the state. If the oath were administered to a "wicked man," Williams claimed, it would "cause him to take the name of God in vain."[36] In addition, he now preached that "regenerate" men should not pray in the presence of the "unregenerate," even their own wives and children.

When the pastor of Salem died, the congregation openly defied the Massachusetts magistrates and appointed Williams. The magistrates warned Salem that Williams's "erroneous" and "dangerous" opinions would lead their church into "heresy, apostasy, or tyranny." The magistrates then held up Salem's request for a land grant in Marblehead Neck, explicitly holding it hostage unless they agreed to dump Williams. Decrying this manipulative tactic as a violation of the sacred Puritan principle of congregational independence, Williams mounted a public attack on the magistrates, condemning their "heinous sin" in a letter circulated to all Massachusetts churches.[37]

At this time, Williams fell ill. From his sickbed he sent a written ultimatum to his Salem congregation: as the churches of Massachusetts had become "full of antichristian pollution," either Salem must separate herself from all the other churches in Massachusetts or Williams would have to separate himself from Salem.[38] The good people of Salem were "grieved" at this request, according to Winthrop. They were not willing to go so far as to follow Williams into "holy isolation."

In October 1635, Williams was dragged before the court for the last time. He recanted nothing, but instead stood as "adamant as Luther at the Diet of Worms," according to Morgan.[39] John Cotton later wrote a letter telling Williams that he had "banished himself." Morgan agrees: "By the time the sentence was delivered there was no alternative. The people of Massachusetts could scarcely have carried out their commission and allowed Williams to remain."[40]

In a published tract seven years later, Williams would answer Cotton's charge that he had banished himself. Williams presented himself as a Christ-like figure persecuted by contemporary Pharisees. He accused the Massachusetts magistrates of "persecuting the witness of the Lord" who was "presenting light unto them."[41] Williams described himself as a "poor despised ram's horn," a prophet "in sackcloth," cruelly "exposed to the mercy of a howling wilderness, in frost and snow." All of these images shed light on the grandiose religious imagination of the hypomanic. It was not just a figure of speech when he compared himself to Christ and the prophets of the Old Testament. The hypomanic truly sees himself in such exalted terms. He is destined to change the world, and those who oppose him are, like the Pharisees, wicked, blind, and on the wrong side of history.

The Massachusetts magistrates thought they were being charitable when they allowed Williams to delay his banishment for a few months to sit out the exceedingly harsh winter and recover from his illness. They had only one condition: he could not "draw others to his opinions." In January 1636, it was discovered by the court that he had violated this condition by preaching privately in his own home.[42] The court then decided to take sudden action and forcibly deport Williams back to England, where he most probably would have been imprisoned or killed, especially if it had become known to the king of England that Williams had publicly called him a liar and a blasphemer. The court dispatched Captain John Underhill to arrest Williams and carry him forcibly aboard his ship. But when Underhill arrived at Williams's home, the house was empty. Williams had been tipped off and fled Salem for Narragansett Bay three days ahead of Captain Underhill's arrival.

Who helped Williams escape? The last man you would have expected: John Winthrop. Williams couldn't live in Massachusetts anymore. But John Winthrop didn't have it in him to condemn the palpable saint to death. The ultimate effect of Williams's banishment was that he and Winthrop became neighbors. Williams founded and then governed Rhode Island for most of the next thirty years. The two men remained friends and stayed in touch by letter. They even went in together on a small piece of Rhode Island property for sheepherding. After Winthrop died, Williams continued the correspondence with his son John Winthrop, Jr., governor of Connecticut.

Soul Liberty in Rogue Island

The principles of religious freedom that Williams is famous for were a total reversal of his previously extreme separatism. Central to the nature of hypomanics is that they are both excessive *and* unstable, so that even their most intensely held views are subject to radical 180-degree change without notice. Williams had taken separatism to its furthest limit. By the time he left Salem, he refused to take communion with anyone but his wife. However, when he founded Rhode Island, he went to the opposite extreme, allowing people of all religious convictions to join him. Winthrop could only shake his head in amazement: "Having a little before refused communion with all, save his own wife, now he would preach to and pray with all comers."[43] There were even shocking rumors that "in their smoky huts" Williams had participated in the religious rites of his Native American neighbors.* According to Morgan, this was "the very thing to be expected from a man like Williams, who leaped always from one extreme to another."[44] The doors of "Rogue Island," as some Massachusetts Puritans liked to call it, were thrown open to every religious misfit, heretic, eccentric, and dissenter who wanted to live there. As long as they obeyed the civil laws, Williams ordered that "no man should be molested for his conscience."

As nutty as it seemed at the time, Williams had a breakthrough of religious genius through his erratic reversal. There is a long precedent for this among prophets. Think of St. Paul, who persecuted the early Church before a blinding revelation made him its chief evangelist. Williams's new insight was that throughout history, those who most sincerely sought God had been persecuted by the state, "and the more godly the more persecuted."[45] Prime examples were the early Christians, Martin Luther, the English Puritans, and now, of course, himself. When the Puritans erected their own society, "the persecuted of England became the persecutors of New England," in the words of Perry Miller.[46] The common denominator, according to Williams, was that state-controlled churches were *always* corrupt, linked as they must be to temporal power, politics, and privilege. "It is impossible for any man or men to maintain their Christ by the sword and worship the true Christ."

Williams traveled to London in 1644 to obtain a patent granting

---

* Williams became a trusted friend of the local Indians, the Narragansetts, even adopting a boy from their tribe to raise as a son. Through these good relations Williams saved Massachusetts from Indian attack several times, more than repaying Winthrop's generosity in saving his life.

Rhode Island possession of her land and standing as a colony. The Rhode Island charter proclaimed: "No person shall be in any wise molested, punished, disquieted or called in question for any difference in opinion in matters of religion."[47] Williams had written a rough draft of the First Amendment.

The practical import of the Rhode Island charter was that Williams gave all of colonial America's diverse dissenters a place to go. One New Amsterdam minister wrote that "all the cranks of New England retired there" because they were "not tolerated in any other place."[48] In his view, that made Rhode Island "New England's latrine." By modern standards, it represented a bold step for human freedom—the first society in history to guarantee in its charter both religious freedom and separation of church and state. The creation of Rhode Island was "a critical turning point in the evolution of America," according to Paul Johnson.[49]

Williams summarized these ideas in his most famous work, *The Bloody Tenet of Persecution*. The book was published in 1644 in England, where it was both banned and publicly burned. Fortunately, Williams was safely on the boat back to Providence with his charter in hand when the book hit the stands. The book's breathless style exposes the racing thoughts of a hypomanic. Edmund Morgan describes Williams's work as a bewildering, "hasty, helter-skelter torrent of words," which nonetheless shows the workings of a "rarely original mind."[50] Ideas pour out of hypomanics, a mix of the ridiculous and the brilliant. Williams had espoused a string of ridiculous notions, then finally had one great idea. The fruition of all his spiritual struggles was summarized in one phrase: every human was entitled to "soul liberty." Williams, who defined himself as a "seeker," was safeguarding not the *content* of religious truth, as other religious leaders had done, but the *process* whereby each individual could seek God in his or her own way. The residents of Rhode Island were the first people in history unfettered by law in their pursuit of holiness.

"Follow your bliss," some business gurus like to say. Americans more than any other people have given themselves permission to follow their utopian dreams.

THE FRIENDS OF GEORGE FOX

In 1656, the Quakers arrived. The first ship bearing two Quaker women had landed in Boston a year earlier. The authorities had stripped them naked, burned their books, and deported them. When an entire shipload of Quakers from England landed in Boston, it was decided, "by prudent care of the government," not to allow them to disembark. Virginia and New Amsterdam also refused to accept the Quakers. Those who did enter Massachusetts were savagely persecuted. "Quakers were commonly tied to cart's tails in Massachusetts, stripped to the waist and whipped out of the colony."[51] They were also starved, had their ears cut off, holes bored in their tongues, and three were even hanged.

The other colonies begged Rhode Island to close its doors to the Quakers as well, but Roger Williams refused. As a result, the followers of George Fox flooded into Rhode Island in such numbers that by the 1670s they made up the majority of the population and took over most of its political offices, much to Williams's irritation.

In the summer of 1672, George Fox, British founder of the Quaker sect, visited Providence. Consistent with the pattern described by James, Fox suffered a series of depressive breakdowns throughout his life, punctuated by experiences of religious elation. "Up and down, up and down, up and down marked the course of his emotional life," wrote biographer Homer Ingle.[52] At age nineteen, in 1643, overwhelmed by agitation and despair, Fox cut his ties with his family, fashioned himself a peculiar outfit made of leather, and wandered about the English countryside fasting and reading the Bible. "No matter what he did, whether remaining long closeted in his room or moping in the countryside, he could not throw off this despair that plagued him."[53] Fox felt as though he were drowning in an "ocean of darkness and death." [54] James, a great admirer of the Quaker religion, offers Fox as an example of a profound religious mind that also manifested severe psychopathology. Fox would frequently do impulsive bizarre things in obedience to inner promptings that verged on the hallucinatory. As James noted, Fox's journal abounded with entries such as the following, describing an incident in Litchfield, England:

> I was commanded by the Lord to pull off my shoes. I stood still for it was winter: but the word was like fire in me. Then I walked on about a mile, and as soon as I got within the city, the word of the Lord came to me again, saying: Cry, "Wo to the bloody city of Litchfield!" So I went up and down the streets, crying with a loud voice, "Wo to the bloody city of Litchfield!" And no one laid hands on me. And thus as I went crying through the streets, there seemed to me a channel of blood running down the streets, and the market place appeared like a pool of blood. [55]

These euphoric revelatory "openings," as Fox called them, lightened "the weight of his depression," according to Ingle. More generally, they became the basis for a philosophy that formally raised the authority of personal revelation over institutional authority. Fox believed in divine guidance by one's subjective sense of God's inner light.* Karl Marx's assessment of Luther's revolutionary impact could just as easily apply to Fox: "He destroyed faith in authority by restoring the authority of faith." [56] Fox argued that there was now no need for any church hierarchy or structure whatsoever: "The Lord would teach his people himself." [57]

Williams fought for the Quakers' right to come to Rhode Island, despite their theological opinions. But simultaneously he felt com-

---

* The notion that every person should be guided by personal revelation is a recurring theme in American religious history. Anne Hutchinson was banished from Massachusetts not long after Williams for preaching a similar gospel.

pelled to publicly oppose what he saw as their errant views. "Blasphemy! Blasphemy!" he cried. Like any good Puritan, Williams believed that man knew God through the Scriptures, not by a self-indulgent "inner light." Fox was encouraging man to make himself "equal in power and glory with God," he protested.[58] A few months short of his seventieth birthday, Williams challenged Fox to a public debate in Providence. Fox later claimed that he hadn't received the challenge until he was aboard ship heading back to England. Williams contemptuously retorted that Fox had "run for it," afraid to face him in a public debate.[59]

Not to be denied, Williams arranged to debate the local Rhode Island Friends in their own meetinghouse. There was an eerie eclipse of the sun on the first day of the debate, but Williams talked on and on in the dark. His scheduled two-day debate stretched to four days. Williams apologized for his "prolixity" but kept talking till the Quakers were exhausted. The Friends stopped arguing theology and began begging for a time limit to the debate. While manics suffer *involuntarily* from a symptom called "pressured speech," a runaway train of rapidly spoken words equally difficult to understand or interrupt, hypomanics *voluntarily* use their torrent of words to pressure others. Almost everyone has bought something from a "high-pressure" salesman, one who wouldn't stop talking until you purchased his product. On that day, it seems unlikely that Williams sold his views to many Rhode Island Quakers, though it wasn't for lack of trying.

Williams followed up by writing an insulting tract entitled *George Fox Digg'd out of his Burrows,* a pun on the name of Edward Burroughs, a prolific Quaker pamphleteer. Fox responded to this "envious and wicked book" with an equally vituperative attack on Williams entitled *A New England Firebrand Quenched.*[60]

What is important is that these cantankerous prophets crossed pens, not swords. The Quakers were whipped with the lash and driven out of Massachusetts, but in Rhode Island they were given a home and subjected only to a tongue-lashing by an elderly Roger Williams.

WILLIAM PENN AND THE CITY OF BROTHERLY LOVE

Finally, it was the Quakers' turn to try their hand at building a City of God. William Penn was born in 1644 and grew up during the English Restoration. A Puritan revolution, led by a bipolar leader, Oliver Cromwell, had dethroned the king of England. But the revolution failed and a Stuart king was put back on the throne. One of the people who helped reinstate him was Admiral Penn, William's father. The admiral had won several brilliant naval battles for the king. His Highness was on such intimate terms with the Penn family that he received young William in his bedroom wearing only his nightshirt.

While at Oxford, going through a phase of "melancholic introversion," young Penn became very excited by an address he heard by Quaker Thomas Loe.[61] He became a Quaker and was thrown out of Oxford for his religious beliefs, decrying the school as "a den of hellish sin and debauchery."[62] The admiral threatened to disown him and then sent young William on a long vacation to France. It seemed to work. He returned to England a vain, affected dandy, no longer interested in religion. But Penn met Loe again years later in Ireland. This time Penn converted for good. He traveled widely with George Fox, preaching around the world and writing tracts, producing more written work than any other early Quaker. As a result of his proselytizing, he went to prison four times and his estates were confiscated.

Penn proved to be an irrepressible evangelist. When the Friends were outlawed from meeting in their meetinghouse, Penn began preaching in the street. He was arrested for disturbing the peace. At his trial Penn refused to be silenced. Even as he was dragged to the back of the courtroom, he made an impassioned speech that swayed the jury. A man's soul was beyond the reach of the state, he proclaimed. When the jury found Penn innocent, the enraged judge had the jury jailed, and still its members refused to change their verdict. Eventually they were released, establishing in English law the precedent that a jury's verdict cannot be compelled or punished.

Despite all the trouble young William caused, the king still felt a sense of obligation to the son of his old friend. He owed a huge debt to the deceased Admiral Penn, not only morally but financially. Young William had in hand a valid £16,000 IOU signed by the king. Giving young Penn a huge tract of land in America concluded the king's business with the Penn family. The land was exchanged for cancellation of the debt. Penn was fortunate in his timing. The king had recently defeated the Dutch, claiming all their territory in North America. To solidify his hold on the land he was promoting an aggressive settlement policy. While populating his colony with Englishmen, the king was now able at the same time to unload a bunch of unruly Quakers, whom he otherwise might have had to imprison at government expense. If they wanted to practice their odd religion there, that didn't matter to him. Penn saw that, "The government was glad to be rid of us at so cheap a rate as a little parchment to be practiced in the desert 3,000 miles off."[63] The king honored his old friend the admiral by insisting that the new colony be named for him. William had wanted to call it Sylvania, so Pennsylvania was adopted as a compromise.

In 1681, Penn's "holy experiment" began. Roger Williams had opened the door to religious dissenters by not "molesting" them, but William Penn put out the official welcome mat. He guaranteed total freedom of religion in the colony's charter—actively inviting, not merely tolerating, people of all faiths. All freeholders were given the right to vote, regardless of religion. This new standard of tolerance attracted all sorts of believers. Philadelphia became the center of colonial Jewish life, for example. And it did not hurt that

Penn offered cheap land on easy terms. Rhode Island had been a place to escape to in desperation. Pennsylvania was a destination.

In Philadelphia, Penn built a city such as no one had seen. "Everything in Pennsylvania was big from the start," wrote Paul Johnson. It had unusually wide streets, lined with trees, paved, and organized in a massive symmetrical grid. Hypomanics always think big, and in this case the city's very urban design announced the ambitious intentions of its founder. This was a modern city of the future, big enough for its diverse people. That was the idea behind the City of Brotherly Love, and it would become the model of a new nation. Historian Edward Channing called Penn "the founder of the United States."[64] It was William Penn's model, far more than John Winthrop's, that the framers of the Constitution followed. Johnson agrees: "Quaker Pennsylvania was the key state in American history."[65]

Not coincidentally, the religiously radical Quakers were also excellent entrepreneurs and quickly turned Philadelphia into the center of American commercial life, outstripping both Boston and New Amsterdam. Most of its new immigrants were simple laborers who transformed themselves into self-employed farmers. Almost anyone could get a hundred acres of rich land there. And soon "the bread colony" was exporting large agricultural surpluses. The Quakers were "well dressed, they ate magnificently, and they had money jingling in their pockets."[66]

The formation of Pennsylvania should have been a brilliant entrepreneurial venture for William Penn as well. He owned "the largest piece of real estate ever legally held by someone other than a monarch, and he was given authority to run it like a feudal lord."[67] But feudalism was dying in England and would never take root in America. His tenants did not pay their nominal rents to Penn, who took such a steep loss on the project that he ended up in debtors' prison at the end of his life. Obstreperous, independent-minded Pennsylvanians, such as Benjamin Franklin, would challenge the financial and political authority of the Penn family at every turn.

But if William Penn's personal affairs floundered, the city he built more than prospered. It became the cultural heart of America, serving as its first official national capital. And not coincidentally, Philadelphia was the town where both the Declaration of Independence and the Constitution were written and signed.

In 1776, Thomas Jefferson sat at his desk in a Philadelphia hotel room, trying to write the Declaration of Independence. At some point, he must have gazed out the window. His genius was that he *saw* what he was looking at: a nation of seekers, each chasing his vision of the future, be it religious, economic, or whatever a human being can imagine. The greatest liberty America could give them beyond the basics was the chance to chase those dreams. The Declaration guaranteed a right no one had even heard of before: the *pursuit of happiness*. Looking at the fast-paced, bustling streets of eighteenth-century Philadelphia, it was "self-evident" to Jefferson that this unheard-of right to pursue our obsessions and wildest ambitions was "inalienable." That's because the freedoms Jefferson was putting on paper were already facts on the ground (though, sadly, only for whites) in the new world Winthrop, Williams, and Penn had built. Jefferson saw that there was room enough in this giant land for us all to pursue our calling, no matter how wacky it might be.

Alexander Hamilton

Father of Our Economy

No other Founder rose so far, so fast, and from so far away—
beginning life as a bastard, a penniless orphan, and an immigrant.
And none crashed as hard as Alexander Hamilton. The prodigy
was a constant one-man charge who relentlessly attacked
America's biggest problems: winning a revolution, adopting a
constitution, and, as his final act, single-handedly designing her
economy. But Hamilton took one charge too many when he ran
into an angry, unstable Aaron Burr. Hamilton lived by his hypomania, and he died by it.

Hamilton's life looks different through the eyes of a clinician.
Though biographers resist attaching "diagnostic labels" to their
subjects, to a mental health professional there is no doubt that
Hamilton was a bipolar type II—someone whose hypomania al-
ternated with major depression. While the evidence of his illness
can be found in their pages, Hamilton's biographers do not even
discuss the possibility that he might have been bipolar. James
Flexner calls Hamilton "by far the most psychologically troubled
of the founders," even a "semimadman" at times—without wondering if this form of semimadness has a name.[1] Biographer
Richard Brookhiser wrote that Hamilton was subject to "moods,"
which could be "noisy and destructive as firecrackers" or "dark and
depressed."[2] But when we spoke, he was cool to the idea of diagnosing him as having any kind of mood disorder. Most recently,
Ron Chernow has described Hamilton as a "volatile personality"
who makes an "irresistible psychological study." An "exuberant genius," he worked at a "fiendish pace" and got himself in trouble
through his "arrogance," "womanizing," and "egregious failures
of judgment." He was also not infrequently "prey to depression."[3]
Yet despite this lively description of bipolar symptoms, Chernow

doesn't mention bipolar disorder as a possibility worth considera-
tion in his psychological study.

The one exception to this rule is Arnold Rogow, who wrote that
Hamilton showed "clear signs of mania and depression" and was
apparently "never entirely free from the symptoms of manic-
depressive illness."[4] Yet even Rogow insists that we cannot know for
certain that Hamilton was *really* bipolar because, "However plausi-
ble these assessments might be, a clinical diagnosis almost two hundred years later that approximates those of modern medical science
is not possible."[5] Rogow is not alone in his skepticism. Can one establish a valid psychiatric diagnosis for a historical figure?

Clinicians normally diagnose living patients. Obviously, I can't
conduct a psychiatric interview with Alexander Hamilton, nor ad-
minister any psychological tests to him. But interviewing a patient is
not the only way mental health professionals establish diagnoses. A
diagnosis can also be determined by *history* if we know enough details
about someone's past behavior. One way of gathering that information is by interviewing people who know the subject well, usually a
family member in the case of a patient. Asking *informants* a systematic set of questions about the presence of specific behavioral symptoms is one of the methods psychiatrists use to establish a valid
diagnosis. But who can serve as an informant for a man long dead?

The only valid informants I could think of were his biographers.
They know him well and, in an indirect way, have spent a lot of
time with him. It struck me as risky, trying to validate my diagnosis
of Hamilton by interviewing writers who had evidenced a strong
resistance to diagnosing him. But I went searching for biographers
nonetheless. I found seven still alive. I was able to contact five, and
they all generously agreed to participate in my study.*

---

* This study was completed before the publication of Ron Chernow's 2004 biography,
Alexander Hamilton. My subjects were Roger Kennedy (*Burr, Hamilton and Jefferson: A Study in
Character*), Arnold Rogow (*A Fatal Friendship: Alexander Hamilton and Aaron Burr*), Noemie
Emery (*Alexander Hamilton: An Intimate Portrait*), Thomas Fleming (*Duel: Alexander Hamilton,
Aaron Burr and the Future of America*), and Richard Brookhiser (*Alexander Hamilton, American*).

There are *observable behavioral criteria* that define every psychiatric diagnosis, so I sought the biographers' observations of Hamilton's behavior. I told the writers I was studying a particular psychological "type," without naming it, and asked them to help me determine if Hamilton fit the "profile." I read them a narrative description of a hypomanic, which I had composed, drawing on both the diagnostic criteria of *DSM-IV* and the larger clinical literature:

He is filled with an unusually high degree of energy. He is restless and impatient. He is unusually active at work and other pursuits. He is quick-thinking. Thoughts race through his head, and he jumps from idea to idea. He can be distracted. He talks fast. He talks a lot. And he aggressively dominates conversations. He sets goals that seem grandiose, yet he appears supremely confident of success. He feels like a man of destiny—maybe even destined to change the world in some way. He is so excited about what he believes he will achieve that he is elated or even a little high. Because his mood is infectious, his confidence can make him charismatic, persuasive and attractive. He can be charming, witty, gregarious and good at making people laugh. He dresses in ways that create an impression and get attention. On the other hand, minor obstacles or delays can easily irritate him, and his temper can be unpredictably explosive. He can be suspicious and hostile towards people he feels are thwarting his plans. He is impulsive. As soon as an idea occurs to him, he urgently wants to act on it, without first thinking through the realistic consequences. He is a risk taker in general. He is a financial risk taker, often overspending in his business and personal life. He can be a physical risk taker. He is unusually sexually active, and can be risky in his sexual behavior. He not infrequently works on little sleep, for example, rising early in the morning full of pep and working till late at night.

I then asked the biographers if this description sounded like Hamilton. Biographers rated their level of agreement using a standard 5-point scale (1, strongly disagree; 2, disagree somewhat; 3, neutral; 4, agree somewhat; 5, strongly agree). In answer to my first question, "Overall, how well does this description fit Alexander Hamilton?," *all* the biographers agreed strongly or somewhat that Hamilton fit the hypomanic profile (the average rating was 4.6 out of a possible 5 points). I also asked them how well *each* trait fit Hamilton (for a summary of the biographers' ratings, see the appendix). They endorsed more than enough criteria to make a diagnosis. In addition, they all strongly agreed that he had suffered from recurrent and sometimes severe depressions—making Hamilton a bipolar type II by definition.

I hope not only to show that Hamilton was bipolar, but more important, that if he hadn't been, he couldn't have led the charge to launch a nation. Hamilton's hypomania was an essential ingredient in his accomplishments. And his accomplishments were an essential ingredient in the creation of America.

THE RISE OF YOUNG HAMILTON: I WISH THERE WAS A WAR

A Foreign Bastard

Hamilton was born out of wedlock on the Caribbean island of Nevis, near Saint Croix. "In all the forty-seven crowded years of his life, Alexander Hamilton was never allowed to forget that he was a bastard."[6] John Adams famously called him the "bastard brat of a Scotch peddler," and Jefferson thundered, "It's monstrous that this country should be ruled by a foreign bastard!"[7] No other founder was an immigrant or came from such humble beginnings. He was "the archetype of the self-made man in early American history," according to Adam Bellow.[8]

Hamilton's pedigree doesn't look promising by twenty-first-century psychiatric criteria, either. Both of his parents were unstable, restless, impulsive types, and they fought constantly. Hamilton rarely mentioned his parents, but he once wrote, "It's a dog's life when two dissonant tempers meet."[9] Acting out and affective disorder ran throughout his family tree. Among Hamilton's antecedents, "adultery, theft, suicide and lawsuits proliferated."[10]

James Hamilton, Alexander's father, was the black sheep of a noble Scottish family, a restless wanderer who traveled far from the family manse and landed in Saint Croix. He was also an unsuccessful entrepreneur. Hamilton recalled bitterly that his father had been reduced to a "groveling condition" by becoming "bankrupt as a merchant."[11] Young Hamilton vowed that he would never allow this to happen to him. James escaped his problems by wandering away from his new family, just as he had from his family of origin. When Alexander was nine, his father got onto a ship and sailed away. Hamilton learned of his whereabouts only as an adult. He offered to bring his father to America, but James didn't come. They never saw each other again.

Alexander's mother, Rachael, was a spirited, beautiful woman. Before she met James Hamilton, she had been married to Peter Lavien, a merchant from Nevis. Rachael appears to have been hypersexual and ill advised in some of her sexual liaisons, as her son Alexander would later also prove to be. Rachael had numerous affairs and, after five years, walked out—leaving behind not only Lavien but also their son, Peter. Lavien used every means at his disposal to force Rachael to come back to him. He had her jailed on charges of "abandoning her family" and "twice committing adultery"—prosecutable crimes, at least for women. But his vindictive attempts at coercion made her rebel even more. Ultimately, he gave up and sought a divorce, charging her with "whoring with everyone." Under the rules of the island, Lavien was free to remarry, but Rachael was not. Thus, she and James Hamilton were legally prohibited from producing legitimate offspring.

After James Hamilton sailed out of their lives, Rachael needed to find a way to survive with her two sons. She rented a small house and opened a retail store, selling food and imported items to the local plantations. "She bought her goods on credit . . . kept her books in good order and made her payments punctually."[12] Rachael's ability to establish and maintain good credit kept her family alive—a lesson that would not be lost on young Alexander, who helped her in the store. He later would establish the good credit of another growing concern—the United States of America.

At one point both Alexander and his mother fell ill. Together they lay feverish and incapacitated in the only bed the family owned. Alexander recovered. But Rachael did not. On February 19, 1768, she died.

At age thirteen, Alexander Hamilton was a destitute orphan.*

Within an hour after Rachael expired, there was a knock at the door. Five members of the probate court marched in, seized the family's meager belongings, locked them away in closets, sealed the doors, and marked them with the king's crest. Four days later, the probate court met in the Hamilton home. Lavien claimed the "estate," such as it was, in the name of Rachael's legitimate son, Peter. The town judge had to lend Alexander's brother, James, money to buy shoes for their mother's funeral.

The Hamilton boys became wards of Rachael's nephew, Peter Lytton. That solution proved to be unstable. After a year, Lytton committed suicide. Alexander and his brother were thus hurled into what Hamilton called "this selfish rapacious world," with absolutely no family at all.[13]

James was apprenticed to a carpenter, and Alexander was sent to work as a clerk for Nicholas Cruger, a merchant from New York who ran an import-export company. Cruger was the man who had

---

* There is historical ambiguity concerning the year of Hamilton's birth. He may actually have been only eleven at this time.

lent his mother merchandise on credit. He had seen Alexander working hard in her store and thought the boy could be of use.

While working for Cruger, Alexander was sent to live with a family named Stevens, whose son Edward was said to look so much like Hamilton that "they could have been brothers."[14] Young Hamilton is described as a dashing golden boy with a "charismatic glow, noticeably Scottish in appearance: his skin fair and ruddy, but given to freckling; his hair sandy; his eyes of a blue that admirers later described as almost violet." His frame was slight but "electrified by a gallant spirit."[15] Edward and Alexander were best friends and felt as though they were brothers. Ned, as Hamilton affectionately called him, wrote Hamilton tenderly "of those vows of eternal friendship, which we have so often mutually exchanged."[16] But the fact that they weren't brothers was driven home painfully when Ned was whisked off to New York to receive a private college education, while Hamilton was stuck as a clerk in Saint Croix.

I Condemn the Groveling Condition of a Clerk

Alexander was miserable when Ned left for college. Pouring out his heart, he revealed to Ned that he longed for glory: "To confess my weakness, Ned, my ambition is so prevalent that I condemn the groveling condition of a clerk or the like, to which my fortune condemns me. . . . I would willingly risk my life, though not my character, to exalt my station."[17] He concluded the letter, "I wish there was a war." Why a war?

The one book Hamilton prized most from his mother's collection was Plutarch's life of Julius Caesar. "There is no danger to which he [Caesar] did not willingly expose himself because he coveted honor," wrote Hamilton.[18] War had been his path to greatness, and Hamilton imagined it could be his, too. Every hypomanic child or young adult has a larger-than-life historic figure with whom he identifies, who becomes the raw material for a secret grandiose identity. With religious conviction they maintain their steadfast belief, even if the facts suggest otherwise, that they are destined to be like their hero. In contrast to normal people, hypomanics do not outgrow these childhood fantasies.* As a young man Hamilton vowed to live by the "code of Caesar." As a mature adult, he would frighten republican idealist Thomas Jefferson when he proclaimed that the dictator Julius Caesar had been "the greatest man who ever lived." Hamilton had "Julius Caesar in him," said John Adams.[19]

When Alexander was only sixteen, Cruger suddenly left the country for emergency medical treatment, leaving young Hamilton in charge of the business for six months. Hamilton took over with haughty aplomb, as he would do again in so many situations. For example, when a pack of emaciated mules arrived, Hamilton refused to send them on their way as the ship's manifest dictated. He demanded that the grizzled captain lead the starving herd out to pasture to fatten them up before they could be shipped and sold. The captain didn't appreciate taking orders from a sixteen-year-old boy, but he moved the mules. Hamilton also countermanded written instructions from Cruger's brother, the other principal partner in the firm, who was too cheap to purchase cannon for the ship's protection. Hamilton ordered the captain to "hire four guns." He fired the company attorney and hired a new one. And he freely signed Cruger's name to his correspondence.

When Cruger returned, Hamilton confidently told him everything he had done, adding that he was certain Cruger would have done the same. Cruger must have been grateful and a little amazed to find his business intact and running quite well. But once he returned, there was little room for Hamilton to advance in the two-person office, and he was demoted back to clerk. Saint Croix was too small for a teenager dreaming of glory and empires.

* Biographers agreed that, from the very beginning of his life, Hamilton felt "like a man of destiny, maybe destined to change the world" (average 4.8) and that he was "grandiose" (average 4.4).

On August 31, 1772, Saint Croix suffered a devastating hurricane. The Sunday after the disaster, Hamilton heard the Reverend Hugh Knox warn his congregation that the disaster was God's judgment upon the island: "God had spoken from the whirlwind."[20] Soon after, Hamilton published a poem in the local newspaper, eloquently echoing Knox's central theme: "Where now, O vile worm is all thy boasted fortitude? . . . What is become of thine arrogance and self-sufficiency? . . . Despise thyself and adore thy God."[21] It was humbly signed "a youth of this island." As Saint Croix's white society was a small one, Hamilton's identity as the author was certain to be discovered. As might be expected, the Reverend Hugh Knox read the poem and liked it very much. Historians have noted that the poem's religious theme was very out of character for Hamilton. However, using writing to impress powerful older men and advance his career would prove to be very much part of Hamilton's modus operandi. Hamilton knew that Knox had helped other worthy boys, considering it his "calling" to be a "patron who draws genius out of obscurity."[22] Though Knox had no money, he had influence. Trained at the College of New Jersey (now Princeton University), he was socially connected to some of the most elite American families. Hamilton indeed was a genius who was very eager to be drawn out of obscurity. Bringing himself to Knox's attention with his poem accomplished that objective. Knox convinced Cruger that as a "joint project" (i.e., a combination of Knox's friends and Cruger's money), they should send young Hamilton to America for an education. Hamilton thus managed to get the two things he wanted most: a ticket to America and a scholarship to college—just like Ned.

The Prodigy Comes to America

When Hamilton arrived in the new world, he was introduced to a network of aristocratic New Jersey families deeply involved in the American drive for independence, people such as Elias Boudinot (future president of the Continental Congress) and William Livingston (first governor of independent New Jersey). Hamilton was hardly starstruck by these eminent people. On the contrary, he announced that he had no intention of "groveling" to anyone.[23] He would ultimately join their revolution and help run it as if it were Cruger's store.

Hamilton was placed in the Elizabethtown Academy to prepare for the entrance examinations for the College of New Jersey. For a foreigner with little schooling, these exams were nearly impossible. In fact, few modern Princeton graduates would have the slightest chance of passing these tests. Applicants were expected to have mastered at least the following: common branches of English literature and composition, elocution, mathematics, and geography, plus the ability to write Latin prose and translate Virgil, Cicero, and the Greek gospels, together with a commensurate knowledge of Latin and Greek grammar.[24]

The young prodigy completed his preparations in less than a year.*

John Witherspoon, the legendary president of the college, examined Hamilton personally. Duly impressed, he warmly welcomed Hamilton into the great fortress of American Presbyterian education and breeding. One might have expected humility and gratitude from the Saint Croix waif, who longed to lay claim to his aristocratic Scottish descent. Instead, the arrogant prodigy made demands, insisting that he be able to study at his own pace as he had done at Elizabethtown. An eyewitness recalled, "Mr. Hamilton then stated he wished to enter . . . classes to which his attainments would entitle him . . . with the understanding that he should be permitted to advance from class to class with as much rapidity as his

---

* All biographers strongly agreed (average 5.0) that Hamilton was "quick-thinking." However, they did not think that he was distractible (average 1.75) or that he jumped "from idea to idea" (average 3.0). Thus, though Hamilton's ability to absorb information and generate ideas was clearly accelerated, it was combined with a laserlike focus.

exertions would enable him." [25] After consulting with the trustees, Witherspoon thoughtfully but firmly told Hamilton he'd have to take regular classes, just like all the other boys. Hamilton found Witherspoon's offer unacceptable. This was just one example of the stunning arrogance Hamilton displayed throughout his life, even early on, when he was a complete nobody.

Alexander traveled to New York City to meet with President Cooper of King's College (later Columbia University). Cooper accepted the upstart on his own terms. As Hamilton predicted, he completed the course of college study in two and a half years.

Hamilton fell in love with New York immediately. It was the first real city he had ever seen, the first place where people moved almost as fast as he did. "New York's style—intense, commercial, go-getting—reflected his vision of America." [26]

Hamilton bonded with his college roommate, Robert Troup, who would become a lifelong friend. Troup was amazed by Hamilton's "extraordinary displays" of "genius and energy of mind." [27] He also noted a peculiarity in his roommate: when walking alone he would talk to himself continuously. This became a running joke among their friends. It was almost as if his thoughts exploded with such force that they demanded motoric expression.

Patriot Leader

All his life Hamilton had wished for a war, in which a man of action could achieve glory and rise above his station. He saw immediately that the American Revolution was the opportunity he had been hoping for, and he wasted no time. After the Boston Tea Party, Hamilton traveled to Boston to meet the patriot leaders. When he returned to New York, he hurled himself into the movement for independence, determined to elbow his way to the front of its ranks, in some cases literally. Soon after his return from Boston, he happened upon a revolutionary rally in progress on the street. Unbidden, he pushed his way onto the stage and launched into a fiery patriotic address. "It is a collegian!" members of the crowd shouted in awed astonishment.[28]

Frantically, he began writing revolutionary tracts for New York newspapers, pumping out sixty thousand words in two weeks. Hamilton would write in "spasms of energy" like this throughout his life.[29] He worked at a "fiendish pace," according to Chernow, who claimed that Hamilton "produced the maximum number of words a human being can scratch out in forty-nine years."[30]

In fact, Hamilton is just one example of a more general link that has been found between hypomania and literary productivity. Kay Jamison studied a sample of elite British writers, selected because they had won Britain's most prestigious literary awards. A third of her subjects reported histories of severe mood swings and had received treatment for an affective disorder. Jamison charted the relationship between the writers' moods and their periods of intense productivity. More than 70 percent reported a decreased need for sleep, along with increased enthusiasm, energy, self-confidence, speed of thought, and euphoric mood during periods of heightened creative productivity.[31]

His best-known collegiate work was a rebuttal of a Tory minister who went by the nom de plume "A. W. Farmer." One gets a flavor of the smug prodigy's withering, facile arrogance in this introduction to *A Farmer Refuted:*

> Sir, I resume my pen in reply to the curious epistle you have been pleased to favor me with. . . . It has been a source of abundant merriment to me. The spirit that breathes throughout is so rancorous, illiberal and imperious; the argumentative part of it so puerile and fallacious; the misrepresentation of facts so palpable and flagrant; the criticisms so illiterate, trifling and absurd; the conceits so low, sterile and splenetic that I will venture to pronounce it one of the most ludicrous performances which has been exhibited to public view during all the present controversy.[32]

Hamilton's articles were attributed to revolutionary leaders John Jay and John Adams. The mistake is understandable. Hamilton employed pen names, as was common practice at the time, but described himself as one of the "patriot leaders."

In these tracts, Hamilton prophesied that America was destined to become an empire wealthier and more powerful than Britain. England had better treat us properly, he warned, because someday she would need to rely on America's might. Marius Willet, a leading New York radical, recalled, "Hamilton after these great writings became our oracle." [33] Through his writing, Hamilton became the patriot leader he had claimed to be.

When a local newspaper condemned President Cooper for his British loyalties, an angry mob of "Liberty Boys," the militant fringe of prerevolutionary New York, marched on Cooper's house. When the mob smashed through the college's front gate, Hamilton awoke to see the torch-carrying rabble. He dashed toward the presidential mansion, dragging Troup behind, pushed his way through the crowd, and hurled himself onto Cooper's front porch, placing his body between Cooper and the mob. Troup recalled that in an effort to save Cooper, Hamilton spoke "with great animation and eloquence." He did "harangue the mob on the excessive impropriety of their conduct, and the disgrace they would bring to the cause of liberty." [34] Cooper's porch became at once Hamilton's stage and bully pulpit.

Cooper could not hear Hamilton because his windows were closed. But seeing his student on the porch, he mistakenly thought that he was leading the lynch mob. Just as Hamilton was pleading for Cooper's life, Cooper raised his window and yelled to the crowd, "Don't mind what he says. He's crazy!" [35] which brought on gales of laughter. The delay allowed Cooper time to escape out the back door and onto a British ship, never again to be seen on American soil.

The Liberty Boys were impressed with Hamilton's mettle and included him in their most daring raid—an attempt to steal British cannon from the Battery in lower Manhattan. On August 23, 1775, they planned to drag these guns, weighing tons and resting on squeaky old wheels, uphill from Bowling Green to Wall Street. To add an extra degree of difficulty, these old cannon sat a few feet across the water from a massive thirty-four-gun British warship, the *Asia*.

Their only asset was the element of surprise, but the Liberty Boys made such a loud racket that their mission was not secret for long. The *Asia*'s captain paused, assuming that the hooligans would desist once they realized they had been detected. When they did not, he opened fire with all thirty-four guns. The massive explosion sent everyone fleeing, with the exception of Hamilton, who continued patiently dragging his cannon up the hill, handing his rifle to a fleeing companion for safekeeping. At the top, his friend Hercules Mulligan sheepishly admitted that he had dropped Hamilton's gun while running for cover. To Mulligan's amazement, Hamilton turned back toward the wall of exploding cannons, walked calmly down the hill, and retrieved his weapon "with as much unconcern as if the vessel were not there," reported the astonished Mulligan.[36] Hamilton had nerve. He wasn't so much brave as unafraid. As with most hypomanics, the meaning of risk simply failed to register with him emotionally.

The daring raid of the Liberty Boys would be for naught. The Provincial Congress of New York was embarrassed by this attempt to provoke the British. There was, as yet, no declared war. Local pride, however, would not allow the guns to be returned. As a compromise, they were left where they were, uselessly stranded (but also prominently displayed) in the town square, where they looked, according to one local, "as conspicuous as a herd of elephants."[37] In that light, the situation took on the comic aspect of a college prank. Hamilton aspired to be more than a Liberty Boy.

Two newly appointed generals in the inchoate Continental Army asked Hamilton to be their assistant. He refused them both. His ambition was to captain his own artillery company (the same position from which Napoleon would later rise), and he achieved his aim, breezing through the gunnery exam after a long weekend of cramming. His first day of command was a rude shock. The young collegian faced an unruly group of ruffians with no skills, no discipline, no uniforms, and a lousy fife-and-drum corps. Hamilton quickly took command. He discharged a few insubordinates, recruited better musicians, and spent the final installment of his funds from Saint Croix outfitting his men in a fashion that made them Yankee Doodle dandies indeed. An advertisement for the return of a deserter from Hamilton's company stated that he had last been seen chicly dressed in "a deep blue coat turned up with a buff, a pair of leather breeches, and a new felt hat." [38] For himself, Hamilton bought even finer duds, including a three-cornered hat, a blue swallowtail coat with shiny brass buttons, and striking white pants.* Hamilton drilled his troops mercilessly, "with indefatigable pains," as Troup recalled. He estimated that Hamilton's company "was esteemed the most beautiful model of discipline in the whole army." [39] There wasn't much competition among the ragtag ad hoc militia. Just by having uniforms they stood out—which of course was Hamilton's intention. Hypomanics are driven to call attention to themselves. They crave attention, not only for the considerable pleasure it brings them, but because one must be noticed to advance.

Then Hamilton got his childhood wish. There was a war. And in 1776, it came to him.

Washington's Boy

Washington's Continental Army flooded into New York City in the spring of 1776. Hamilton's company was engulfed and annexed by this larger force, and Hamilton came under Washington's com-

---

* All but one biographer agreed that Hamilton liked to dress "in ways that create an impression and get attention" (average 4.2).

mand. Washington's first review of the troops was on May 15. All companies mustered on a field for inspection. As Hamilton had hoped, the snap, energy, and precision of his men caught Washington's attention. He assigned Hamilton command of the guns at Fort George at the lower tip of Manhattan. Day and night, Hamilton stood next to his cannons, looking out over the water and scanning for British warships. Washington expected the British fleet to sail right toward him. Hamilton commanded the front line in the impossible defense of New York.

On August 7, 110 warships emerged out of the fog. The slow, majestic stampede of floating mammoths was terrifyingly beautiful, huge white sails puffing gracefully, wide brown bodies cutting proudly through the water, bright cannons gleaming, Union Jacks flying. More and more, they kept coming and coming until they filled the entire horizon. And they didn't fire a shot. The American militia was but a pack of flies to them. One warship had more firepower than Washington's entire army. They silently turned north and sailed unmolested up the Hudson.

Faced with this stunning display of power, the rebels could do little but watch, with the exception of Hamilton, who yelled, "Fire!" The very idea that his few guns could even scratch the most massive armada the world had ever seen was entirely irrational. They didn't land a single blow against the enemy, but four of his own men were killed when one of their own cannon blew up. The gun probably hadn't been fired since the French and Indian War.

The Continental Army began to realize with sickening horror the overwhelming size of the force it was facing. It was defending a city, surrounded by water, against the most powerful navy in the world. And unless rowboats counted, it didn't have a single ship. At first, the Continentals tried desperately to hold the American fortifications in Brooklyn Heights. Washington saved his army from total destruction only by quietly evacuating his troops in rowboats (which came in handy after all) across the East River into Manhattan one moonless night. Had he not escaped, the war would have been over on its first day. Washington learned from his mistakes and began leading his troops like the guerrilla army they were.

On Christmas night, Washington and his troops quietly crossed the Delaware River in small craft in a blinding snowstorm. Hamilton crossed with him, steadying his cannon in the icy boat. They took two thousand hungover Hessians in Trenton by surprise. General Charles Cornwallis then led a British force to Trenton on a retaliatory raid. When Cornwallis went out looking for the revolutionaries, Washington doubled back and attacked the English headquarters at the College of New Jersey in Princeton. Legend has it that Hamilton fired a cannonball that decapitated a portrait of the King of England.

After these two minor victories, Hamilton was euphoric. The "dawning of that bright day . . . broke forth with such resplendent luster," he wrote.[40] With his irrational hypomanic optimism, Hamilton seemed to believe that they had practically finished off the British. "Such is the present situation that another Trenton affair will amount to a complete victory on our part, for they are at too low an ebb to bear another stroke of that kind."[41] Such an assessment was beyond overconfident; it was absurd. The revolutionaries had embarrassed the British but done no real damage to their forces.*

After this exhilarating victory, Hamilton collapsed into "a long and dangerous illness."[42] He would periodically break down physically after superhuman exertions of energy into illness or an exhausted "funk."[43] While still recovering, in January 1777, Hamilton received what has been called The Letter: an invitation from George Washington to serve as one of his aides-de-camp. It was this relationship that made Hamilton a Founder.

Washington's team of assistants was a special breed: bright, ambitious young men eager to risk their lives for fame—a pretty

* There was general agreement among the biographers that Hamilton was often "elated" about what he thought he would achieve (average 4.6).

hypomanic lot. For example, the Marquis de Lafayette, a French nobleman descended from ten generations of soldiers, ran away from his family to fight in the Revolution. He threatened to burn his own ship when it appeared that it might be captured by the British before crossing the Atlantic. When first touching American soil, he uttered an "oath to conquer, or perish in the cause."[44] "You ask me when I first longed for glory," he wrote in his memoir. "I can recall no time when I did not love stories of glorious deeds, or have dreams of traveling the world in search of fame."[45] Young men of such ambitions made up Washington's staff.

The aides slept together every night, "like a pack of blood-hounds" on the floor, or two or three to a bed, in the homes and farmhouses that served as their temporary quarters.[46] They called themselves a "band of brothers" and found kindred spirits in one another. Though from vastly diverse backgrounds, they shared the same genetic temperament.* "This was the closest thing to a family Hamilton ever had," biographer Roger Kennedy told me.

And Washington ran his camp like a family, addressing his aides as "my boy." Washington, who never had any biological children, sublimated his paternal drives toward his "beardless boys."[47] In turn, Washington's aides worshiped him. One might think that Hamilton, the orphan, would have been eager to bask in Washington's paternal warmth. But Hamilton was deeply conflicted. Most of his fellow aides, "whose backgrounds were less troubled, responded easily to this overwhelming paternalism."[48] From a psychodynamic perspective, a good father figure was a terrifying

---

*John Laurens, Hamilton's closest friend, was another interesting bipolar Washington aide. He suffered from depression but also had energetic idealistic schemes. Laurens had the racially progressive idea of organizing slaves as soldiers, which was bold for a boy from South Carolina whose father was the president of the Continental Congress. Hamilton worked with his friend to win acceptance for the idea, but it was rejected. Laurens recklessly got himself killed by rushing back to the front and engaging in a fatal exchange of fire after the war had been declared over.

prospect for a young man who had learned to deny such longings: "He was drawn to it, but he feared it."[49] Hamilton defensively claimed that he had no need for fatherly love and said he consciously cultivated an "air of distance" in his relationship to the commander in chief.[50]

> For three years past I have felt no friendship for him and have professed none. . . . The pride of my temper would not suffer me to profess what I did not feel. Indeed when advances of this kind have been made to me on his part, they were received in a manner that showed at least I had no inclination to court them, and that I wished to stand rather upon a footing of military confidence than of private attachment.[51]

As they moved from place to place, Washington and his aides stayed in the homes of private families, often wealthy ones who had sufficient room. Evenings might be spent in competitive banter. Hamilton thrived in this atmosphere.* Meanwhile, nights offered competition of a different sort. Hamilton was notorious for being successful in bedding the ladies. His hypersexual behavior was apparent to those who knew him. Martha Washington, who witnessed some of Hamilton's conquests when staying with the general in camp, made a sly reference to them when she named a tomcat impregnating all the local females "Hamilton." The more puritanical John Adams was offended by Hamilton's unspeakable "debaucheries" and "audacious and unblushing attempts upon ladies of the highest rank and purest virtue."[52] Adams seriously wondered if Hamilton's overweening ambition was caused by "a superabundance of secretions which he could not find enough

---

* Biographers agreed that he was "charismatic" (average 4.6), "charming, witty, gregarious and good at making people laugh" (average 4.8), and interpersonally "attractive" (average 4.8).

whores to draw off."[53] Though Hamilton married Elizabeth Schuyler during the revolution, the bonds of matrimony couldn't contain his sexual appetites. As secretary of the Treasury, Hamilton would become the subject of the government's first sex scandal.*

Hamilton rose to become Washington's de facto chief of staff. One could hardly think of a more important position for a young man from nowhere, but Hamilton was frustrated. He longed to distinguish himself in battle. He had wished for a war. Here it was, and he was missing it, "chained to the desk's dead wood." Many times Hamilton implored Washington for a combat command, and every time he was turned down. The commander in chief made the judgment that he needed his talented chief aide at headquarters, even if Hamilton was jumping out of his skin itching for action.

In the Battle of Monmouth, Hamilton finally got his chance. After months of hiding from his superior enemy, Washington finally planned to attack the Redcoats. As protocol would dictate, the attack was to be led by his most senior ranking general, Charles Lee. An eccentric character, Lee said he disapproved of the entire operation and declined the command. Hamilton was delighted! Command then passed to Hamilton's camp brother, General Lafayette, who would surely include him. But even as the marquis, "in raptures with his command and burning to distinguish himself," was being congratulated, Lee reappeared to rescind his refusal, ending the celebration. Then Lee changed his mind again, and yet again. Finally, Washington "grew tired of such fickle behavior" and told Lafayette to proceed.[54] He chose Hamilton as his principal aide. "Our personal honor" is at stake, Hamilton wrote to Washington.[55]

Lafayette and Hamilton rode out together in the morning. They spent the day spying on British troops, moving men, and commu-

---

* Biographers agreed that Hamilton was "risky in his sexual behavior" (average 5.0) and was "unusually sexually active" (average 4.8).

nicating with headquarters and each other. Just as the operation began to unfold, Lafayette received a discouraging letter from Washington. Lee's "uneasiness" at having refused command was "increasing" rather than "abating."[56] Incredibly, Washington was giving Lee yet another chance to lead the attack, just as it was being launched. "Hamilton and Lafayette's personal adventure was over."[57]

But under Lee's ambivalent leadership the attack dissolved into a chaotic retreat. After his last-minute insistence on leading the attack, Lee once again reverted to his initial instincts and refused to attack on Washington's order. Washington is reputed to have sworn so hard he "shook leaves from the trees." Washington, Lafayette, and Hamilton worked together frantically to regain control and avoid a rout. When General Lee seemed to be retreating, Hamilton rode to the scene "in great heat" and confronted the general. To the contrary, Lee insisted, he would be the last man to abandon the hill he was defending. Hamilton jumped off his horse, drew his sword, and proclaimed that no one was to retreat. Neither he nor Lee would abandon that hill. "I will stay here with you, my dear General, and die with you! Let us all die rather than retreat! We will die here on this spot!"[58]

At his court-martial for his lack of aggressiveness at Monmouth, a trial Hamilton had worked to initiate, Lee described Hamilton's demeanor on the battlefield as "a frenzy of valor." Even to his friends Hamilton appeared to straddle the boundary of bold and suicidal. Fellow aide-de-camp Jack Tilghman praised Hamilton's energy and courage at Monmouth: "He was incessant in his endeavors during the whole day in reconnoitering the enemy and rallying and charging." However, he also noticed that Hamilton seemed "to court death under our doubtful circumstances."[59] Hamilton and his fellow beardless boys had a "desperate desire for great risk,"[60] wrote biographer Noemie Emery, an addiction "as lethal and compelling as a drug."[61] According to the code of

Caesar, "life was just a coin to purchase fame."* A compulsion to take risks is another classic sign of hypomania.

Four years after Hamilton joined Washington's family, a dramatic break between them occurred on February 16, 1781. The commander and his aide passed each other on the stairs at headquarters in New Windsor. "He told me he wanted to speak with me," Hamilton recounted in a letter to his father-in-law. "I answered that I would wait upon him immediately." Hamilton posted a letter and was stopped on the way back by Lafayette, with whom he conversed for a few minutes. When he returned, he found the general waiting for him at the top of the stairs. "Accosting me in an angry tone, Washington said, 'Colonel Hamilton . . . you have kept me waiting these ten minutes. I must tell you sir you treat me with disrespect.' "

Hamilton's response to this rebuke was to resign on the spot: "I am not conscious of it sir; but since you have thought it necessary to tell me so, we part." Washington's angry retort was "Very well sir. If it be your choice." [62]

Hamilton stamped downstairs, venting his rage to Lafayette, who was horrified by Hamilton's impetuous action and tried to convince him to rescind his resignation. Like most hypomanics, Hamilton often evidenced "egregious errors in judgment that left even his keenest admirers aghast." [63] Brilliant creativity and gross lapses in judgment often have shared roots in hypomania.

After cooling down for an hour, Washington did the decent, reasonable thing. He sent Hamilton a note, "assuring me of his great confidence in my abilities, my integrity, usefulness etc., and of his desire, in a candid conversation, to heal a difference which could not have happened but in a moment of passion." Washington signed his note "Sincerely and affectionately yours."

* With the exception of one biographer, all agreed that Hamilton was a "physical risk taker" (average 4.0). There was strong agreement that he was "a risk taker, in general" (average 4.8).

Washington reached out, but Hamilton would not accept the olive branch. "This resolution was not to be revoked," Hamilton told Washington by letter. He did not wish to have a private conversation, as it would be "mutually disagreeable." He would serve Washington until his other aides returned. In the meantime, he instructed, they should act toward each other as if the incident had not taken place. Hamilton graciously offered to do nothing to undermine Washington's popularity. Did the obscure young aide really believe that the nation's confidence in its hero and commander in chief would be diminished by his surly resignation? "Never did the megalomania that haunted the uncontrolled part of Hamilton's mind present itself more conspicuously."[64]

Hamilton's resignation was clearly an impulsive self-destructive act and the sign of an increasingly troubled mind. "Somewhere in the middle of 1779, Hamilton's nerves had started to give way," Emery wrote.[65] I have found that whenever historians use a phrase including any form of the word "nerve"—nervous exhaustion, attack of nerves, nervous breakdown—it is a code for a psychiatric problem. Hamilton was depressed, irritable, and agitated.* Not only was his personal desire to fight thwarted, but the revolution he was trying to manage was in permanent stall. The Continental Army was dreadfully undersupplied and undermanned and lacked the tools to win the war. He wrote from Morristown in 1780 that "unless some expedient can be instantly adopted, a dissolution of the army for want of subsistence is unavoidable."[66] Men were losing feet for lack of boots. Hamilton had treated Cruger's mules better. He quickly understood that this lack of resources was a national political problem. The weak Continental Congress had no authority—and worse, no source of revenue. It received a mere pittance in alms from state politicians, who were greedy to protect

---

* Biographers split over whether Hamilton was irritable (average 3.8) or prone to explosions (average 3.6). The two biographers who disagreed acknowledged that he was irritable and explosive at times but disagreed because this was not typical of his overall behavior.

their local power and privilege. Because the states starved the Continental Congress for funds, Washington's troops were literally starving.

Everyone's morale was low, but Hamilton's was closer to suicidal. In a letter to Laurens, he wrote, "I hate Congress—I hate the army—I hate the world—I hate myself." In an earlier letter to Laurens, he wrote that he would choose a "brilliant exit" rather than endure this intolerable situation.[67] "It was not the first time Hamilton had glancingly alluded to suicide," wrote Chernow.[68] Classically, most people think of mania and depression as two opposite states that alternate, but they often coexist simultaneously— a "mixed" mood state is one that combines depressive affect with manic or hypomanic impulsivity. Hamilton was in intolerable pain and felt he had to *do* something.* *Action* made him feel better— even if it took the form of self-destructive acting out.

The Product of Some Reading

After the break with Washington, Hamilton had no job, but this did not stop him from trying to save America. The country's root problem was its fiscal insolvency. During the war, Hamilton had been privately collecting and reading economics books. Now that he was unemployed, he put his thoughts on paper and mailed them to Robert Morris, the newly named superintendent of finance for the Continental Congress.

It was a great relief to the Continental Congress and the country that Morris, a successful Philadelphia merchant, had accepted the position. Prior to his taking office, there had not been *one* person in charge of America's fiscal affairs. Finances had been mismanaged by a committee of men, none of whom was proficient in economics or finance. Hamilton, among others, hoped that Morris's appoint-

---

* Biographers agreed that Hamilton was "restless and impatient" (average 4.4).

ment would change that and offer new life to the Revolution and the country.

Hamilton wrote in his letter to Morris that he did not "pretend to be an able financier." [69] The ideas he was sending Morris were "the product of some reading on the subject of commerce and finance" and "occasional reflection on our particular situation." [70] The many-thousand-word report was filled with detailed economic statistics, extensive quotations, and astoundingly innovative ideas.

The money issued by Congress was "no more a currency than the ragged end of a kite," Hamilton complained. The notes were "dead beyond resuscitation." [71] This Morris already knew. Protest marchers in Philadelphia were wearing Continental currency in their hats and even gluing it to their dogs to protest its complete devaluation.

Using England as a model, Hamilton suggested the creation of a National Bank of the United States that could lend money to the government to make war, as the Bank of England did. This bank could also issue a solid currency backed by solid capital and, equally important, solid capitalists. Hamilton proposed that shares in the bank be sold to wealthy private investors, who would then have a personal incentive to see the bank succeed. "The safest reliance of every government, is on men's interests. . . . The only plan that can preserve the currency is one that will make it the *immediate* interest of the moneyed men to cooperate in its support." [72]

Most creative of all, Hamilton came up with a remarkable scheme to make an asset out of America's biggest liability. Each of the individual colonies and the Continental Congress were drowning in millions of dollars' worth of debt. Hamilton proposed that they consolidate these many debts, have the Continental Congress assume them all—and make it a *national* debt. "A national debt, if it is not excessive, will be to us a national blessing," Hamilton declared. Unlike other Founders, such as Jefferson, Hamilton had a vision of one powerful nation, not the loose federation of states that then existed. A federal debt would require federal taxation and finally guarantee a stream of income for the United States of America. The debt could become "powerful cement to our union." [73]

Morris sincerely thanked Hamilton for his "performance" and for "the good intentions and pain you have taken," but he was called to the more pressing practical problem of juggling Congress's bills.[74] He didn't have time to contemplate experimental theories about national debt. Morris pled inexperience: "My office is new and I am young in the execution of it." Nonetheless, he did wish to talk with this prodigy further: "Communications from men of genius and abilities will always be acceptable." [75]

Charge!

After submitting his plan, there wasn't much more Hamilton could do for the American economy. He desperately wanted to get back into the war. There was just one obstacle in his way: George Washington—the commander in chief he had so peevishly offended—made all combat assignments. Hamilton beseeched Washington by letter to give him a combat command. Washington sent back a refusal that same day, offering a reasonable explanation: that such an action would jump Hamilton ahead of field officers with seniority. Washington took pains to point out that he had done this once before; it had created hard feelings, and he had resolved not to violate this protocol again. Washington assured Hamilton that there was no vindictiveness in his decision: "My principal concern arises from an apprehension that you will impute my refusal . . . to other motives than those I have expressed, but I beg you to be assured I am only influenced by the reasons I have mentioned." [76] Hamilton sent back a churlish reply, countering Washington's arguments. Washington *had* done it before, so why not for him? And if he lacked seniority in the field, that was Washington's fault. He had repeatedly denied Hamilton's requests for combat duty.

Having begun his charge, Hamilton would not be turned back. On July 8, 1781, Hamilton simply arrived at Washington's headquarters. He had a letter delivered to Washington's tent tendering his resignation from the army. "I wrote the General a letter and enclosed my commission." [77] Washington knew that this dramatic gesture was a Hamilton tantrum aimed at manipulating him. Despite this, Washington still felt a residue of affection and gratitude toward Hamilton, as did his fellow aides, who missed him terribly. And Washington may have felt a trace of guilt, too, as he had impeded his chief of staff's most ardent ambition for combat. Washington "could not allow Hamilton to stamp away from military life, blaming ingratitude," without "hurting his own conscience." [78]

Washington said yes.

Washington "pressed me to retain my commission, with an assurance that he will endeavor by all means to give me a command," Hamilton wrote to his wife, adding that he felt honor bound to rise above personal feelings and accept the assignment—as if he had not demanded it.

As fate would have it, Hamilton's histrionic personal moment could not have come at a more dramatic historic moment. The Continental Army was about to fight the decisive battle of the war at Yorktown.

Hamilton's performance during the Battle of Yorktown illustrates what makes a Washington different from a Hamilton in a combat situation. Bipolar military leaders take inspired risks that seem brilliant in retrospect—if they work. They fire up their troops with their charisma and fearless aggression. In contrast, a general like Washington relies on his judgment and wisdom and is trusted for his rock-steady reliability. In the best wars, these two types of generals work together, and the bipolar is *not* in charge. For example, during World War II, George Patton was America's bipolar general. His nonbipolar superiors were army buddy Dwight Eisenhower and Omar Bradley.* During the Revolution, fortunately for America, George Washington ran the army. But in the Battle of Yorktown, his charging young aide, Alexander Hamilton, was set free to attack at last. The way he did so helps illustrate how he and Washington fundamentally differed in their style of military leadership.

The British general Cornwallis was holed up inside the fortified walls of Yorktown with a large part of the British army. The first stage of the American offensive had been to lay siege. French engineers condescendingly instructed the Americans in the fine points of siege warfare, which began with digging trenches. Heavy guns buried in the earth could shoot up with accuracy, while enemy gunners on the fortifications practically had to hit a hole in one to land a ball in a trench.

The French dug one trench and the Americans the other. When the time came for the American trench to be occupied, Hamilton's light infantry company was given the honor of leading the procession. With flags flying and drums beating, they ceremoniously

---

* One could have guessed how Patton would lead an army of tanks by watching how he fought with a saber in the 1912 Olympics. A one-man attack machine with extraordinary energy, Patton virtually never used a defensive stroke. "Patton's offensive-mindedness with the sword was a harbinger of his future generalship on the battlefield," wrote biographer Carlo D'Este. "Throughout his career disdain for defense was a Patton trademark. To attack was to succeed, to defend was to invite defeat." "My attack will go," Patton asserted in defiance when ordered to stop fighting.

Patton claimed to have conscious memories of all the great historic military battles from experiences garnered during his past lives. He had the grandiose notion that he was an eternal superwarrior destined to fight in all the great wars of history. In war he felt energized, alive, indefatigable. Between World Wars he was depressed to the point of incapacitation.

In World War II, we were very lucky to have Patton. The Germans thought he was our best general. But we were equally lucky to have Eisenhower over him. After the war, Patton wanted to invade Russia, and Eisenhower wisely fired him. Only two men have been crazy enough to invade Russia, and both were full-blown manic-depressives: Hitler and Napoleon (see D. Jablow Hershman and Julian Lieb, *A Brotherhood of Tyrants: Manic-Depression and Absolute Power*). Unfortunately, neither of them answered to a higher rational authority.

marched into the trench under heavy cannon fire and disappeared from view. Hamilton was unhappy that "his advance was invisible to the thousands of watchers in all three armies."[79] But, of course, the purpose of first digging a trench and then occupying it is to be invisible.

It was at this moment that Hamilton gave an "extraordinary order," as Captain James Duncan called it. Hamilton ordered his men to climb out of the trench and onto the open ground, where they were nakedly exposed to the British cannons. Lining them up as if on a parade ground, he put them through drill of arms. The action was so bizarre that the enemy was momentarily dumbfounded. Instead of shooting them to pieces, the British stopped firing altogether. "Although the enemy had been firing a little before, they did not now give us a single shot. I suppose, their astonishment at our conduct must have prevented them, for I can assign no other reason," wrote Captain Duncan. In response to what must have been an impulsive inspiration, Hamilton created a moment of defiantly brave drama. But it was reckless. That he risked the lives of his young soldiers for his little display shows a complete loss of judgment. Captain Duncan shook his head: "Although I esteem him one of the first officers in the American army, I must beg in this instance to think that he wantonly exposed the lives of his men."[80] Clearly, this is not something Washington would have done.

The enemy's fortifications were battered by the trench cannons for a week. Two powerful redoubts dug deeply into the earth were the most forward British position. When the time came to storm those redoubts and transform the siege into an attack, those chosen to lead the daring charge would have the highest honor. Needless to say, Hamilton wanted it more than life itself.

Military etiquette dictated that one redoubt be attacked by the French and the other by the Americans. The American leader, to be chosen by Hamilton's longtime friend General Lafayette, came down to a choice between two commanders in Lafayette's light infantry: Hamilton and Jean-Joseph Sourbader de Gimat. Gimat was a fellow Frenchman who had joined the American army with Lafayette. Lafayette chose the more battle-hardened Gimat, reasoning that he had more experience. Hamilton went ballistic, storming into Lafayette's tent, shouting that he had more seniority than Gimat, and adding that technically he was "officer of the day." Lafayette "excused himself by saying the arrangements had been sanctioned by the commander-in-chief."[81]

Hamilton wrote a "spirited and manly letter" to Washington. And when that didn't work, he charged into *his* tent. Hamilton was lucky once again, as his crisis of personal honor aligned in this instance with American honor. It had escaped no one's attention that both of the officers chosen to lead the charge were French. This time, Washington was only too happy to give Hamilton the command he demanded. When Hamilton emerged from Washington's tent, he was ecstatic. He embraced his friend and assistant, Major Nicholas Fish, almost jumping into his arms and shouting "We have it! We have it!"[82]

The plan for the assault was simple. Under the cover of night, on a secret signal—five bursts of cannon fire—the French and American soldiers were to sneak up on the redoubts. Because those were surrounded by wooden barbed wire, pioneers with axes were to go ahead of the soldiers to clear the path.

Hamilton was so overeager that when he looked up in the night sky and saw Jupiter and Venus, he thought it was the signal and almost jumped. When the real signal came at last, Hamilton asked his men for a few brave volunteers. Twenty men stepped forward. At that, Hamilton took off at a mad run, sprinting toward the enemy without looking back to see if anyone was behind him. He ran so fast that he reached the walls before a single shot was fired— far ahead of the pioneers with their heavy axes. Hamilton and his men squeezed through the sharp thicket pell-mell in whatever manner they could. "The ardor of the troops" would not allow them to wait, Hamilton later explained. That ardor was no doubt a response to the infectious enthusiasm of their fearless leader. This ability to infect others with enthusiasm is an essential component in charismatic leadership.

In contrast, when the French troops reached their redoubt, they waited, as ordered, for the pioneers. While they stood around, exposed to close-range enemy fire, they suffered heavy casualties. The French followed procedure, while the Americans hurtled ahead, improvising as they went. Paradoxically, breaking the rules and recklessly surging forward at top speed was the safest course.

The outlying British and Hessian garrison of about sixty men surrendered to Hamilton quickly. "From the firing of the first shot by the enemy to their surrender was less than ten minutes," wrote Hamilton.[83] Meanwhile, the French were still mired in their assault, and the Americans were only too happy to graciously offer their assistance.[84]

Cornwallis surrendered at Yorktown, and the war was essentially over. Hamilton put Major Fish in command of his battalion and rode triumphantly home to his family. He rode at such a fast pace that he exhausted his horse and had to switch it for another. Once home, he collapsed and was very sick for two months.

Hamilton was furious that Congress offered him no formal recognition for what he considered his great heroism at Yorktown, though it was, after all, only one battle in a long war. His bravery, however, had not escaped the attention of the one man who mattered. Washington praised Hamilton's "intrepidity, coolness and firmness of action."[85] Hamilton won Washington's respect at Yorktown, and "the commander-in-chief and the former aide were free to reapproach each other on a more equal footing."[86] Hamilton was Washington's boy no longer. He was a gentleman of recognized honor and valor, just as he had always dreamed of being.

CONSTITUTIONAL WARRIOR

Losing It in Philadelphia

The war was over. America was no longer a colony, but it was not yet a country. It is precisely at this point that most revolutions stumble, and it was by no means inevitable that ours would succeed. Washington saw disaster unfolding before his eyes. In 1786, he wrote to Madison, "No morn ever dawned more favorably than ours did, and no day was ever more clouded than the present."[87] America continued to stumble along under the Articles of Confederation, a loose constitution of sorts drafted hastily in 1777. It had numerous flaws: most notably, it provided no way to fund the federal government with anything but voluntary contributions from the states. In recent years, even those had dried up. By 1787, only two or three states paid anything at all. Most state assemblies wouldn't even discuss financial requests from Congress. It was too politically unpopular while the country was in an economic depression. Hamilton said, "Things are continually growing worse: Having long kept Congress on short rations, the states seem about to deny it sustenance altogether."[88] Washington had characterized the country as limping along under the Articles of Confederation, "always moving upon crutches and tottering at every step."[89] By 1787, it was not merely tottering but falling down the stairs.

One man who was happy to give it a shove was George Clinton, governor of Hamilton's home state of New York. Clinton was the archetype of the party boss. "The old Irishman" ran New York like a personal fiefdom, dispensing thousands of patronage jobs to his extended family and supporters. He had no desire to surrender any power to a federal government. Hamilton was determined to stop Clinton from sabotaging the country.

Twice, Congress had tried to obtain authorization to open a stream of federal revenue—a 5 percent tariff on all imports, called an impost. All thirteen states needed to agree. Rhode Island had blocked the impost bill in 1781. In 1783, the one spoiler to derail the impost was Clinton's New York. Now, in 1786, Congress was making a third, desperate attempt. Twelve of the thirteen states had approved it, and New York was once again the sole holdout.

In January 1787, now a New York assemblyman, Hamilton stood on the floor of the assembly. He made an impassioned brilliant speech lasting several hours in support of the impost that "left him doubled up in pain and exhaustion."[90] Though it must have been a moving scene, the Clintonians were unmoved, literally. No one bothered to rise from his chair to refute Hamilton. They didn't have to. A voice vote was called—as if Hamilton hadn't even spoken—and the impost was killed.

New York's defeat of the impost seemed to be the "death knell to the confederation."[91] Quite simply, the federal government could no longer function. An incensed Henry Knox, then secretary of war, exclaimed, "Every liberal good man is wishing New York in Hell!"[92]

Ironically, it was New York's defeat of the impost that created the utter desperation in 1787 that was necessary to generate momentum for a Constitutional Convention. The Articles of Confederation were now broken beyond repair. America needed a new constitution, or it would fail.

In 1786, Hamilton and James Madison had issued a formal call for a Constitutional Convention at a sparsely attended planning meeting in Annapolis. Madison had been taken aback when Hamilton pulled a draft constitution out of his pocket dated 1784. Hamilton had been planning this for a long time. As early as 1780, when he was an aide-de-camp, he had written to lawmakers, urging them to form a new government. Historians credit Hamilton with being the first American to call for a Constitutional Convention. Among all the Founders, Hamilton had the most radical and unswerving vision of a strong federal government at the head of a colossal, vigorous nation. Just as he dreamed of glory and power, he wished nothing less for America. He had not been born a Virginian or a New Yorker and did not feel his primary loyalty as being to a state but rather to a nation.

The Constitutional Convention of 1787 should have been one of Alexander Hamilton's finest hours. As Emery wrote:

> The Constitutional Convention was Hamilton's child. No one had wanted it more than he did, or had fought for it so long. It was his hope for the transformation of his country from its state of disgrace and impotence into the great and mighty nation of his dreams.[93]

None of his biographers can fully explain what happened to Hamilton at the Constitutional Convention in Philadelphia. More than one has suggested that he was in a disordered mental state of some kind. "It's like he was on something," Kennedy told me. Emery wrote that Hamilton was "restless and depressed" during the Convention, which suggests that Hamilton was once again in a mixed state: hypomanic and depressed at the same time. It was at these moments that he was most apt to do something self-destructive. The reason for his despair was much the same as it had been during the Revolution: he was watching America self-destruct and, despite his heroic efforts, felt helpless to do anything about it.

Governor Clinton had to appoint Hamilton as a delegate to the Constitutional Convention, as it was widely known that Hamilton was the New Yorker most qualified to go. But Clinton outsmarted Hamilton and his allies by sending him to the Convention as one member of a three-man delegation. Under the rules adopted by the Convention, the states voted as a unit, and within his own delegation Hamilton was outvoted at every turn. Hamilton, a man of action, "was forced to watch in silence as the New York vote went for measures he despised."[94] Robert Yates and John Lansing, the two Clinton delegates, delighted in mocking Hamilton as they obstructed his plans for America.

To make matters worse, the national delegates were choosing

between two inadequate plans: the "Virginia plan," drafted by Madison, and the "New Jersey plan," which was little better than the Articles of Confederation. The stronger Virginia plan was missing a very necessary ingredient: an executive branch with any significance. After defeating the king of England, these politicians were so worried about potential dictators that they were almost paranoid. The Virginia plan proposed that one—or, even worse, possibly three—chief executives be elected by Congress for a one-year term.

Hamilton had hoped that Washington, president of the Convention, would back him in his nationalist proposals. But Washington "confined his participation to rulings and to formal votes." Knowing that he would be the first president, Washington was paralyzed by an "agony of self-consciousness" for fear of "seeming to vote himself more power."[95] Thus, Washington and Hamilton were unable to function as a team, despite the fact that they were on the same side of the battle and sitting only a few feet apart. Without Washington's modulating influence, Hamilton was prone to make errors in judgment. "Hamilton in his political career was seldom able to function effectively without Washington as a guide and a reference. That guidance and restraint were missing here."[96]

For the first three weeks, Hamilton said little on the floor of the Convention, which was odd in itself.[97] Though he was silent, his mind was racing. In his notes he often couldn't finish a sentence without starting a second and then a third—evidence that a flight of ideas strained his ability to think clearly.[98] Hamilton felt "impatient and restless."[99] He had to *do* something.

He impulsively decided on a "bold stroke": he would present the Convention with a "solid plan." The heat was stifling that day, but Hamilton spoke for an astounding six-hour stretch without a break, by far the longest speech at the Convention.* He proposed

* Biographers generally agreed that Hamilton talked "a lot" (average 5.0), talked "fast" (average 4.5), and tended to "aggressively dominate conversations" (average 4.4), though two said they didn't know. "It's not as if we have him on tape," one told me.

ideas that he admitted were "radical." More than any other delegate, Hamilton had a vision of an "energetic" federal government.
In his speech he proposed that the president and senators be
elected for life. In his notes he wrote, "ought to be hereditary," but
fortunately he had the presence of mind to omit that comment.[100]
He lavishly praised the British system of constitutional monarchy
as "the best in the world."[101] And he hinted at abolishing all state
power. "If the states were extinguished," he pronounced, it would
be no loss. In one speech he managed to sound every possible
alarm. Hamilton's close friend Gouverneur Morris described the
speech as an "indiscretion" that "subjected him to censure."[102]
The speech would indeed "plague him for the rest of his life."[103]
His enemies branded Hamilton a "monarchist."[104]

There was concern that Hamilton had damaged not just himself
but the cause. "That speech was full of what we would call today
killer sound bites for the opposition," Emery told me. Immediately
after Hamilton spoke, Madison and the other nationalists jumped
up to reassure the Convention that Hamilton did not speak for
them. Hamilton had become a minority of one.

Hamilton then abruptly left the Convention "with no explanation beyond some oblique note to Washington."[105] While some
of the most important decisions in our history were being made
in Philadelphia, Hamilton was attending to comparatively triv-
ial legal work in New York. It wasn't like Hamilton to leave the
field in the middle of battle. Clearly, he was not his normal self.
As the meeting in Philadelphia began to look doomed, Washington missed his charging aide-de-camp. On July 10, Washington
wrote to Hamilton, "I am sorry you went away. I wish you were
back."[106]

In the end, Washington's strategy of dignified silence triumphed.
The Convention awarded the president the power he enjoys to this
day, because, when imagining a president, they looked across the
room and saw George Washington. One delegate wrote that America would never have had an executive branch "had not the mem-

bers cast their eyes towards General Washington as President; and shaped their ideas of the powers to be given to a president, by their opinion of his virtue." [107]

Hamilton returned to Philadelphia briefly to sign the completed Constitution, even though the finished product did not meet his specifications. "No man's ideas were more remote from the plan than mine," [108] he declared contemptuously. It was, he said, merely "better than nothing." [109] But if the country failed to ratify the Constitution, there would be no America. As Gouverneur Morris put it, the only decision left was: "Shall there be a national government or not?" [110] The choice was between "anarchy and convulsion on the one hand, and the chance of good" on the other, wrote Hamilton.[111]

Hamilton's mind cleared. He could see the redoubt he had to storm, and it was time to charge.

Cranking Out *The Federalist Papers*

Hamilton, Madison, and John Jay combined forces to sell the Constitution to the public and, more important, to the ratifying conventions convening in each state. Jay fell ill after writing only a few letters. With one comrade fallen in battle, it was left to Madison and Hamilton to pick up the flag and continue. The result of their efforts, *The Federalist,* is regarded as one of the jewels of American political thought. *The Federalist Papers,* as they are now known, were not the bound volume of august political theory we find today. They were op-eds printed in the newspapers of every state and read by serious citizens across the country. In a new frenzy of hypomanic activity, Hamilton wrote fifty-one of the eighty-five letters, under deadline, often penning text as the type was being set.* Originally, the letters were to be published twice a week.

---

* Biographers agreed that Hamilton was "filled with an unusually high degree of energy" (average 4.8), and that he was "unusually active" (average 4.4).

Hamilton vowed to double the pace. "Let any anti-Federalist try to match that output. None did, but the effort nearly killed him." [112]

Hamilton presented two starkly contrasting possible American futures: together we could become a wealthy and powerful nation; or, as a loose confederation of states, we would war among ourselves, as European states had done for centuries. And those same predatory European nations would exploit this disunity to divide and conquer America.

Hamilton and Madison's words were in the minds of the delegates at each of the thirteen constitutional ratifying conventions. The hardest to convince would be the delegates of New York.

Fighting the Battle of Poughkeepsie

George Clinton organized a nationwide campaign to defeat the proposed federal government. Without New York, he swore, there would be no Constitution. The New York State constitutional ratifying convention of 1788 in Poughkeepsie lies among history's many obscure moments, but it was one of Hamilton's best and one of the nation's most crucial. Hamilton stood like David before the Goliath of Governor Clinton and his machine. Anti-Constitution forces went into the New York ratifying convention with a two-to-one majority. Hamilton's slingshot was the power of his voice. Just as he had once exhorted General Lee to do on that hill during the Battle of Monmouth, Hamilton would stand on the Constitution in Poughkeepsie, defending it to his last breath. This is a vivid demonstration of the power of hypomanic pressured speech. Day after day, Hamilton barraged the members of the ratifying convention with his verbal assault.

Hamilton spoke with passion, elegant reasoning, and haughty eloquence, appealing to the hearts, minds, and patriotism of his fellow delegates. He speechified the better part of every day for *six weeks*. In addition, at night, he held meetings with and wrote speeches for the other pro-Constitution delegates. Meanwhile, the Clinton machine cranked out amendments to the Constitution. Clinton presumed that these amendments would be rejected, allowing New York to abort the union without being directly to blame for its premature death. Hamilton kept talking and Clinton mocked him: Was Hamilton writing a new edition of *The Federalist*? he asked. Hamilton's jeremiad went on unabated—a one-man filibuster, even if his speech did nothing to stop the delegates from voting out one Clinton amendment after another to destroy the union.

Madison sent word to the New York delegates that this was an up-or-down vote—no amendments would be considered. He would vote no, Clinton declared defiantly. "The advocates of the Constitution are determined to force us into a rejection. . . . If convulsions and civil war are the consequence, I will go with my party." [113]

Hamilton redoubled his attack and made it personal. Everyone knew that Clinton preferred a weak federal government to better preserve his own powers of patronage. [114] In the beginning of the first Federalist paper, Hamilton had written that the greatest obstacle to the Constitution would be "the obvious interests of a certain class of men in every State who resist all changes which may hazard a diminution of the power, emolument and the consequences of office they hold under the State association." [115] In Poughkeepsie, Hamilton declared that "corruption's poison administered to a single man, may render the efforts of the majority totally vain," leaving no doubt who that poisonously corrupt man was. [116]

Then the news came that Virginia, the last major holdout state, had ratified. Madison had led that battle with Jefferson and Washington at his side. Then New Hampshire ratified, achieving the necessary quorum of nine states to form the United States of America. There was no stopping America now. Was New York in or out? Hamilton threatened that some in New York City would attempt to secede from the state to join the Union if the convention failed to act. The tide was turned. A handful of Clinton delegates crossed over, publicly apologizing to their visibly enraged boss and patron. As they explained in deeply emotional speeches, they could not live with their conscience any other way. Hamilton's words had pierced enough stony hearts to bring New York into the Union. Ratification passed 30 to 27 in Poughkeepsie.

In New York City on July 27, there was a parade celebrating the adoption of the Constitution. Hamilton was finally "the hero of the day." [117] The most memorable float was a wooden battleship named the *Alexander Hamilton,* a replica in every detail of a real seafaring vessel. Adorning the bow was a statue of Hamilton holding the Constitution in his right hand and the Articles of Confederation in his left. Fame was depicted as a woman, crowning Hamilton with a laurel wreath while blasting her trumpet. One witness wrote that the S.S. *Alexander Hamilton* "made a fine appearance sailing with flowing sheets and full sails down Broadway, the canvass waves dashing against her sides." [118]

In the parade a man dressed as a farmer drove a plow drawn by six oxen. It was Nicholas Cruger, Hamilton's old boss from his boyhood in Saint Croix. The clerk he had sent to America for an education—just sixteen years ago—had led the charge to create a nation. What must Cruger have been thinking that day?

The bastard did all right.

THE HEIGHT OF POWER:
FIRST SECRETARY OF THE TREASURY

In 1789, Washington rode to New York City to begin his presidency. En route, he stopped at the Philadelphia home of Robert Morris on an important mission. The top priority on Washington's to-do list was to persuade Morris to join his cabinet as the first secretary of the Treasury. Washington told him, "The treasury, Morris, will of course be your berth," assuring him that "no one could challenge his worthiness." Morris respectfully but firmly declined. He wanted to make money in the private sector (ironically, he would make terrible investments and die broke). But Morris said he knew whom Washington should appoint: "My dear General, you will be no loser for my declining the secretaryship of the treasury, for I can recommend you a far cleverer fellow than I am for your ministry of finance, in the person of your former aide-de-camp, Colonel Hamilton." [119] Washington was stunned. During the time Hamilton had worked for him, Washington had known nothing of Hamilton's private economic studies, nor was he aware of the proposal Hamilton had sent to Morris. Washington's stepson recalled, "The President was amazed and continued, 'I always knew Colonel Hamilton to be a man of superior talents, but never supposed he had any knowledge of finance.' " To which Robert Morris replied, "He knows everything, Sir; to a mind like his nothing is amiss." [120] Hamilton was the first cabinet member chosen for Washington's administration.

The finances of early America were truly desperate. When Washington began his first term, America was in a "state of utter fiscal chaos." [121] Here is a partial list of leading economic indicators to consider: (1) The government was bankrupt and had no source of revenue. (2) Both the federal government and the state governments were defaulting on the massive debts incurred to win the Revolution, driving American credit down. (3) There was no viable currency. The $200 million in paper money the Continental Congress had printed was worthless. "Not worth a Continental" had become a popular expression. (4) Although the economy had been on the upswing since the Constitution had been adopted in 1787, it had a long way to go. The country was just recovering from a depression.

Alexander Hamilton solved all of these problems by the time he left office in 1795. For good reason, *New York Times* economics columnist Paul Krugman once praised President John F. Kennedy's council of economic advisers by saying that "they were the greatest collection of economic minds to sit in one room since Alexander Hamilton pondered alone."

Establishing America's Credit

Much was accomplished through the scheme for a national debt that Hamilton had tried to explain to Robert Morris by letter during the Revolution. Immediately upon taking office, Hamilton threw himself into a fury, producing his forty-thousand-word *Report on Public Credit* in a three-month "surge of desperate speed." [122] As always, "his capacity for hard work was almost superhuman." [123]

Hamilton could not endure watching America become a shameful bankrupt, as his father had been. He moved quickly to prop up the nation's plummeting credit. All the states had war debts, but few had ideas about how to repay them. The federal government had no means to repay the $67 million the Continental Congress had borrowed from French and Dutch bankers. Thousands of revolutionary soldiers sent home with government IOUs in lieu of pay weren't going to get paid anytime soon either, and some of the veterans' protests were becoming violent. The government even had a lottery to raise money and then didn't pay the winner.

Hamilton's solution was that the federal government should assume *all* these debts and consolidate them into one large national debt. The total was too massive to be paid in one lump sum. Rather, Hamilton proposed that the restructured debt be serviced with monthly payments. The reliability of those payments would establish America's credit, just as his mother's regular payment to Nicholas Cruger had kept her in business. Today, the world trusts U.S. Treasury bonds more than any other financial instrument short of cash itself. In more than two hundred years, the U.S. government hasn't missed a payment. And just as Hamilton envisioned, that has guaranteed America's credit.

Well-publicized rumors of Hamilton's plan for the assumption of debts sparked "America's first bull market." Government debt instruments had become almost worthless, selling for 10 cents on the dollar. A quick 900 percent profit would be realized if they were redeemed at full value by the federal government. Those in the best position to cash in on this boom were those in government, who knew what was coming. Northern congressmen became big buyers of government securities. Hamilton was delighted, as he craved their votes for the assumption plan. His master plan to empower America had always been to align the interests of the wealthy with those of the nation. John Adams should have listened to his wife, Abigail, when she begged him to invest in government bonds (he bought land instead). If he had, their net worth would have been substantially higher. Large European investment houses were also buying up American debt, typically working through American partners who were feeding them inside government information. Hamilton couldn't have been happier to see such foreign investment in the United States. Finally, he encouraged his New York friends to invest. Not surprisingly, Hamilton became "the hero of the New York business community." [124]

Hamilton was shocked to find his brilliant plan stalled in Congress, and even more so when he learned who was stalling it: his old friend James Madison. Madison had been one of the few people Hamilton had trusted enough to show a draft of his report. His betrayal came as a surprise.* During Washington's administration, a Virginia power bloc, led by Thomas Jefferson, coalesced into the Republican Party, which would dominate early American politics. Madison had become Jefferson's able lieutenant. For Virginia gentry, "Land, not fluid measures of capital, was their ultimate measure of wealth. Investment bankers and speculators, as they saw it,

---

* Biographers split over whether Hamilton was "suspicious" (average 4.0). The one biographer who disagreed said, "Maybe he wasn't suspicious enough," given the power and determination of his enemies.

made no productive contribution to society." [125] Madison was disgusted that speculation in government debt notes had become "the sole domestic subject of conversation" and found it particularly repulsive that unsuspecting Revolutionary War veterans were being induced to sell their government IOUs at a steep discount. [126] Jefferson would later write that those "infected with the mania" of "licentious commerce and gambling speculation" should be "excluded from our territory, as we do persons infected with disease." [127] The Virginians also saw that Hamilton's plan would strengthen federal power, something they were extremely opposed to. Although both Madison and Jefferson had fought for the Constitution, once it was enacted, they regressed to defending their regional interests.

Hamilton was fortunate in his timing. He had jumped off the starting block with his report on public credit even before Jefferson had returned from France to take his position as secretary of state. Hamilton immediately asked for Jefferson's help in mediating the conflict with Madison, before Jefferson had time to give the matter much thought. In this brief honeymoon period, everyone in Washington's cabinet hoped to be able to work together. To settle this conflict quickly, Jefferson invited Hamilton and Madison to his home for what Joseph Ellis has dubbed "The Dinner." A deal emerged: If Hamilton would throw his support behind the Potomac area as the home of the new nation's capital, Madison would desist from actively obstructing Hamilton's economic plan. Locating the capital there would be good for Virginians. Perhaps equally important, it would be good for Madison, who had joined Henry Lee in a "grandiose speculation to acquire lands on the falls of the Potomac." [128] It is probably no coincidence that the four congressmen who agreed to switch their votes in favor of Hamilton's financial plan all hailed from districts bordering on the soon-to-be-booming Potomac.

This would be the last thing Thomas Jefferson would ever do to help Alexander Hamilton. Jefferson soon came to believe that Hamilton was "something of a demon," Hamilton biographer

Thomas Fleming told me. In Jefferson's mind, Hamilton's efforts to build a strong central government looked like a counterrevolutionary plot to bring back monarchy. His efforts to hasten America's commercial and industrial development signaled the death of Jefferson's rural ideal. "For Jefferson and his followers, wedded to their vision of an agrarian Eden, Hamilton was the American Mephistopheles, the proponent of such devilish contrivances as banks, factories, and stock exchanges." [129]

Jefferson's campaign to destroy Hamilton began early in Washington's first term. Too well mannered and clever to attack directly, he worked secretly through minions. "He was a very, very devious man," said Fleming. Jefferson hired Madison's College of New Jersey classmate Philip Freneau, putting him on the State Department's payroll as a "translator." His real mission was to publish a newspaper to malign Hamilton personally and discredit his policies. Defending his honor and his mission always gave Hamilton a new surge of energy. He slashed back, publishing numerous letters and newspaper articles refuting the Freneau attacks. Jefferson complained to Madison that Hamilton was single-handedly outpublishing their whole organization. "He is a host unto himself," replied Madison in defense.

In another scheme to get Hamilton, Jefferson worked secretly through Virginia congressman William Branch Giles. Jefferson saw to it that a nine-point report accusing Hamilton of corruption was submitted to Congress. But Hamilton parried that attack too. "Working feverishly through two days of all-night sessions, Hamilton composed a defense and was acquitted." [130] The whirling dervish spun out of their trap.*

In 1792, the Republicans finally struck pay dirt when they caught Hamilton in an adulterous affair with a twenty-three-year-old

---

* Three of the biographers agreed that Hamilton often worked "on little sleep" (average 4.6) and that he rose early, full of energy, even after working late (average 5.0). Two felt there was insufficient information about his sleep habits.

woman named Maria Reynolds. Her husband had blackmailed Hamilton for $1,000 to keep the affair quiet. When later arrested on other charges, Mr. Reynolds offered to exchange false damning information against Hamilton for leniency. He claimed that Hamilton had conspired with him to speculate in government securities. James Monroe, along with two other Republican congressmen, confronted Hamilton with the charges. Hamilton confessed to the affair, believing that as gentlemen they would keep it secret, but offered convincing evidence that he hadn't been involved in any impropriety outside his personal life.* When the affair was made public, Hamilton came close to demanding a duel with Monroe, who he believed had leaked the secret. Monroe had. He told Jefferson, who secretly paid yellow journalist James Callender to publicize the scandal, along with the unsubstantiated accusations of corruption. Hamilton counterpunched again. Against the strenuous advice of his friends, Hamilton published a tract freely admitting to the improper sexual relationship but denying the charge of corruption. The pamphlet became a best-seller. Hamilton's personal reputation was slightly tarnished, but suspicions of official misconduct were dropped.

Bancomania

The second stage of Hamilton's economic plan was the creation of a national bank. The bank would print paper currency, providing society with the liquid capital needed for virtually every commercial transaction. Currency would also facilitate the collection of taxes by the Treasury. There was great suspicion of paper money at that time, and some farmers vowed to boycott it. The bank could also lend the government money in emergencies such as war. It would regulate the national banking system. And, as Hamilton had

---

* Hamilton was much more greedy for fame than money. Biographers split on whether he was a "financial risk taker" (average 4.2) who overspent (average 3.8).

indicated in the plan he had mailed to Morris, it would issue shares of stock.

Compared to the assumption of state debts, the bank sailed through Congress, but the vote followed North-South lines. Nineteen of the twenty "no" votes were southern states. Jefferson, Madison, and Attorney General Edmund Randolph—all Virginians—urged their fellow Virginian, President Washington, to veto the bill on the grounds that it was unconstitutional. They pointed out that nowhere in the Constitution did it explicitly mention the authority to create a bank. The notion that the federal government was prohibited from doing anything not explicitly mentioned in the Constitution was such a rigidly strict interpretation that it would not only have killed the bank but destroyed the federal government's ability to govern.

To Hamilton's alarm, Washington seemed to be swayed by these absurd arguments. He told Hamilton he was leaning toward vetoing the bank bill and even asked Madison to draft the text of the veto. Hamilton was dumbfounded. "He had never dreamed of Washington's doubting." [131] Hamilton threw himself into writing-frenzy mode to compose a response. He stayed up all night on February 22, 1791, and had the document on Washington's desk the next day. The ability to work on little sleep is one of the more concrete diagnostic criteria for hypomania. Though we know little of Hamilton's sleep habits generally, he was always able to forgo sleep when necessary. Hamilton's response argued that the federal government was vested with the *implied* powers required to conduct its business effectively. Those powers were limited only by what was *prohibited* by the Constitution, a position that would later be supported by John Marshall, first chief justice of the Supreme Court. Forty-eight hours after receiving Hamilton's report, Washington signed the bank bill.

If the assumption of state debts had sparked rampant speculation, it was nothing compared to the mania that swirled around stock in the Bank of the United States. All twenty thousand shares issued in July 1791 were sold within an hour. A brisk market in bank shares sprang up immediately, with furious buying and selling—a "delirium of speculation." [132] In the grips of this "Bancomania," as one newspaper called it, shares quickly quadrupled in value. "The National Bank stock has risen so high, so enormously above its real value, that no transaction in the annals of history can be found to equal it," wrote one newspaper. It was America's first speculative bubble.

At first, Hamilton was delighted to see the brisk demand for shares in his bank. But as the bubble expanded, he could see disaster on the horizon. He wrote a colleague, "These extravagant sallies of speculation do injury to the government and to the whole system of public credit by disgusting all sober citizens, and giving a wild air to everything." He feared that chaos would ensue when the bubble burst.

It did.

The domino that made all the others fall was Hamilton's trusted friend, Assistant Secretary of the Treasury William Duer.[133] Hamilton saw that Duer was speculating wildly in bank bonds, risking both his reputation and that of Hamilton's department. He wrote to Duer that he had gone "further than was consistent either with your own safety or the public good. My friendship for you, and my concern for the public cause, were both alarmed." [134] Hamilton would have been far more alarmed if he had known how far Duer had gone. In March 1792, Duer borrowed hundreds of thousands of dollars to purchase huge amounts of stock on margin. Had the market risen, Duer would have become the richest man in America. But the market dipped, and Duer couldn't cover his positions. His failure set off a chain reaction. His rich partners couldn't cover their positions either. As they discovered too late, Duer had stolen their money, along with a quarter-million dollars from the U.S. Treasury, to place his gigantic wager. Duer was whisked away to prison, where he eventually died. The collapse of so many prominent financiers set off a panic. Jefferson wrote to Thomas Randolph with some satisfaction that the "gambling scoundrels" were going down like "nine pins." Overstating the case, he wrote that "every man concerned in paper was broke," including most of New York.[135]

The "panic of 1792" has the distinction of being the first financial panic in American history, yet somehow Hamilton knew what to do. The head of the U.S. Treasury marched into the marketplace and bought thousands of shares, promising further repurchases. Prices recovered. The market stabilized. "Hamilton saw no inconsistency in continued Treasury purchase of bonds. The bull market was good for business, attracted foreign capital to America, and gave the new government an aura of confidence and success."[136]

In May 1792, as a direct response to the Duer disaster, a group of twenty-five merchants decided to bring some order to this chaotic trade in government securities by organizing a "stock market." They met daily to trade bonds under the shade of a large buttonwood tree on Wall Street in Manhattan. They formalized their association in a document quaintly called "The Buttonwood Agreement." One day this group would name itself the New York Stock Exchange.[137] Eventually it would trade in public companies as well as government securities, providing capital for canal companies, then railroads, then automobiles, forever fueling America's expansion. The creation of the stock market was just one result of Hamilton's miracle.

Alexander Hamilton issued his final recommendation for the American economy—*Report on Manufactures*—in 1791. He wrote that Americans had a "peculiar aptitude for mechanic improvements," which, along with Americans' "spirit of enterprise," would someday make the American economy the "admiration and envy of the world."[138] Hamilton's recommendations as to how government could strengthen industry were contemptuously ignored. "Instead of being forced or fostered by public authority it [manufacturing] ought to be seen with regret," wrote Madison.[139] To Jefferson, who believed that "those who labor in the earth are the people of God," industrialization was the apple in the American

Eden. A decade later, even Jefferson was forced to admit that growth in American manufacturing was necessary to avoid a crippling dependence on Europe. He conceded the point most reluctantly: "Our enemy has the consolation of Satan on removing our first parents from Paradise: from a peaceable and agricultural nation, he makes us a military and manufacturing one." [140]

During Hamilton's tenure, the American economy took off. Exports and shipping doubled—100 percent economic growth! Hamilton exuberantly called his economic miracle "a spectacle of national happiness never surpassed, if ever before equaled, in the annals of human affairs." [141]

In 1801, Jefferson would occupy the White House. The Virginia Republicans would maintain control over that piece of valuable Potomac real estate for twenty-four years—a generation. Years later, Jefferson would bitterly regret having hosted The Dinner and having made that deal with Hamilton on the federal assumption of debt. He claimed that it had been "the worst political decision he ever made." [142] But by then it was too late. Hamiltonian economics had saved America.

THE FALL OF ALEXANDER HAMILTON: THIS AMERICAN WORLD WAS NOT MADE FOR ME

During Washington's two terms in office, Hamilton was the president's chief adviser. And Hamilton's own power flowed in large part from his special connection with Washington. Hamilton was "filled with bitterness" when in 1799 he learned that Washington had died. It was not just a matter of personal grief. Washington "was an aegis very essential to me"—*aegis* is the Greek word for "shield." [143] With Washington gone, Hamilton lost his protector. Unlike Jefferson, who had built a national party, Hamilton had no political organization. "He had admiring colleagues, but no Praetorian Guard," said Kennedy. Furthermore, without Washington's steady hand, Hamilton began to make mistakes. He shot himself in the foot with his own party, the Federalists. In opposition to President Adams, who was seeking reelection in 1800, Hamilton backed another Federalist candidate: Charles Pinckney, a second-rate South Carolina politician who had nothing to offer except that he could be controlled by Hamilton. The result was that he split the Federalist vote, handing his enemy Jefferson the presidency. It was arguably the worst mistake of Hamilton's political career. Members of his own party were understandably furious with him. An enraged Adams called Hamilton "the most restless, impatient, artful, indefatigable and unprincipled intriguer in the United States, if not the world." [144] The Republicans were now poised to destroy everything Hamilton had built, or so he thought, and it was to a large extent his own fault.

Suddenly, it seemed that he was despised in the very country he had helped create. "There is something terrible going on in this country," he brooded, when "a man can be turned into a demon." [145] The depth of his depression is revealed in this letter addressed to his friend Gouverneur Morris:

> Mine is an odd destiny. Perhaps no man in the United States has sacrificed or done more for the present Constitution than myself. . . . Yet I have the murmurs of its friends no less than the curses of its foes. What can I do better than withdraw from the scene? Every day proves to me more and more that this American world was not made for me. [146]

For the first time, Hamilton was leading a one-man retreat.

Hamilton also faced the worst kind of personal tragedy. In 1801, his oldest son, Philip, was killed in a duel. He was defending his father's honor against the libelous attacks of George Eaker, a Republican Party hack and friend of Aaron Burr. The dashingly handsome Philip was his father's favorite, "the flower of the family." [147] Philip was killed because, as an act of gallantry, he fired his first shot into the air, thus demonstrating his willingness to defend his father's honor without taking a life. Eaker shot to kill. To make matters worse, Alexander Hamilton may have advised his son to take this noble, self-destructive course of action. Some biographers contend that Hamilton had known nothing of the duel until Philip was dead. But Hamilton's grandson, Allan McLane Hamilton, claimed in his biography of Hamilton that his grandfather had dispensed this fatal advice to Philip. Thomas Rathbone, a former classmate of Philip, was quoted in the *New York Post*—a newspaper founded and published by Hamilton—as saying that Hamilton had given his son instruction "to reserve his fire until after Mr E. had shot, and then discharge his pistol into the air." [148] If that were true, Hamilton's guilt and nauseating horror must have been intolerable. When he heard of Philip's death, Hamilton fainted. And he nearly fainted again at the funeral. "Never did I see a man so completely overwhelmed with grief as Hamilton has been," wrote his college friend Robert Troup. [149]

As if that weren't devastating enough, Hamilton's beautiful and musically talented eldest daughter, Angelica, became incurably insane with grief. She acted as if Philip were still alive, speaking to him as if he were sitting next to her. Alexander Hamilton's grandson wrote:

> Upon receipt of the news of her brother's death in the Eaker duel, she suffered so great a shock that her mind became permanently impaired, and although taken care of by her devoted mother for a long time there was no amelioration in her condition, and she was finally placed under the care of Dr. MacDonald of Flushing and remained in his charge until her death at seventy-three. During her latter life she constantly referred to her dear brother so nearly her own age as alive. [150]

Not only was Hamilton facing the loss of his son and his unbearable guilt over it, but each day he had to witness its destructive impact on his shattered daughter. It was beyond endurance. "The roof fell on the guy. He was very, very depressed," Fleming told me. Though Hamilton was "no stranger to depression," after Philip's death he "tumbled into bottomless despair," accompanied by a severe physical lethargy that had not been present in his previous depressive episodes, according to Chernow. "It is indisputable that in Hamilton's final years he was seriously depressed." [151]

It was after the election of 1804 that Alexander Hamilton fatally collided with Aaron Burr, another bipolar politician in political decline and in the midst of a severe depression. Burr and Hamilton were longtime peers and rivals. During the Revolution, when serious doubt had begun to arise about Washington's leadership, Burr had been one of the officers who had supported General Lee, the fickle general from the Battle of Monmouth. After the war, Burr, also a New Yorker, had gone into politics as a Republican and rose to become Jefferson's vice president in 1800. Had it not been for Hamilton, Burr would have become president in 1800 due to a flaw in the election procedures. Though everyone knew the ticket was Jefferson-Burr, the votes for president and vice president were not marked separately. Technically, each man had the same number of votes, and the election was thrown to the legislature to decide. To block Jefferson, the Federalists in the legislature were leaning toward choosing Burr, who was secretly courting them. As much as Hamilton hated Jefferson, he thought Burr to be truly dangerous and convinced his colleagues to vote for Jefferson. Ironically, Thomas Jefferson became president only through the active lobbying of Alexander Hamilton, the mortal enemy he had tried to destroy with his dirty tricks.

Historians often point out that Hamilton and Burr came from origins that couldn't have been more different. Burr was an "American aristocrat," with ancestors going back to the *Arabella*.[152] He was the son of a College of New Jersey president and the grandson of Jonathan Edwards, the famous evangelist who had led the "Great Awakening." But Burr, with the blood of Protestant prophets running through his veins, was as bipolar as Hamilton. And in this important regard their origins were more similar than different.

For example, Burr was even more hypersexual than Hamilton. During his vice presidential years, Burr had mistresses in Philadelphia, New York, New Haven, and Boston. "Vice President Burr had carried sexual liberation to an extreme that troubled even his closest friends." [153] Mathew Davis, editor of Burr's memoirs, marveled, "His intrigues were without number. His conduct most licentious."

Even Hamilton's grandiosity was no match for Burr's megalomania. Ironically, Adams and Jefferson both referred to Hamilton as the "American Bonaparte," and Jefferson seriously feared that Hamilton might try to take over the country by military coup. As it turned out, Aaron Burr was the one Jefferson should have kept his eye on.

The "Burr conspiracy," which would unfold after the duel with Hamilton, was a mad, grandiose scheme from the beginning. The plan was that Burr would ride west with a thousand armed men, take over the Western Territory, which Jefferson had acquired through the Louisiana Purchase, and declare it a separate country, with Burr at the helm. Then they would invade the Spanish territories of Mexico, Texas, Florida, and even South America to create a new empire. The plan was crazy. Kennedy described Burr as being "manic" during this time.[154] Burr rode to Washington and personally threatened Jefferson, warning him that he was "in the mood to do him harm." [155] Jefferson, who had long since cut Burr dead politically, said he wasn't worried. He should have been. "What could be more delicious than to whisk President Jefferson's Louisiana Purchase out from under his nose and convert it into a vehicle for the fame of Aaron Burr?" [156]

The plot was foiled, and Burr was put on trial for treason. Chief Justice Marshall risked being impeached by Jefferson when he found that there was insufficient evidence to convict Burr. But Burr was guilty, and everyone knew it. Legally exonerated but disgraced, Burr became suicidally depressed.[157] Ultimately he fled to Europe, but he never gave up his mad dreams of conquest. He lobbied the British to join his plan to invade the West. When that failed, he approached Napoleon himself. After Napoleon declared war on Spain, Burr tried to interest him in a foray against Mexico. "In lengthy written proposals" submitted to the emperor through intermediaries, he never ceased pitching the idea.[158]

Burr and Hamilton had one more feature in common. Thomas Jefferson wanted to destroy them both. The occasion for Burr's final confrontation with Hamilton was Burr's failed attempt to become governor of New York in his race against Morgan Lewis in 1804. Burr campaigned hypomanically, "twenty-four hours a day." [159] Lewis didn't campaign at all. Working behind the scenes as usual, Jefferson had joined forces with Clinton in an alliance against Burr. As Clinton's reward, he was chosen to replace Burr as Jefferson's second vice president. Burr not only lost the election, he lost by the widest margin in the state's history and was humiliated. The Republican newspapers, by now a well-oiled character assassination machine, battered Burr day after day and didn't stop even after he had lost. "If, in 1804, Burr had to shoot someone to square accounts, his victim might properly have been Thomas Jefferson." [160] But, of course, Burr couldn't challenge the president of the United States to a duel.

After the governor's race, Burr went into a tailspin. He became a "profoundly depressed and angry man." [161] It was when Burr was in this frame of mind that a rather obscure letter, published two months earlier in the *Albany Register,* was mentioned to him by a friend. The author, Dr. Charles Cooper, claimed that this had been a private letter, never intended for publication. How it got to the newspaper is unclear. Cooper had written that Hamilton had made disparaging remarks about Burr at a private dinner. Exactly what Hamilton said is not even mentioned, except to say that it communicated a "despicable" opinion of Burr.

Burr fired a letter to Hamilton, demanding that he disavow the offensive word "despicable." In the code of gentlemen, such character-besmirching phrases were fighting words. He was clearly demanding that the offensive stain on his character be removed or it would come to pistols. Hamilton was not even quoted as having used the word "despicable" (even though it accurately described his opinion of Burr). "Therefore, all Hamilton had to do at this propitious moment was to deny having said anything that could possibly fit that description, then express his personal regret that such slanderous insinuations had been attributed to him in the press. Burr would have had little choice but to accept his explanation." [162] Unfortunately, Hamilton engaged in a debate over the meaning of the word "despicable." The word, Hamilton wrote, "admits to infinite shades, from the very light to the very dark. How am I to judge the degree intended?" [163] The tone of his response was arrogant and insulting, almost as if he were trying to provoke Burr. "Hamilton's fate was sealed once he sent this letter." [164]

In the series of letters that went back and forth, Burr upped the ante, in effect demanding that Hamilton renounce anything negative he had ever said about him. If Hamilton had complied with that demand, he would look like a coward, recanting his long and publicly held opposition to Burr just to avoid a duel. Now he was trapped.

Was the duel a form of suicide? When I spoke with Thomas Fleming, whose book *Duel* focused exclusively on the deadly Burr-Hamilton encounter, he said that the idea that Hamilton committed suicide via duel was "absolutely silly." Roger Kennedy differed strongly: "I think he was suicidal at the end." In his book, Kennedy called the duel "assisted suicide." [165] This was not a new idea. John Adams's grandson, Henry Adams, had claimed it was suicide long before. Even if the duel was not a conscious suicide attempt, Kennedy believes that suicidal impulses were an invisible guiding hand in Hamilton's unconscious motivation. Even Fleming admits that "on a certain level in his mind he longed for death." [166] Hamilton had to feel at least partially responsible for his

114

son's death. Whether or not he had instructed his son to waste his fire, his son had died defending Hamilton's honor on the very field where Hamilton would meet Burr. In some part of his mind, Hamilton had to feel he *deserved* to die there, too.

Though Hamilton had been mired in a deep depression, his mood took a dramatic upswing immediately before the duel. It is well known to mental health professionals that patients who are severely depressed frequently become euphoric just before committing suicide. The final decision to die is experienced as a relief. There appears to be an end in sight to their intolerable, interminable pain. The agonizing conflict between their warring impulses to live and die being resolved, there comes a paradoxical sense of peace. All the people who met Hamilton during that time were struck by how unusually happy he seemed. Oliver Wolcott, who succeeded Hamilton as secretary of the Treasury, was "stunned" when he heard news of the duel.[167] Wolcott had just met with Hamilton the day before and had found him to be "uncommonly cheerful and gay."[168] On that same day, Hamilton visited his ailing friend Robert Troup, who remarked on his "composure and cheerfulness of mind."[169] One week before the duel, Hamilton and Burr sat next to each other at a Fourth of July dinner honoring Revolutionary War veterans. Burr was "brooding and silent."[170] But "Hamilton was strangely ebullient. He laughed and joked with numerous friends in the group."[171] Toward the end of the evening, he leaped onto the table, broke into song, and began to dance. In hindsight, the lyrics he sang seem prophetic:

> Why, soldiers, why
> Should we be melancholy boys?
> Why, soldiers, why
> Whose business, 'tis to die![172]

Hamilton may have felt euphoric, not because he intended to die, but because his existential problem was going to be solved—

one way or another, through death or triumph. Either way, "he was going to resolve life's dilemmas," said Kennedy. Practicing the code of Caesar yet again, he would either make a brilliant exit or catapult himself back into the public spotlight. Hamilton had charged his way into danger and out of depression throughout his career. The duel may have been, as Ellis put it, just "one more gallant gamble." [173] Hamilton was energized to storm what would prove to be his last redoubt.

In the final letter Hamilton left for posterity, he promised to "reserve and throw away my first fire." [174] He could behave no less honorably than his fallen son Philip. Hamilton fired into the air. Burr did not. Usually both parties survived duels. Guns were still too crude to be accurate. But Hamilton was killed by a stroke of bad luck: A one-ounce ball hit him in the rib and ricocheted into his vital organs. Had the bullet been a centimeter higher or lower, he would have survived.

What would Hamilton's future have looked like then? "There's no doubt in my mind that if Hamilton had lived, he would have become president in 1808," Fleming told me. Jefferson's second term ended in disaster, and the Republicans were vulnerable. If that's true, then Hamilton missed the Mount Rushmore–sized fame he'd fought for all his life by a fraction of an inch. But his Rushmore-sized ambitions for America came true, thanks in no small part to his hypomanic drive and creative genius.

Alexander Hamilton was buried in a church graveyard on Wall Street, a most fitting resting place for the founder of America's economy. Before Hamilton, Wall Street was just a street.

IV Andrew Carnegie

Industrial Revolutionary

Only four generations after Alexander Hamilton's death, America surpassed Great Britain to become the world's preeminent manufacturing economy, just as Hamilton had prophesied. There is no better illustration of how this miraculous success was achieved than the life of Andrew Carnegie.

Carnegie came from a long line of hypomanic Scottish rebels. The men of his parents', grandparents', and great-grandparents' generations were socialist revolutionaries. It might seem ironic that the grandson of one of Scotland's first socialists became one of history's most famed capitalists, or that the nephew of a strike organizer became a notorious strikebreaker. But this genealogy illustrates that the same genetically inherited temperament that makes a left-wing political revolutionary can make an industrial one. It is the *temperament* of a revolutionary that is genetic. What an individual does with his biology is up to him. Hypomanic energy can be directed toward any mission. The content of revolutions are as varied as human thought.

We normally think of "robber barons," as the industrial titans of the nineteenth century were dubbed, as the epitome of rapaciousness: brutal, ruthless, practical men of action. Carnegie was all those things. According to stereotype, such a man could never be a wild-eyed idealist chanting "Peace now." But Carnegie was that, too. Carnegie was no less idealistic than his forebears. The older and more successful he became, the more frankly messianic he grew, until he became convinced that he would personally spread the gospel of democracy across the earth, speed up evolution, and bring everlasting world peace.

He didn't succeed in that final mission, a failure that broke his indomitable spirit, but he enriched America beyond measure. In

119

his lifetime, and in part because of his hypomanically driven achievements, America took the global economic lead and never looked back.

THE MAKING OF A HERO

A Family of Prophets

"Agitation is the order of the day" was the rallying cry of Thomas Morrison. Carnegie's maternal grandfather was an electrifying speaker who rode up and down the roads of Fife preaching his radical political gospel. One of Scotland's first socialists, he called for the redistribution of land under the slogan: "Each shall possess, all shall enjoy." And he published the country's first radical newspaper, *The Precursor.*[1] Morrison lived in Dunfermline. Once the capital of Scotland, it was a picturesque town on a hill overlooking a bay. Its skyline was dominated by a majestic abbey, where Robert the Bruce and other Scottish kings had been buried centuries earlier. The local aristocrats who owned the land surrounding the abbey were incensed at Morrison's strident call for the abolition of inherited privilege. Although they opened the grounds to the public once a year for a festival, they decreed that neither Morrison nor any of his descendants would ever be allowed to set foot there. Morrison died on the road in 1837, "haranguing the public" till the end. In his *Autobiography,* Carnegie said he had "inherited" his style of public speaking from Grandpa Morrison, who had died when he was only two. Those who lived long enough to hear both men speak swore it was true.

Morrison's son Tom was another eccentric revolutionary. He carried a walking stick "as big as a post," pounding it loudly on the ground when he wished to emphasize a point.[2] With his large, bushy beard and a tall chimney-shaped hat, he was difficult to ignore, especially at political meetings, where he would heckle speakers with a "strange cuckoo song." The conservative *Dunfermline Journal* declared his behavior "an abomination to any well regulated mind."[3] In all, "he gave the appearance of a wild man," wrote Carnegie biographer Joseph Frazier Wall.[4] Uncle Tom's cause was the People's Charter, a proposed British constitution that would give the vote to "every man over twenty-one years of age, of sound mind not undergoing punishment for a crime."[5] Morrison organized a general strike, urging that workers "not resume the production of wealth until the People's Charter becomes law."[6] Troops and cavalry were sent into the streets of Dunfermline. "I remember as if it were yesterday," wrote Carnegie in his *Autobiography,* "being awakened during the night by a tap on the back window by men who had come to inform my parents that my uncle . . . had been thrown into jail because he dared to hold a meeting which was forbidden."[7] The Charter would suffer defeat in the House of Commons in 1838 by a vote of 235 to 46.

On Carnegie's father's side, rebels can be traced back three generations. His great-grandfather was arrested for sedition against the local gentry during the Meal Riots of 1770. His grandfather Andrew, after whom he was named, was known for leading subversive meetings. A self-taught intellectual, he organized a "college" among his fellow weavers that consisted of a cottage with a handful of books in the center of town where the men would meet, "well fortified with malt whiskey," and denounce aristocrats.[8] Andrew Carnegie, Sr., was an exuberant man with an infectious love of life, dancing, and practical jokes. He was fond of the Scottish proverb "Be happy while you are living because you are a long time dead."[9] From this grandfather, "whose name I am proud to bear," Carnegie claimed he inherited "my optimistic nature, my ability to shed trouble and to laugh through life."[10] Carnegie's hypomanic optimism was a force of nature that would prove essential to his meteoric rise. "Next to Carnegie, Norman Vincent Peale was a clinically depressed pessimist," wrote Richard Tedlow in *Giants of Enterprise.*[11] There was nothing Carnegie thought he could not accomplish. "That he could ever fail in life, that any possible ambition could not be achieved—such doubts never entered Carnegie's mind," wrote biographer Burton Hendrick.[12]

The Humiliation of Will Carnegie

Carnegie's father, Will, was a third-generation weaver who moved to Dunfermline because it was the center of the damask-weaving trade. Damask weaving was unique—an intricate craft in which elaborate patterns, such as thistles, unicorns, even portraits were embedded in a satin weave of cotton, linen, or silk. Two thirds of Dunfermline's 11,500 residents made their living through the handloom. Among his peers, Will was acknowledged as a "master weaver," an artist among artisans.

Will Carnegie's temperament was almost the opposite of his father's. "It was always difficult for strangers to believe that the quiet shy William could be the son of the irrepressible Andrew."[13] Though different in temperament, William quietly shared his father's political beliefs, which explains how he came to marry Thomas Morrison's daughter. When he moved to Dunfermline, he became attached to this great radical family. They in turn took a liking to him and brought him under their wing. Over many family dinners, Will became smitten by Margaret Morrison, Carnegie's mother.

Their first son, Andrew Carnegie, was born on a bleak day in November 1835. His hypomanic impatience was evident almost from birth: His aunts recalled that as an infant "he preferred to have two spoons going at once."[14]

Will carved out a life of "working-class opulence" in Dunfermline. When Andrew was a baby, the family moved to a bigger house because Will needed room to expand his business. He bought new looms, took on apprentices, and dedicated the ground floor to production, while the family lived upstairs in accommodations that seemed spacious compared to the house they had moved from. Young Andrew's ambition was to become a great weaver like his father, his first hero.

Carnegie also drank in colorful stories of Scotland's historic heroes told by his uncle Lauder, who owned a small store on High Street, where Andrew and his cousin Dod spent much of their time. William Wallace, the Scottish freedom fighter known to most Americans through the movie *Braveheart,* topped his pantheon. Wallace, who emerged from obscurity to lead a rebellion against the English king Edward I in 1297, was anointed "guardian of Scotland" and ruled the country briefly before being decapitated by the king's men. "Wallace of course was our hero. Everything heroic centered in him." [15] Wallace played much the same psychological function for Carnegie as Caesar had for Hamilton, forming the core of a grandiose self-image. "If the source of my stock of that prime article—courage—were studied, I am sure the final analysis would find it founded on Wallace, the hero of Scotland. It is a tower of strength for a boy to have a hero," Carnegie wrote. [16] Of course, it is perfectly natural for young boys to have heroes, but Carnegie's identification with Wallace was so intense that it became a guide for his actions for the rest of his life. When faced with a difficult situation, he wrote, "I was not beyond asking myself what Wallace would have done. . . . A real disciple of Wallace or Bruce could not give up; he would die first." [17]

Though Will Carnegie was a believer in political change, he could not adapt to technological change. The Industrial Revolution began in Britain with the introduction of steam-powered looms. By 1835, there were more than 110,000 power looms in Britain, mostly dedicated to the manufacture of cotton sheets and textiles. Cotton, once a luxury fabric like silk, could now be manufactured inexpensively. This increase in efficiency put cotton hand weavers out of business. Will Carnegie didn't believe the same thing could happen to him and the other skilled craftsmen who made the linen. He was wrong. The Jacquard loom, which could be programmed with punch cards to make intricate designs, was invented in 1825.

Their speed transformed damask linen from an expensive work of art into a cheap commodity, too. There were more than 84,560 handloom linen weavers in Scotland in 1840 and only 25,000 by 1850. Eventually, they would become extinct. "The change from handloom to steam-loom weaving was disastrous to our family. My father did not recognize the impending revolution," Carnegie re-called.[18] For a period of time buyers still purchased Will Carnegie's linen, but increasingly they expected to pay steam-loom rates. The price the market would bear spiraled downward, and so did the fortunes of Will Carnegie and his family. "Shortly after this I began to learn what poverty meant."[19] One day in the winter of 1847, Will Carnegie returned from a fruitless sales trip and announced quietly to his son, "Andra, I can get nae mair work."[20] This moment shaped the course of Andrew Carnegie's life. He saw his proud family plummeting into poverty, and his father could do nothing to stop it. "Then and there came the resolve that I would cure that when I became a man."[21] Will's moment of humiliation became Carnegie's moment of determination: The mission toward which Carnegie would direct his hypomanic energies was set.

The entire community of Dunfermline weavers was eventually put out of work by the steam loom. In 1847, after a bubble in rail-road stocks burst, a market panic sank the entire British economy into depression and produced massive unemployment. The potato famine in Ireland brought the more ominous risk of starvation. Be-tween 1845 and 1850, 1,300,000 people left the British Isles for America. Like so many others in 1848, the Carnegies decided to see if their luck would be any better in America. Notably, it was Margaret who made the decision. They sold their furniture at auc-tion for nearly nothing. Will's precious handloom, which he had once played like a musical instrument, sold for no more than the price of the wood. "The proceeds of the sale were most disappoint-ing," remembered Carnegie.[22] Only the charity of a family friend gave them the final £20 they needed to pay for their passage.

The night before the family set sail, Will's sister found him sitting

124

alone in the dark in his empty cottage with his head in his hand: "His attitude was verra sad," she said.[23] The forty-three-year-old master weaver had become a "tired and defeated man," sinking into a depression from which he would never emerge.[24] America would prove to be the final chapter in his personal tragedy, "the end of the catastrophe." But for his son Andrew, America was the beginning of an epic adventure.

Eager Young Man in a Vital Young Land

Andrew watched heartbroken, "with tearful eyes," as the spire of the Dunfermline Abbey faded into the distance. He vowed to return someday. Though still in mourning for the loss of his home, Andrew adapted to the new world with extraordinary speed and enthusiasm. For most, the ocean crossing was an ordeal of anxiety and discomfort, but to Andrew it was fun. The boat excited him, and he peppered the sailors with constant questions. Within twenty-four hours, "the small tow-haired boy was the one person that every sailor knew, and he was soon adopted as an informal messenger and mascot."[25] "I left with sincere regret," wrote Carnegie. "Undoubtedly, Andrew was the only passenger aboard who held to that sentiment."[26] The family had to endure another three weeks on a slow steamship to Pittsburgh, where they were met at the dock by Andrew's Aunt and Uncle Hogan, relatives who had emigrated ten years before.

The family settled in "Slabtown," a slum in Allegheny, a few miles outside Pittsburgh. Will borrowed a handloom from his brother-in-law. Finding no commercial buyers, he had to lower himself to peddling tablecloths door to door. "The returns were meager in the extreme," wrote Carnegie.[27] Margaret, the indomitable survivor, obtained work sewing shoes for $4.00 a week. "There was no keeping her down," Carnegie wrote admiringly. Gradually, she replaced Will as Andrew's central hero. Will Carnegie's "wife and son clearly thought him a failure," according to biographer Harold Livesay.[28] He could no longer provide for his family's most basic needs.

The $4.00 a week his mother earned was not sufficient to keep them alive. The family needed at least $7.50 a week to eat. There was no question: the thirteen-year-old Andrew would have to work. He obtained a job in a textile factory as a "bobbin boy" for $1.20 a week. "It was a hard life," Carnegie recalled.[29] He arrived before daybreak and left after sunset, working twelve hours a day, six days a week. Hard as it was, it was better than the alternative: "The prospect of want had become to me a frightful nightmare."[30] To Andrew, who always looked at the bright side, "the cloud had a silver lining, as it gave me the feeling that I was doing something for my world—our family."[31]

Andrew found freedom from drudgery in books. He traces this to the generosity of a Colonel Anderson ("I bless his name as I write"), who opened up his personal library free of charge to "working boys." "The windows were opened in the walls of my dungeon through which the light of knowledge streamed in. Every day's toil and even the long hours of night service were lightened by the book which I carried about with me."[32] Having a book in his pocket gave Carnegie hope. When the library narrowed the definition of working boys to include only apprentices, Andrew wrote a letter to the *Pittsburgh Dispatch* "urging we should not be excluded," and the definition was changed. With little formal education, Carnegie became an autodidact. Colonel Anderson's library launched a lifetime of learning.

One day, Uncle Hogan was playing checkers with the manager of the Pittsburgh telegraph office, who mentioned that they needed a messenger. Hogan suggested his young nephew for the job. Although Will worried about his son walking alone to Pittsburgh, Andy jumped at the chance. Carnegie's excitement was understandable: it gave him a desperately needed raise in pay to $2.50 a week and got him out of the dreaded factory. It also placed him, albeit at the lowest level, conveniently at the nexus of business and progress in a young Pittsburgh, then America's "gateway to the West." Carnegie claimed that he *knew,* then and there, that his job as a messenger was the beginning of bigger things: "I was lifted in paradise, yes, heaven as it seemed to me. . . . I felt that my foot was upon the ladder and that I was bound to climb."[33] His ascent felt predestined. One of his fellow messengers recalled that Carnegie's "mind seemed to be towards bigger things."[34] Carnegie's ambition was gargantuan from the start.

Carnegie hurled himself into his messenger job with enthusiastic abandon. To better discharge his duties, he spent his evenings memorizing every street, every firm, and every businessman in Pittsburgh. His hustle paid off. One day, when distributing the monthly pay to the messenger boys, the boss pushed past Carnegie, as if he were not to be paid. Carnegie panicked, fearing he had made a terrible mistake and lost his job. Instead, the boss pulled him aside after the other messengers went home to tell him that he "was worth more than the other boys."[35] He gave him a $2.25-a-month raise, to $13.50, and assigned him the additional responsibility of managing incoming messages. "He was now earning almost half of the $30 required monthly for their family to live with reasonable comfort."[36] Carnegie ran the two miles home without stopping.

He managed to keep his secret for an entire night, confiding only in his younger brother, Tom, as they went to sleep. "I sketched to him how we would go into business together; that the firm of 'Carnegie Brothers' would be a great one, and that father and mother should yet ride in their carriage."[37] The next morning, when he produced the extra money, his parents were astounded:

On Sunday morning with father, mother, and Tom at breakfast, I produced the extra two dollars and a quarter. The surprise was great and it took some moments for them to grasp the situation, but it soon dawned on them. Then father's glance of loving pride and mother's blazing eyes soon wet with tears, told their feeling. It was their boy's first triumph. . . . No subsequent success or recognition of any kind ever thrilled me as this did. . . . My whole world was moved to tears of joy.[38]

Young Andrew was finally a hero.

Carnegie may have been his family's savior, but his greatest regret was that he failed to save his father. One of his final memories of his father was seeing him return by boat from another disappointing sales trip:

> I waited for the boat, which did not arrive till late in the evening, and went down to meet him. I remember how deeply affected I was on finding that instead of taking a cabin passage, he had resolved not to pay the price, but to go down the river as a deck passenger. I was indignant that one of so fine a nature should be compelled to travel thus. But there was comfort in saying:
>
> "Well father, it will not be long before mother and you ride in your carriage."
>
> My father was usually shy, reserved, and keenly sensitive, very saving of praise (a Scotch trait) lest his sons might be too greatly uplifted; but when touched he lost his self-control. He was so upon this occasion, and grasped my hand with a look which I often see and can never forget. He murmured slowly:
>
> "Andra, I am proud of you." . . . He was kindness itself. . . . Alas! He passed away soon after returning from his western tour just as we were becoming able to give him a life of leisure and comfort.[39]

This poignant scene with his father on the dock was simultaneously one of the saddest and one of the most triumphant moments in Carnegie's private Oedipal drama. Freud claimed that every young boy competes with his father, especially for his mother's affection.[40] Carnegie was an "oedipal victor," triumphing in both these aims. At a young age, he was a success compared to his father. And his claim to have exclusively possessed his idealized mother was rather undisguised:

Perhaps someday I may be able to tell the world something of this heroine, but I doubt it. I feel her to be sacred to myself and not for others to know. No one could ever really know her—I alone did that. After my father's early death she was all my own. The dedication of my first book tells the story: It was: 'To my favorite heroine, my mother.' "[41]

Being a mother's favorite has its rewards. Freud observed: "A man who has been the indisputable favorite of his mother keeps for life the feeling of a conqueror, that confidence of success that often induces real success."[42] In Carnegie's inner narrative he was born to win, and throughout his life he acted the hero he believed himself to be. On the other hand, Margaret Carnegie possessed Andy as much as he did her. His mother extracted a vow that he would not marry till she died. Carnegie's fiancée, Louise Whitfield, who was forced to endure a long, secret engagement, understandably thought Carnegie's favorite heroine was "the most disagreeable woman she had ever known."[43] Carnegie finally married Louise in 1886, when he was fifty-one, six months after his mother died.

As satisfying as it was to surpass his father, it was devastating for Carnegie to see this man he loved—a man with "one of the sweetest, purest, kindest natures I have ever known"—laid low.[44] Who had done this to his father? Manufacturers, with their power looms, had crushed him with their superior technology. It was a lesson Carnegie would never forget. He would become an infamously ruthless competitor, who used cutting-edge technology to destroy his rivals with the ferocity of an avenging William Wallace.

My Andy

Every morning Andy went into the telegraph office early before work to sweep up. While he was there he taught himself Morse code. Messenger boys were never allowed to touch the equipment when the line was open for business, but one day a message came

129

in when all the operators were out. The "supremely confident Andrew could contain himself no longer."[45] He risked his job and took the message. This experience became the basis of one of his business maxims: "The rising man must do something exceptional, and beyond the range of his special department. HE MUST ATTRACT ATTENTION."[46] Attracting attention, of course, is one of the things hypomanics do best.

Instead of firing him, his boss was pleased and let him man the telegraph machine when the regular operators were on break. Not everyone welcomed the young upstart. In those days a telegraph operator worked with a "copyist," who would record the patterns of dots and dashes on paper before they were decoded. Copyist Courtney Hughes "resented my presumption and refused to 'copy' for a messenger boy." Andrew then did something that astounded old Courtney, along with everybody else: "I shut off the paper slip, took pencil and paper, and began taking the message by ear. I shall never forget his surprise." Carnegie had mastered the ability to transcribe letters directly from sounds—one of only a handful of people in the country who could do so at the time. After that, "there was never any difficulty between dear old Courtney Hughes and myself."[47] James Reid, the office superintendent, recalled, "Though he was little he was full of spirit."[48] Carnegie became a full-time telegraph operator for $4 a week. The Carnegies purchased a home from Uncle Hogan for $550. By this point, Carnegie wrote, "future millionairedom seemed to be dawning."[49]

It was obvious to Carnegie that America was a land of opportunity. In a letter to Uncle Lauder, he explained, "If I had been at Dunfermline working at the loom it's very likely I would have been a poor weaver all my days, but here, I can surely do something better than that, and if I don't it will be my own fault, for anyone can get along in this country."[50] Andrew's letters to Scotland were so enthusiastic that his cousin Dod took exception and challenged him to debate America's merits. Carnegie began by mailing Dod a copy of the Constitution and asked to see England's (it had none). "We have the charter which you have been fighting for for years."[51] The reforms their relatives had struggled unsuccessfully to achieve were "in successful operation here." The immigrant to America found "no royal family," "no established church," and "no aristocracy" to keep him down.[52] Furthermore, Americans were not just politically free; their minds had been "freed from superstitious reverence for old customs."[53] America emanated an intangible vitality, energy, and creativity that young Carnegie attributed to its youth. "Everything around us is in motion," he wrote his cousin in wonder. "Old England" was epitomized by "the lassitude of old age," while "young America showed the vigor of manhood."[54]

In Carnegie's eyes, America was the utopian new world his family had fought for. Andrew "worshiped his adopted country like it was a living breathing hero," according to biographer Peter Krass.[55] The only bad thing Carnegie could say about America was that slavery was "the greatest evil in the world." He declared himself to be an "ultra-abolitionist." "One man trafficking in the flesh of another" and "women and children lashed like cattle" sickened him.[56] But even in the face of this great evil, he was optimistic: something so terrible couldn't last long in such a great country. He predicted it would soon die out of its own accord.

Visitors to the Atlantic and Ohio Telegraph Company couldn't help but notice the "buoyant, hustling white-haired Andy."[57] One customer who noticed him was Tom Scott, regional superintendent of the Pennsylvania Railroad, the largest and most complex railroad of its day. To manage the routing of its trains, the Pennsylvania had just strung its own telegraph wire, and it needed a telegraph operator. Scott offered the job to Andy at $35 a month. This would prove to be Carnegie's big break. He was lucky to be the right young man at the right place at the right time. Railroads were among the most revolutionary technologies of the nineteenth century; they "increasingly drove the American economy, both literally and figuratively." [58] Carnegie began with the Pennsylvania in February 1853. A year later, the company breached the Allegheny Mountains for the first time, connecting Pittsburgh to the eastern seaboard and starting a local economic boom. The journey to Pittsburgh, which had taken his family three weeks by boat, now required a mere fifteen hours. That "ought to satisfy the fastest of this fast generation," wrote the *Pittsburgh Gazette*.[59]

As in the telegraph office, Carnegie leaped at any opportunity to distinguish himself. One morning, he came into work to find that a train had derailed, the entire system was gridlocked, and Scott was nowhere to be found. "No one but the superintendent himself was permitted to give train orders," wrote Carnegie. There was good reason for this rule: an incorrect order could result in enormous property damage or even fatalities. "I knew it was dismissal, disgrace, perhaps criminal punishment for me if I erred. But finally, I could not resist the temptation to plunge in, take the responsibility, give 'train orders,' and set matters going. 'Death or Westminster Abbey,' flashed across my mind." [60] Frantically, he rerouted trains with telegraph messages signed with his boss's initials. "All was right" when Scott arrived—a virtuoso performance. "In less than a year, he had achieved complete familiarity with the most sophisticated railroad operation in America." [61] Carnegie was afraid he might be fired, but Scott was pleased and even bragged to his boss about what "his white-haired Scotch devil" had done. Scott promoted him and gave him a raise, and soon Carnegie was routing all the trains.

Scott was only too happy to enable the rise of the young man he affectionately called "my Andy." Carnegie did an outstanding job, but there was another reason Scott took him under his wing. Hypomanics have a hidden talent which is integral to their success. They have an uncanny ability to make other people feel good about themselves. Carnegie idealized Scott, hailing him as a "genius." "He was my great man and all the hero worship that is inherent in youth I showered upon him." [62] Hypomanics' energetic flattery, just one manifestation of their infectious enthusiasm, induces a state of heightened self-esteem in others—a powerful tool in securing their help. It transforms bosses into mentors and employees into disciples.

THE GOOSE THAT LAYS THE GOLDEN EGGS

In 1856, Scott offered his protégé a chance to purchase ten shares of a package-shipping company—Adams Express—for $500. For Carnegie this was an astronomical sum. "Five hundred cents was much nearer my capital. I had not fifty dollars saved for investment but I was not going to miss the chance of becoming financially connected with my leader and great man."[63] Carnegie claimed in his autobiography that his mother mortgaged their home, but historians believe that Scott must have lent Andy the money. Carnegie quickly saw a return on his investment in the form of a $10 dividend check. Opening that envelope was a revelation about the wonders of capitalism. "I shall remember that check as long as I live . . . it gave me my first penny of revenue from capital—something I had not worked for with the sweat of my brow. 'Eureka!' I cried. 'Here is the goose that lays the golden eggs.' "[64] Andrew triumphantly displayed the check to all his friends. "The effect produced upon my companions was overwhelming. None of them had imagined such an investment possible."[65]

Just like Carnegie, Scott had risen in both wealth and position through the patronage of an older man: J. Edgar Thomson, president of the Pennsylvania Railroad. Thomson introduced Scott to a surefire way to make money. What made the pair so successful was a method of investing that is illegal today. As senior officers of the Pennsylvania Railroad, Scott and Thomson knew which companies the Pennsylvania would do business with before anyone else, as they were the men who made those decisions. So, with little risk, they invested in companies they were in a position to benefit. "The insider investment technique was 100 percent guaranteed and there were no laws preventing it." [66]

T. T. Woodruff built the first sleeping car in 1856. When he approached Thomson and Scott about obtaining a contract from the Pennsylvania, they immediately recognized the potential of this new invention and persuaded Woodruff to form a partnership with them. Young Carnegie was once again brought along for the ride, and his fortune began with the Woodruff Sleeping Car Company in the late 1850s. For just over $1,000 he received one eighth interest. Once again, he laid out no money of his own. He was required to come up with only $200 in cash, which he borrowed from a bank. The balance was "subtracted from his dividends." When the more aggressive Pullman Company absorbed Woodruff, the combined entity cornered the sleeping car market. The return on Carnegie's minimal investment was astronomical.

Carnegie would later convince himself that he had personally discovered Woodruff. Thirty years later, Carnegie wrote in his book *Triumphant Democracy,* "A farmer looking kind of man ... wished me to look at an invention he had made." According to Carnegie, Woodruff pulled a model train sleeping car out of a green burlap bag, and the moment Carnegie laid eyes on it, "like a flash the whole range of discovery burst before me. 'Yes,' I said, 'that is something the continent must have.' " [67] Carnegie claimed that he had then promptly alerted Scott and Thomson to this magnificent invention. Carnegie's version was pure fantasy. Woodruff had met directly with Thomson and Scott after they saw him demonstrate a working prototype. That Carnegie believed his own embellished story is suggested by the fact that he proudly sent an autographed copy of the book, with warmest regards, to none other than T. T. Woodruff himself, who became understandably incensed when he read this fictional account of his life. "Your arrogance spurred you to make up statements," he wrote back in rebuke. [68] The old man took to the newspapers to refute Carnegie's claim. Carnegie's grandiosity could distort his reality testing—a problem that would get worse over time.

Carnegie's next major investment *was* his own idea. He formed the first company in America to specialize in building iron railroad bridges, Keystone Bridge. He included Scott and Thomson as partners and big customers. He then hired the best bridge builders in the country and made them partners, too.

Carnegie had hitched himself to a rising star in Tom Scott. Scott was promoted to vice president of the entire Pennsylvania Railroad, and he convinced Thomson to give his old job as superintendent of the Western Division to Carnegie, despite Thomson's reservations about Andy's age. Needless to say, Carnegie had no reservations about accepting his chance at "glory," as he put it. The twenty-four-year-old stood at the epicenter of transportation and communication in "one of the most challenging jobs in the country."[69] Under his management traffic quadrupled, costs fell, and productivity rose.

To achieve this, he pushed his men almost as hard as he pushed himself, which is to say "full throttle every minute."[70] It was a job that often required "twenty-four hour attention."[71] Fortunately for Carnegie, he had the hypomanic ability to work on little sleep:

> At one time for eight days I was constantly upon the line, day and night, at one wreck or obstruction after another. . . . Never knowing fatigue myself. . . . I overworked the men and was not careful enough in considering the limits of human endurance. I have always been able to sleep at any time. Snatches of a half an hour at intervals during the night in a dirty freight car were sufficient.[72]

A Great Cause

As it turned out, Carnegie's ability to work without sleep proved fortunate, not only for him but for the nation. Soon after the Confederates fired on Fort Sumter, they sabotaged the tracks of the Baltimore and Ohio Railroad that led to Washington and cut the telegraph lines as well. The capital was cut off from the North, unable to receive either troops or information, while the Confederates massed to their south. Maryland's governor, a Confederate sympathizer, ordered all federal troops out of the state and had the railroad bridges burned to ensure that no more soldiers arrived. Washington was defenseless and in mortal peril.

Scott was quickly appointed assistant secretary of war in charge of transportation. Carnegie was not exaggerating when he wrote, "It was one of the most important departments of all in the beginning of the war."[73] Washington's survival would depend on whether they could get the trains moving again. Scott sent Carnegie to lead a team of engineers by steamship to Annapolis to effect repairs. After "three 24-hour days of grueling work," they had repaired both the tracks and the telegraph lines, with Carnegie pushing the pace. "I gloried in being useful to the land that had done so much for me, and worked, I can truly say, night and day."[74] Andy rode exuberantly into the capital with the first trainload of soldiers, "astride the engine like a gallant knight," tooting the horn and proudly displaying his "battle scar" (his cheek had been cut by a telegraph line).[75]

Washington had been saved.

Sleepless repair-athons continued apace. Carnegie's crew rebuilt the Long Bridge in Alexandria in seven twenty-four-hour days. Then, while they were in Alexandria, there was another call for help.

The North had been cruising to what appeared to be an easy victory in the Battle of Bull Run, validating hopeful predictions that the war would be brief. But when General Stonewall Jackson and his Virginia riflemen joined the battle, the rebels rallied. A few hours later, the Northern troops were retreating in panic. Lincoln and his war secretary, hunched over their telegraph, were stunned. So was Carnegie. "We could not believe the reports that came to us," he wrote. "It soon became evident that we must rush every engine and car to the front to bring back our forces. The closest point then was Burke station. I went out there and loaded up train after train with the poor wounded volunteers."[76] There were 950 wounded and 625 dead, and Carnegie helped put them all onto the trains at a frantic pace, working until Burke station was overrun by the enemy and finally hopping the last train out.

"I was all aflame for the flag," Carnegie wrote, elated to be an important player in this battle between good and evil.[77] After the Battle of Bull Run, Carnegie wrote a friend in exultation, "How gratifying to lie down at night and think by George you are of some use in sustaining a great cause."[78] With typical Carnegie optimism, he took the Northern rout as a good thing: "Depend upon it, the recent defeat is a blessing in disguise. We shall now begin in earnest. Knowing our foes, the necessary means will be applied to ensure their overthrow."[79]

Scott and Andy were put in charge of the War Department's telegraph office. Every day Lincoln visited them, anxious for the latest news from the battlefield. Carnegie was awed, not by his office but by Lincoln the man. Though his features were "homely," "intellect shone through his eyes and illuminated his face to a degree which I have seldom or never seen in any other." Lincoln embodied the egalitarian ideals of his grandfathers. He was democracy in the flesh:

> His manners were perfect because natural; and he had a kind word for everybody, even the youngest boy in the office. His attentions were not graduated. They were the same to all, as deferential in talking to a messenger boy as to Secretary Seward. . . . I have never met a great man who so thoroughly made himself one with all men as Mr. Lincoln. As Secretary Hay so well says, "it is impossible to imagine anyone a valet to Mr. Lincoln; he would have been his companion." He was the most perfect democrat, revealing in every word and act the equality of all men.[80]

Respect for Lincoln aside, Carnegie had no inhibitions about offering his advice to the president. On one occasion, Tom Scott was called to an emergency cabinet meeting. The crisis of the day was whether to return two Southern prisoners taken from aboard a British ship. Britain viewed this as a territorial violation—British ships were protected under her sovereignty—and vowed to fight if the prisoners were not returned. Carnegie convinced Scott to tell Lincoln that this was no bluff. "Return the prisoners" was his urgent advice. At the cabinet meeting, Secretary of State Seward made the same argument, and Lincoln was "at last converted," Carnegie wrote. It would not be the last time Carnegie would tell a president what to do. It became a lifestyle. He would aggressively foist his unsolicited wisdom on every president from Abraham Lincoln to Woodrow Wilson—whether the topic was tariffs, Supreme Court nominees, or world peace.

Carnegie was sent back to Pittsburgh, where the Union needed him to help run the Pennsylvania Railroad, which he did during most of the war. The elation of aiding in a great cause faded over the grueling months. Every day, at all hours of the day, tens of thousands of troops and thousands of tons of supplies had to be moved. Carnegie moved them, but things were always verging on chaos. The wounded traveling back from the front were heartbreaking, and as they kept coming the scene became soulnumbing. Carnegie moved 100,000 bloodied boys north, a traumatizing endless parade of carnage. By war's end he was on the verge of a breakdown. He became "dour and gloomy," "burnt out," and physically ill.[81] But he endured. The war changed one thing forever, for Andy and thousands of others: he was a boy no more.

With the war all but won, Carnegie requested and was granted a three-month leave of absence. After twelve years, he returned to his beloved Dunfermline for the first time. "I felt as if I could throw myself upon the sacred soil and kiss it."[82] But he was shocked by how much smaller everything seemed. In his child's memory High

Street was as big as Broadway, but "here was a city of Lilliputians." When he entered Uncle Lauder's store, he exclaimed, "You are all here; everything is just as I left it, but you are now all playing with toys." [83] Not only was the town smaller, the aspirations of its people seemed small, too:

> My dear old Auntie Charlotte, in a moment of exultation ex-
> claimed: "Oh, you will just be coming back here some day *and
> keep a shop on High Street.*" To keep a shop in the High Street
> was her idea of a triumph. Her son-in-law and daughter . . . had
> risen to this great height, and nothing was too great to predict for
> her promising nephew.[84]

After the war, Carnegie focused on Keystone Bridge. He won contracts to span the Mississippi and Missouri rivers, tying together the eastern and western United States with bridges bigger than anyone had ever seen. "The transcontinental railroads generated enormous enthusiasm; they seemed to fulfill the vision of 'manifest destiny'—'tying the nation together with sinews of steel.' " [85] Keystone rode the postwar railroad boom—railroad mileage nearly doubled from 1865 to 1872.

In a few years Carnegie had parlayed his borrowed $500 into more than $400,000, one of the largest fortunes in America. In 1865, Thomson offered Carnegie the chance to become the general superintendent of the entire Pennsylvania Railroad. He declined. He was twenty-nine and never needed to work for anyone else again. When a friend asked him how things were going, he exuberantly exclaimed, "I'm rich! I'm rich!" [86] He bought his mother and brother a house in the country, hired a servant, and bought a horse. Margaret could now indeed "ride in her carriage," as he had always promised. Little Andy was his own man, even if he was still a mama's boy.

MAN OF STEEL

A Dark Night of the Soul

Carnegie accelerated the pace of his financial deals, with Scott and Thomson barely hanging on. It was hard to keep up or even keep count. Carnegie became the driving force in a dizzying network of companies, deals, and schemes. He was involved in sleeping cars, oil, iron, telegraphy, construction, real estate, coal, and bridge building. "Carnegie was frenetic to the point of manic as he pursued, created and promoted moneymaking deals," wrote Krass.[87]

One December night in 1868, Carnegie had a spiritual crisis. As he was sitting at his desk, a "year end melancholy took hold."[88] It was the holidays, and he was a single man living alone in a hotel. Well, not alone, exactly. His mother was in the adjoining room. But he was lonely. For the past year he'd lived in the swank St. Nicholas hotel in New York to be close to the action on Wall Street. Suddenly, as if visited by the ghost of Christmas future, he saw nothing but a worthless life of moneygrubbing in front of him.

He vowed then and there to change his life. He swore to it. He took out a piece of paper and wrote a new plan, a contract with himself:

Dec. '68
St. Nicholas Hotel
N. York

Thirty-three and an income of 50,000 per annum.

By this time in two years I can so arrange all my business as to secure at least 50,000 per annum. Beyond this never earn— make no effort to increase fortune, but spend the surplus each year for benevolent purposes. Cast aside business forever except for others.

Settle in Oxford & get a thorough education making the

140

acquaintance of literary men—this will take three years of active work—pay especial attention to public speaking.

Settle then in London & purchase a controlling interest in some newspaper or live review & give the general management of it attention, taking a part in public matters especially those connected to education & improvement of the poorer classes.

Man must have an idol—The amassing of wealth is one of the worst species of idolatry. No idol is more debasing than the worship of money. Whatever I engage in I must push inordinately therefore should I be careful to choose that life which will be the most elevating in character. To continue much longer overwhelmed by business cares and with most of my thoughts wholly upon the way to make more money in the shortest time, must degrade me beyond hope of permanent recovery.

I will resign business at Thirty-five, but during the ensuing two years, I wish to spend the afternoons in securing instruction, and in reading systematically.[89]

Carnegie felt debased, degraded, and nearing damnation. It was simultaneously a moment of depressive distortion and, paradoxically, a moment of clarity because all bravado and pretense were stripped away. "Whatever I engage in I must push inordinately." That was his hypomanic temperament, which he had inherited from his grandfathers. Carnegie knew he would always be more driven than other men. *How* he used that power, and toward what aim, was his own ethical and existential choice, with permanent consequences for his soul.

Andrew Carnegie did change his life at this turning point, but he did not give up business. Like so many New Year's resolutions, the letter was put into a drawer. His career in business, in fact, was just about to really begin.

Finance was the mere manipulation of paper and people. It

didn't contribute anything of worth to the world. Searching within himself for something of value, he remembered that his father, grandfather, and great-grandfather had *made* things, beautiful things. And he realized that he wanted to make things, too. "My preference was always manufacturing. I wanted to make something tangible," he would later explain.[90] Carnegie decided to sell everything he had and concentrate on one industry. "Put all your eggs in one basket, and then watch the basket" became one of his slogans.[91]

How Carnegie decided on steel is the stuff of legend. The superior properties of steel over iron were well known, but its manufacture was prohibitively expensive. During one of his trips overseas, Carnegie visited Henry Bessemer at his Sheffield steelworks in the spring of 1872. Quite by accident, Bessemer had made a major discovery. By chance some molten iron had been exposed to a blast of cold air. The rush of air had increased the iron's temperature and burnt off the impurities, producing steel. In an instant, Bessemer saw the implications: "What a perfect revolution it threatened in every iron making district in the world was fully grasped by my mind as I gazed motionless at that glowing ingot, the mere contemplation of which almost overwhelmed me."[92] When Carnegie saw what Bessemer had discovered, he really "got the flash," realizing its revolutionary implications in an instant, just as Bessemer had. He was once again in the right place at the right time. Great entrepreneurs often do not create original ideas—they *grasp the significance* of an idea, wherever it comes from, and *leap on it* with everything they have. Carnegie rushed back to Pittsburgh to put all his eggs into a basket of steel.

An Irresistible Force

Carnegie's plan to manufacture steel faced a number of obstacles that appeared insurmountable. "It seemed as though the gods of fate were intent on turning against Carnegie on every front."[93] How he overcame each one is a story in itself.

The first obstacle (and the easiest) was his brother, Tom, who disapproved of the idea as risky. As Andy had promised that night when they were boys, Carnegie Brothers had become a great company. Carnegie had included Tom as his partner in numerous businesses, and Tom served as his right-hand man. It was a very successful partnership, but not an easy one. Like their father, Tom was a shy, cautious introvert. "The fact was that Tom, though fraternally fond of Andrew, was temperamentally unsympathetic," according to William Abbot, who served as president of Carnegie's steelworks for several years. "Tom did not have Andrew's ambition. . . . He disapproved of Andrew's skyrocketing tendencies, regarding him as a plunger and a dangerous leader."[94] If Tom thought Andrew was out of control, Andrew in turn perceived his brother as having been "born tired"—a distorted perception produced by their opposite temperaments. Anyone would look tired compared to Carnegie. Most Carnegie employees found Tom much easier to deal with. He was "forever smoothing over feathers his brother ruffled."[95] Eventually, Andrew left the day-to-day operations to him, while he spent more and more time in Europe and New York. No one was sorry to see Andrew go. When Carnegie told one manager, Bill Jones, that he was relieved to be leaving for his annual summer vacation, his reply was "And you, Andy, don't know what a relief it is for all of us."[96] Behind every successful hypomanic entrepreneur there stands a long-suffering person of normal temperament who must counterbalance and compensate for his excesses. Tom was the human shock absorber.

Ignoring Tom's objections, Carnegie leaped forward, determined to build the largest and most modern steel mill in the world. That he did so during the most dismal economic times was a Herculean task no reasonable person would have thought feasible. In the go-go years of the post–Civil War boom, business in America had been thriving. But in the fall of 1873, the stock market collapsed, banks and brokerage houses failed, the money supply shrank, unemployment hit 25 percent, soup kitchen lines grew, and recovery was six years away. America had entered its "first great depression." The demand for steel plummeted, along with its price. The primary customers for steel had been the railroad companies, which used them for track. No sector's stock had been more inflated than that of railroads, which were the Internet stocks of their day. When the bubble burst, half the railroads in America went bankrupt, and those that did survive were not planning to expand. With his usual irrational optimism, Carnegie considered this macroeconomic disaster a stroke of good luck. Thanks to runaway deflation, he paid less for labor and materials. It became a Carnegie technique to stockpile cash and expand in bad economic times—the opposite of what most businesses do. Still, even at a discount the gargantuan plant was a technological marvel that cost an unprecedented $1.25 million. Carnegie's steel mill was quite literally a concrete expression of his oversize ego—fiery and immense in scale.

Yet another stumbling block to launching his mill was, of all people, his old mentor, Tom Scott. Scott had come up critically short of cash in the market downturn. He had tried to build his own railroad, the Texas & Pacific, with short-term loans—a strategy that Carnegie had advised him against. Now, in the huge national credit crunch, Scott needed Carnegie to cosign a loan to stay afloat. Carnegie was summoned to a hastily called meeting with Scott and his partners. They leaned on him with all their might to cosign the loan. "The arguments lasted all day and all night."[97] Carnegie owed everything he had to his "genius" and "great man." "Yet, I was not tempted for a moment to entertain the idea of involving myself," Carnegie wrote. He knew Scott was heading into bankruptcy, and he wasn't about to go down with him. Thomson, the grandfather figure of the trio, who also had much of his capital sunk into the Texas & Pacific, sent a letter to Carnegie appealing to his loyalty: "You of all others should lend your helping hand."[98] Carnegie would not relent. He was summoned to a second meeting, but he became the immovable object. Carnegie was determined to continue his own ascent even though it meant "cutting the rope that bound him to Tom Scott and letting his friend sink."[99] It was "one of the most trying moments of my whole life," but "nothing in the world would ever induce me" to sign that loan. Carnegie's *true loyalty* was to his own *ambition*. He had attached himself to Scott in the first place only to use him as a vehicle for that ambition. Now that Scott became an impediment to it—well, sorry old friend. Some might justifiably deplore this approach to human relationships. It is ruthlessly narcissistic, but it is a trait common to most people who accomplish great things. Andrew Carnegie had a mission: "All my capital was in manufacturing."[100] Nothing and nobody was more important than that.

If he had cosigned that loan, Carnegie would not have been able to launch his mill. Carnegie's bankers got wind of the Scott situation and, assuming that Carnegie had cosigned, decided to call his loans immediately, to make sure they got paid before Carnegie went bankrupt along with Scott. Summoned to their wood-paneled office, Carnegie was confronted by the bank's officers. They were taken aback. Not only hadn't Carnegie cosigned but he gave them a righteous lecture about financial responsibility for daring to think he would even contemplate something so foolish. They rescinded their demand for immediate repayment. For the rest of his career, Carnegie never had any problem obtaining credit.

The competition was yet another barrier to Carnegie's entry into the steel business. An aristocracy of steel titans conspired through "pools" to fix prices, divvy up business, and keep others out. They looked down at this brash young man who had pushed his way into their company. "Carnegie despised pools" and mockingly called these older men "the Fathers in Israel."[101] Pools offended his competitive spirit, though he participated in them when he thought it to his advantage. When the Fathers in Israel summoned him to a

145

meeting, they announced that they had decided to assign his mill a mere 9 percent of the business. Carnegie leaped to his feet, banged his fist loudly on the table, and thundered threateningly at them: he astounded them by quoting precisely the costs and revenues of each company present (by becoming a small stockholder, he had obtained their corporate reports). After impressing them with his command of real numbers, he then made one up. He threatened to drive them all out of business by making steel for $9 a ton—a whopping lie as his minimum cost was $50. The bluff worked. "The committee at once got off its high horse, stopped snickering at me and met my demands." [102] As Carnegie later told one competitor, "I can make steel cheaper than any of you and undersell you. The market is mine whenever I want to take it." [103] In the end, that was no bluff. "Carnegie was the Napoleon—that is the commander and intuitive genius, who planned campaigns and executed them with a rapidity and boldness that swept all enemies from his path," according to a business associate, John Walker, who was not alone in referring to the five-foot, three-inch Carnegie as Napoleon. [104] At one time or another the greatest industrial titans of the age—Vanderbilt, Rockefeller, Morgan—tried to best Andrew Carnegie. None did.

Finally, the biggest barrier of all was the English. They had almost total dominance of the steel market. The British producers viewed American manufacturers contemptuously; they could safely export their worst steel to America and still compete effectively against America's domestic producers. "American steel" became a nickname for the British producers' grade B product. Carnegie's mill was, coincidentally, built on a field where the famous English general Edward Braddock had been defeated during a decisive battle of the French and Indian War in 1755. Carnegie liked to think of it as a good omen: "There on the field of Braddock's defeat, we began the erection of our steel-rail mills." [105] Carnegie hurled himself into the battle to beat Britain.

Hard Driving

Carnegie had a three-step formula for success: "Cut costs, scoop the market, and run the mills full." The first step was the most important. Lowered production costs made it possible to lower prices. Lower prices allowed one to capture all the business, or "scoop the market." To meet that increased demand he had to "run the mills full," producing economies of scale, which again lowered prices. These three steps created a self-sustaining virtuous cycle. "Show me your cost sheets" was his mantra. Carnegie wasn't interested in profits, which fluctuated with market conditions. "Watch your costs, and the profits will take care of themselves," he said. He knew that "a penny a ton gain in efficiency could translate to millions of dollars." [106] He wanted *everyone* to be focused on *one* thing: cost cutting.

The importance of micromeasuring costs seemed obvious to Carnegie, even though no one had thought of it before. "I was greatly surprised to find that the cost of each of the various processes was unknown." [107] His competitors didn't even know if they were in the black until they balanced their books at the end of the year. Carnegie found it "intolerable to be a mole burrowing in the dark." He kept apprised of the cost of every phase of production, in minute detail, on a week-by-week basis. "I insisted on such a system of weighing and accounting being introduced throughout our works as it would enable us to know what our cost was for each process and especially what each man was doing, who saved materials, who wasted it, and who produced the best results." [108] No one liked this scrutiny. "Every manager in the mills was naturally against the new system," Carnegie wrote. "There goes that damned bookkeeper," grumbled one of the foremen. "If I use a dozen more bricks than I did last month, he knows it and comes around to ask why." Counting every brick gave Carnegie the powerful knowledge of who was saving him money and who wasn't. He announced to his managers that they would be paid commensurate with how much money they saved. The idea seemed bizarre to the people whose bricks were being counted. But it accomplished its intent. The men who worked for Carnegie became almost as obsessed with efficiency as he was.

But Carnegie was hardly cheap. He spent enormous amounts of money for even the smallest technological edge without a second thought. "Older heads among the Pittsburgh manufacturers" criticized his "extravagant expenditures," but he asserted that they would have been a bargain at twice the price. For example, Carnegie was the first to employ a chemist. His competitors said they couldn't afford to hire a chemist. "They could not afford to be without one," he wrote. "Nine tenths of all uncertainties of pig-iron making were dispelled under the burning sun of chemical knowledge. We had the complete monopoly on scientific management."[109] Carnegie never forgot that modern factories had killed his father with their more efficient steam looms. With the largest and most modern factory in America, he planned to be the one making a killing. He put an unheard-of 75 percent of his profits into expansion and modernization, *every year,* which his partners did not appreciate. They would have preferred to see the profits distributed to them as dividends.

Carnegie understood that the more steel he made and the faster he made it, the cheaper each ton would become. To keep the mills running full, Carnegie adopted a procedure known as "hard driving"—firing the furnace full blast twenty-four hours a day (which he did every day but Christmas and the Fourth of July). The British steelmakers thought Carnegie mad. Sir James Kitson, president of the British Iron and Steel Institute, said, "It won't last . . . this continual work at high pressure does not pay in the end."[110] English industrialist Sir Lowthian Bell decried the "reckless rapid rate" of hard driving. At that rate, the interior lining of each furnace had to be replaced every three years.[111] Carnegie's superintendent said in response to Sir Lowthian, "We think a lining is good for so much iron and the sooner it makes it the better." What would Sir

Lowthian have thought if he had known that Carnegie had ordered his men to tear down a brand-new rolling mill, one they had built only three *months* before, when he found a more efficient design? It was readily apparent to Carnegie that the money generated by faster production more than paid for new equipment. To his British competitors, the replacement of properly functioning equipment was a "wicked waste." One of them scolded Carnegie, "We have equipment we have been using for twenty years and it's still serviceable." Carnegie's riposte: "And that is what is the matter with the British steel trade. Most British equipment is in use twenty years after it should have been scrapped. It is because you keep this used up machinery that the United States is making you a back number."[112]

Carnegie himself invented nothing, indeed made no technical contribution whatsoever. So what did Carnegie contribute? He was a human engine pushing an accelerating pace of innovation, driving large groups of men, often mercilessly, toward levels of productivity never imagined. If Carnegie put a strain on his furnaces with all his hard driving, it was nothing compared to the strain he put on his managers and workers. Business historians have hailed Carnegie as a "management genius" and called his organization a "masterpiece."[113] What was his secret? Though the Bible teaches that patience is a virtue, in business hypomanic impatience can be an asset. A stream of memos document that better was never good enough for Carnegie. When one lieutenant wired Carnegie that they "broke all records for making steel last week," Carnegie replied, "Why not every week?" When his blast furnace manager reported, "No. 8 furnace broke all records today," he responded, "What are the other ten furnaces doing?" When a sales agent signed a big contract, Carnegie's reaction was "Good boy! Next!"[114] When Carnegie first started making steel, fifty tons was a good day in any mill. By the time he retired he was producing more than half a million tons a year—a 20,000 percent increase in production.

Carnegie looked for men who could rise to his challenge. The most notable was his superintendent, Bill Jones, a volatile, belligerent Welshman with a "booming bass voice" who felt equal to any man alive (he insolently called Carnegie "Andy"). In response to what he viewed as an insane demand for radically increased production, Jones told Andy to back off and let him handle matters: "Your last two letters have been received. . . . It is utterly impossible to make that amount of rails in the time specified . . . I know what rail making is. . . . Have patience and I think I can show you a thing or two."[115] Asking Carnegie to have patience was like waving a red flag in front of a bull. Carnegie didn't *want* to be patient. He wanted Jones to be impatient, and rather than backing off, he increased his demands. Jones realized he was just going to have to show the Little Boss (as Carnegie was called behind his back) who the real steel master was. He bet Carnegie a new suit of clothes that he could beat the production of their main rival—Pennsylvania Steel. Jones saved time by moving freshly cast ingots from the converter directly onto a train of moving flatcars, carrying their steel to market still warm. Thus, "rapid movement of materials became another hallmark of the Carnegie works, another characteristic that distinguished American mills from their British counterparts."[116] It was this same principle that would ultimately lead to Henry Ford's great innovation: the assembly line.* When Jones won their bet, he crowed to Carnegie, "I guess you had better send that order for a

---

* "Every thing can always be done faster" was Ford's mantra. Day after day, he paced the factory floor shouting, "No, no! Not fast enough!," stopping at every workstation, brainstorming aloud with each worker. The men he employed were smart can-do types, or they were quickly fired. (There was no shortage of talented candidates for Ford jobs. Ford became nationally famous when he announced "Five Dollar Day"—paying his workers $5 a day, twice the going rate.) Ford "couldn't be still," wrote biographer Garet Garrett. His impatience was the secret to his success. The motor inside of him revved so quickly that the world around him seemed maddeningly slow, and he wanted the world to catch up (Ford personally set a world speed record in 1904, driving one of his cars madly across a frozen lake). When Ford began making cars, the industry standard was ten days to produce one vehicle. By the time he finished, a car drove off the assembly line every few seconds.

suit of clothes, for I fear that by the time you have compared our results with that of other works, you will feel sure that I am entitled to two suits. Now in conclusion, you let me handle this nag in this race." [117]

The truth was, William Jones was *born* impatient, just like Carnegie. The son of a Welsh "nonconformist preacher," he too had the restless blood of prophets in his veins. He rose from private to captain in the Union Army in large part because of that restless aggressive energy. "During one particular skirmish, Jones and his company had to wait while engineers erected a pontoon bridge across a river, but impatient to engage the enemy, he cried, 'hanged if I'll wait for the bridge,' and he dove into the muddy river. It was only a few feet deep and he split open his nose." [118] Jones was a "restless experimenter and inventor" who became "the greatest steel maker in American history." [119] Through his continuous tinkering, he doubled the plant's productivity. He is credited with making the Bessemer converter a success in America. In him Carnegie found a kindred spirit—a fellow impatient man.

Carnegie offered a partnership in the company to Jones, who refused it because he distrusted stock. "Just give me a hell of a salary if you think I'm worth it," he said. "All right, Captain, the salary of the President of the United States is yours," Carnegie replied, and matched the salary of the president: $25,000. [120] This was quite a promotion for a man who had started his career as a $2-a-day mechanic.

When asked about such astronomical salaries for managers who performed, Carnegie replied, "I can't afford to pay them any other way." [121] Machines and systems that could increase efficiency were worth their weight in gold, but people who could design, run, and improve such systems were worth their weight in platinum. Carnegie maintained that there was no labor so cheap as the dearest mechanical labor. Paying high wages to the best of his employees *lowered* costs. It seemed incomprehensible to Carnegie that his competitors didn't get this. Jones made him millions. Carnegie couldn't afford to nickel-and-dime him when he knew his competitors were trying to lure him away.

Jones died "with his boots on," as he had always predicted he would, when a vat of molten steel spilled on him. For the rest of his life, Carnegie kept a picture of Jones in his bedroom.

All Gets Better

Carnegie made a partnership in his company available to any employee who proved his worth. "Any ambitious young man had universal opportunity just sitting there waiting to be taken. No barriers." [122] This kind of opportunity was unavailable anywhere else in America. He "kept an eagle eye out for talent in his mills" and promoted from the bottom. "Every year should be marked by the promotion of one or more of our young men," said Carnegie. "We cannot have too many of the right sort interested in profits." [123] In 1889, twenty men were made partners. Each had risen from humble starting positions. "Promote from the ranks should be the motto," Carnegie said, bragging, "Mr. Morgan buys his partners, I grow mine." [124] (Despite all the partnerships he handed out, Carnegie never ceded control. He was always majority partner. And a contract, known as "the ironclad," made sure that *any* partner who left the company for any reason, including death, had to surrender his stock at the original book value, which was nominal.)

When questioned as to whether one man he was planning to promote was really up to the task, Carnegie said he was more than willing to give the boy a "trial." A trial, Carnegie believed, was the best any man could hope for. "That's all we get ourselves. If he can win the race he is our racehorse; if not he goes to the cart." [125] Carnegie's method identified, empowered, and rewarded men who were both talented and hypomanically driven, like Jones. Competition within the organization for these coveted partnerships was intense, and Carnegie was convinced that this spurred men to greater heights of performance. He even had Jones organize the men by department into a softball league, because competing against one another on the field spurred them on to outdo one another in the mill. "It was survival of the fittest in the Carnegie ecosystem." [126]

That was no accident.

Carnegie's gut feelings about competition found validation in a radical new philosophy: Social Darwinism. In the 1870s, Darwin and his theory of evolution were revolutionary. *On the Origin of Species by Natural Selection* was first published in 1865. Herbert Spencer, a British sociologist, adapted Darwin to societal relations. The unvarnished truth was that man progressed through the "ceaseless devouring of the weak by the strong." [127] It was actually Spencer, and not Darwin, as most people assume, who coined the term "survival of the fittest." "One part of the community is industrious and prudent and accumulates capital," Spencer wrote, "the other idle, and improvident or in some cases perhaps, unfortunate." [128] There are winners and there are losers, and that was simply a scientific *fact*. Through this winnowing process, intelligent life had been born, and through it higher peaks of civilization would be reached, according to Spencer.

Carnegie was an agnostic searching for a secular religion. In his search, he pored over Darwin and Spencer, looking for answers to life's biggest questions. "A new horizon opened up for me. . . . I began to view the various phases of life from the standpoint of an evolutionist. . . . The result of my journey was to bring a certain mental peace. Where there had been chaos there was now order. My mind was at rest. I had a philosophy at last." [129]

The term "Social Darwinism" is discredited today as a self-serving rationalization used by amoral nineteenth-century laissez-faire capitalists to justify their exploitation of workers. "With the model of ruthless competition in which only the 'fittest survived,' it thus followed logically that the richest entrepreneurs were the fittest." [130] Rich capitalists could both congratulate themselves on their outstanding success and shed no tears for the losers they devoured—no more than a lion would grieve for its prey. Yet Carnegie never thought of himself as a robber baron. He believed himself to be the most enlightened of employers. His mill was run in a fashion that he thought was evolutionarily correct—offering advancement without prejudice for the most able and the cart for the rest. Carnegie took great pride in this. For him, Social Darwinism was an *idealistic* worldview, not a mere excuse to abuse his fellow men. Carnegie's idiosyncratic interpretation of evolution was wildly utopian. It was nothing less than the path to the advancement of mankind. Like most utopians, Carnegie failed utterly to see the dark side of his philosophy as it was put into practice.

One day he had a revelatory experience in which he *saw* the "truth of evolution":

> I remember that light came as in a flood and all was clear. Not only had I got rid of theology and the supernatural, but I had found the truth of evolution. "All is well since all grows better" became my motto, my true source of comfort. Man was not created with an instinct for his own degradation, but from the lower he had risen to the higher form. Nor is there any conceivable end to his march toward perfection. His face is turned toward the light; he stands in the sun and looks upward.[131]

Carnegie's Darwinian revelation shows that hypomanic and manic revelations are not limited to classic "religious experiences." The *content* of revelation is as varied as human imagination. The *process,* in its essentials, is always the same. Revelation is a life-changing eureka moment that fills the subject with light, joy, and special insight into the workings of the universe and instills in him a new sense of missionary purpose. Carnegie's insight had messianic implications about the special place of his adopted country in world history. Compared to the aristocratic social order that prevailed where Carnegie had been born, American democracy cre-

ated a fairer playing field that didn't interfere with Darwinian competition. A society in which the best man could win would itself win
in the competition between nations because it was more in har-
mony with the principles of evolution and, as such, intrinsically
more efficient. In business, more efficient corporations competed
their rivals into extinction. Carnegie was convinced that democracy
would compete every other form of social organization out of existence. America was leading the peoples of the world in the "march
towards perfection." Carnegie felt destined to be the evangelist who
would bring his gospel to the world.

The Wages of Sin

Carnegie's grandiose idealism blinded him to an important concrete reality: that the conditions in his mill were inhumane. They
have been described as "among the worst in the world." The worst
strain of all was put on the simple laborers, who endured the smoke
and heat of a veritable Hades on Earth to work the furnaces and
roll the steel. There were hundreds of fatal accidents, many due to
fatigue. To run the mill twenty-four hours a day, Carnegie designed
a shift schedule he called "the long term plan," where workers
pulled twelve-hour shifts for twelve days in a row, followed by a
grueling twenty-four-hour shift on the thirteenth day and then a
meager twenty-four hours off on the fourteenth. Once a man
worked the day shift for two weeks, he worked nights for the next
two weeks. Evenly distributing the nights shifts among the workers
was an attempt at fairness, but such shift switching disrupted the
workers' circadian rhythms, producing even greater fatigue. Bill
Jones was enlightened enough to intervene and institute a rotation
of three eight-hour shifts. He could see that the men were working
beyond their breaking points. He argued to Carnegie that the eight-
hour shift would pay for itself, because he would be able to push his
men harder each hour they worked, thus increasing productivity
per man-hour. But when a bad economy demanded cost cuts,

Carnegie foolishly abandoned that progressive experiment. He had little sympathy for men who whined about working twelve hours. *Carnegie* had worked twelve-hour shifts when he was only thirteen years old. The notion of a twenty-four-hour shift didn't seem insane to a hypomanic who could work without sleep.

Also, these overworked men were grossly underpaid. No man could support a family on the 14 cents an hour he paid. But Carnegie had romanticized the grim poverty of his past, even praising it in an essay entitled "The Advantages of Poverty," in which he argued that being poor is the best preparation for a rising young man. The "dark horse" coming from behind would beat his more pampered rivals every time, Carnegie proclaimed. He had worked his way up from bobbin boy and believed that anyone in America could do the same. Furthermore, there was no place in America where that was more true than in Carnegie's mill. What else could the men want?

Perhaps if he had spent more time with his men, he wouldn't have been so clueless. But beginning in the 1880s, Carnegie spent less time in Pittsburgh and more in Scotland and New York. That Carnegie was able to be successful as a partial absentee owner was a testimony to his management team. His racehorses could run. And Carnegie evidenced a remarkable ability to crack the whip by transatlantic mail. Not surprisingly, he wore out managers almost as fast as furnace linings. Tragically, the first casualty was his brother, Tom, who died suddenly in 1886, having drank himself to death. Perhaps the stress of working for Andrew had driven him to it. Longtime partner Harry Phipps took over but then retired out of exhaustion in 1888. Longtime friend David Stewart was elected chairman and died. Carnegie left "a veritable graveyard of destroyed chairmen, presidents and managers" in his wake.[132] Hypomanic entrepreneurs can run through people quickly. Using them up, driving them away, or turning against them are all common patterns among hypomanic leaders.

When Phipps quit, the mantle fell to William Clay Frick in January 1889. Whereas Tom Carnegie had been a shock absorber, Frick was the opposite: "cold blooded and machinelike" and "one of the cruelest employers in the industry," he amplified Carnegie's failings in the human resource department.[133]

When Carnegie left the country in the summer of 1892, he knew there would be a tough labor negotiation at his Homestead Mill while he was gone. The workers' contract expired in July, and he was demanding wage concessions to compensate for a bad market. In those days, wage cuts were standard practice. The price of labor fluctuated with the price of the product. It was a cruel practice, pushing thousands of families below the poverty line. And it was an unfair one, because wages were not raised in commensurate fashion when new efficiencies raised productivity and increased profits. Wage cuts were a fact of life for the nineteenth-century workingman, and in the summer of 1892 everyone at the mill accepted them as inevitable. The only arguments were about how much to cut.

Carnegie doubted that this situation would come to a strike, but if it did he had endured them before. At worst, Frick would have to do what Carnegie had always done so successfully in the past: "Let a little grass grow over the plant," as Carnegie put it. He didn't need scabs. He simply closed down the mill, let the men get hungry, and negotiated from strength. With his millions in the bank, Carnegie could easily outlast workers who lived one paycheck away from starvation. "The policy I had pursued in cases of difference with our men was of patiently waiting, reasoning with them and showing them that their demands were unfair."[134] Carnegie thought Frick was a "positive genius," and he left for vacation with hearty confidence that his manager would sort things out. Unfortunately, his genius turned a petty dispute with a handful of workers into an armed battle forever etched into the annals of American labor history.

Frick intended to handle things his way and intentionally kept Carnegie unapprised of events as they developed. He rolled three miles of barbed wire around the entire plant and set up gun turrets. The workers dubbed it "Fort Frick." He then provocatively hired three hundred Pinkerton guards. Pinkertons were not just security guards then, but dreaded "assassins" who had killed strikers in several previous violent labor disputes around the country. "The Homestead men realized they were fighting a much larger battle that represented all oppressed laborers."[135] They would fire on Fort Frick. Thinking he had the element of surprise, Frick floated the Pinkertons down the river at night in an unmarked barge. An enraged mob was waiting for them. Before they made it to shore, pandemonium broke out. Several people on both sides were killed and more injured.

When Carnegie read about the violence in the newspapers the next day, it was "like a bolt out of the blue." He was mortified. He had created a prominent public persona as an *enlightened* capitalist. He had even published articles supporting the right of workers to unionize, at least in principle. This happening at a Carnegie plant seemed like a shocking betrayal, and the national public backlash was furious. "Three months ago Andrew Carnegie was a man to be envied. Today he is an object of mingled pity and contempt . . . a moral coward . . . without a grain of decency . . . or manhood," wrote the *St. Louis Dispatch*.[136] Some Republicans blamed the presidential victory of Democrat Grover Cleveland on the wave of anti-business sentiment aroused in the populace by the Homestead disaster.

Carnegie was so desperate to clear his name for Homestead that he made things up to put himself in the best possible light. He claimed in his *Autobiography*, "I was traveling in the Highlands of Scotland when the trouble arose" and consequently "did not hear of it till two days after." That was a lie. He read it in the morning papers like everyone else. Moreover, Carnegie insisted that his men loved and trusted him so deeply that, had he been in the loop, they would have worked out their differences peacefully. According to Carnegie's story, his men had cabled him for help, but tragically, he received the telegram too late to intervene. "While in Scotland I received the following cable from the offices of the union of our workmen: 'Kind master, tell us what you wish us to do and we shall do it for you.' This was most touching but alas too late. The mischief was done."[137] Unfortunately, Carnegie, the "kind master," was never able to produce this "touching" telegram, claiming to have mislaid it. In fact, it never existed.

But Carnegie was not lying when he wrote, "Nothing I have had to meet in my life, before or since, wounded me so deeply."[138] Homestead had "a depressing effect on him" that festered for years.[139] To prove to himself and to the world that Andrew Carnegie really was the hero he knew himself to be, he needed to do something bigger and better than the world had ever seen before.

Selling Out

Hard driving took a terrible toll on both men and machines, but Sir James Kitson was wrong. This "work at continuous pressure" did "pay in the end," and not just for Carnegie but for America. When Carnegie began his career, the British owned the world steel market. "As late as 1870, Britain produced more steel than the rest of the world combined. Carnegie made steel his own industry, and he thundered past his native land with the rush of an express train. In 1900, the year before Carnegie's retirement, the United States produced twice as much steel as Britain."[140] Carnegie beat the British, and far worse than had his hero William Wallace. Carnegie's hypomanic pace of relentless innovation dramatically dropped the price of steel, and the positive consequences were manifold. Carnegie's affordable steel rails formed the spine of the continent's developing transportation infrastructure, allowing millions of people to do what Americans like to do best: move. The easy movement of goods and workers stimulated the economy and tied a gigantic landmass into one country. Carnegie's steel built

America's cities. His mills supplied the steel for the Brooklyn Bridge, the New York and Chicago elevated subways, the Washington Monument, and—perhaps most important of all—the first skyscraper. These tall buildings became integral to the rise of America's cities, as millions of immigrants poured into urban centers and population density increased. As Jefferson had feared, America ceased being a predominantly rural nation, and manufacturing was to blame.

Even more important, Carnegie, "the first modern industrialist," created a *method*. His maniacal impatience to go faster produced efficiencies that were imitated, both by his competitors and by manufacturers in other industries, just as Ford's assembly line was imitated. The net result was that it made the production of *all* goods cheaper. The effect of these methods on the American economy is incalculable. Cheaper goods made Americans richer in real wages. America became the first country where the majority of the population was middle-class. Carnegie and Ford couldn't have come at a better time. It was around the turn of the century that immigration truly exploded. Not all of those huddling masses could become rich. But the inexpensive mass production of goods meant that most of them could at least acquire the basic comforts of life. It brought the American dream down to the level of the average American. When Ford entered his industry, cars cost $2,000 to $3,000. Ford dreamed of a $250 car that any man with a job could afford. Achieving his dream didn't just make him the richest man on Earth—it made everyone behind the wheel of a new Tin Lizzie feel like a millionaire.

But Carnegie had finally tired of business. In 1901, when J. P. Morgan offered to buy Carnegie out, he didn't hesitate. He wrote the unheard-of price of $480 million on a scrap of paper, and Morgan did not hesitate to accept. To make the victory complete, the egotistical Carnegie insisted that Morgan travel uptown to his office with the check, rather than Carnegie having to go downtown to Morgan. Morgan was there in a flash with effusive flattery: "Mr.

Carnegie, I want to congratulate you on being the richest man in the world!"[141]

Morgan combined Carnegie's company with his competitors to create the greatest monopoly of all time: U.S. Steel, the world's first billion-dollar company. Morgan was himself a bipolar type II. When suffering from his recurrent depressions he took long sea voyages in search of recuperation. When he was up, Morgan was charismatic, hypersexual, high-living, and free-spending. Appropriately nicknamed "Jupiter," he was Olympian in the force of his personality. Like a god, Morgan held the entire American industrial economy in his hands and molded it to his will, systematically "morganizing" industry after industry into giant trusts.

Paying Carnegie half a billion dollars was not Morgan's first choice. Immediately preceding the buyout, Morgan had tried to squeeze Carnegie out, allying with both his competitors and his customers against him. Carnegie had responded in his typical aggressive fashion by counterattacking. Taking the battle to Morgan, Carnegie had announced his entry into several of the industries, such as steel pipes, that Morgan had already morganized. Morgan didn't think he was bluffing; Carnegie had done things like that before. When he hadn't liked the shipping rates the Pennsylvania Railroad charged him, he built a competing railroad. He may or may not have been bluffing, but just as the "Fathers in Israel" had backed down, so did Morgan. Unable to force him out, Morgan became desperate to buy him out. That was Carnegie's plan all along, many argue.

How desperate Morgan had become, even Carnegie didn't know. A couple of years later, Carnegie ran into Morgan on a transatlantic steamer and told him, "I made one mistake when I sold out to you. I should have asked you for a hundred million more." With a sly grin, Morgan replied, "Well, you would have got it if you had."[142] The conversation didn't make Carnegie angry. His retirement had never been about the money. After he retired, Congressman A. O. Stanley said to him, "I believe you would have captured the steel trade of the world if you had stayed in business." Carnegie replied, confident as ever, "I am as certain of it as I can be certain of anything." [143] Carnegie knew full well that he would have made far more money if he had stayed in business.

But it was time. Carnegie was sixty-five, and it was time to honor the contract he had written in the St. Nicholas Hotel more than thirty years before. Something, perhaps the spirit of Grandpa Morrison, had scared Carnegie that December night into fearing for his very soul. The St. Nicholas compact had been a promise to be true to his radical roots. And he went on to fulfill each of its promises. In his St. Nicholas resolution, Carnegie had vowed to return to Britain to "make the acquaintance of literary men," take "part in public matters," and "purchase a controlling interest in some newspaper [to advocate for] education & improvement of the poorer classes." He would do all those things and more. His progenitors had started a revolution, and Carnegie aimed to finish it.

THE PASSION OF SAINT ANDREW

A Triumphal March into Dunfermline

On that sad day in 1848 when young Andrew Carnegie watched the spire of the abbey recede into the distance, he swore he would return. "What Benares is to the Hindoo, Mecca to the Mohammedan, Jerusalem to the Christian, all that Dunfermline is to me," he would explain. [144]

Two decades before Carnegie sold his business, he had already begun to turn his attentions to his new career as a philanthropist and to his old home. In 1881, when he returned to Dunfermline, it was a triumphant procession. Carnegie rode in a luxurious coach with an entourage of gentlemen and his mother at his side, "riding in her carriage" for all to see. On the outskirts of town, an old man with white hair greeted them. It was Uncle Lauder, who jumped aboard. What awaited them when they entered Dunfermline moved Carnegie to tears:

> At the entrance to the city, a triumphal arch had been built and "Welcome Carnegie" banners graced the streets. Factories and businesses were closed, sidewalks were crowded with men, women and children in their Sunday best, faces pushed through upper story windows, and a mile long parade stretched through the town, following the coach, as some twenty thousand people paid tribute.[145]

One of his traveling companions recalled, "The town was ablaze with flags and mottoes and streaming ribbons." Most amazing, they were *American* flags. "The American stars and stripes waved everywhere, even over the noble old abbey where the Scottish kings lie in their stone coffins," Carnegie's friend recalled with astonishment.[146]

Carnegie had come home to dedicate a library he had donated to the town. He had also built public baths and a recreational center. Carnegie's generosity to Dunfermline would continue for the rest of his life, but perhaps his most satisfying gift came in 1902, when he bought the estate around the abbey, the one his grandfather and all his descendants had been forbidden to set foot in. "What it would have meant to my Grandfather, Father, Uncles," Carnegie crowed triumphantly.[147] Carnegie made it a public park open to the town's inhabitants, not just one day a year but every day.

In the summer of 1898, Carnegie purchased a Scottish castle on a large estate overlooking the water, much like the old abbey. He employed almost every laborer in the region to transform the mere castle into a palace fit for a king. In fact, King Edward stopped by to get ideas for the refurbishment of Buckingham Palace. A series of stained-glass windows that celebrated the different stages of

Carnegie's career, beginning with his job as a bobbin boy, was just one of the extraordinary features. Carnegie was building a cathedral to celebrate himself. A full-time organist was employed to play spiritually uplifting music on a massive instrument Carnegie had installed in the center hall. This was the beginning of a new career as prophet, Andrew Carnegie style.

Speeding Up Evolution

In 1889, in the *North American Review,* Carnegie wrote an essay entitled "Wealth," where he put forth the proposition that "he who dies rich dies disgraced." [148] He argued that it was the duty of every successful entrepreneur to give away his money before he died. The owner and editor of the journal proclaimed it the "finest essay he had ever read." British Prime Minister William Gladstone was so impressed that he had Carnegie's essay reprinted in England under the title "The Gospel of Wealth."

After Carnegie retired, he vowed to practice what he had preached. This grandson of a radical socialist was going to redistribute his wealth in a radical way. Like Roger Williams, Carnegie was going from one extreme to another, from robber baron to Robin Hood. He had already donated money on several occasions, but now the world's richest man publicly announced that henceforth he would devote himself to giving away his entire fortune. He had $360 million, and after making provisions for his wife and daughter, he announced his intention to give away every penny. The news created an international sensation and enormous curiosity. A British syrup company had a contest for ideas: "How should Andrew Carnegie spend his money?" It received 45,000 suggestions, the most common of which was "Give it to me."

Never one to do things in small ways, Carnegie entered philanthropy, as he had steel, on a scale never seen before. He "set the pace of philanthropy in his time—for all time, for that matter." [149] Rockefeller was inspired by him as a role model and turned to

Carnegie for advice on how to become a philanthropist. Carnegie evangelized all his fellow millionaires to follow in his footsteps.

Not everyone stood up and cheered. His motives were considered suspect by some who thought his flashy good works were a way "to satisfy an insatiable desire for attention, notoriety and immortality." [150] Others thought he was assuaging a guilty conscience over Homestead. No doubt these motives were operative. Carnegie certainly loved attention. Fifty-seven towns awarded him their "freedom," the British equivalent of the key to the city, more than any other person in history, including Winston Churchill. Carnegie's British friend John Morley wrote sympathetically that he didn't envy Carnegie's having to publicly accept all these honors and make speech after speech. But Carnegie confessed to Morley that he never tired of it. His appetite for the limelight was indeed insatiable. He surrounded himself with an unending stream of guests at home precisely because he so loved being the center of attention, oblivious of the fact that perpetual entertaining was wearing his wife out both mentally and physically.

Carnegie had a vision that was so ambitious and lofty it made everything he had accomplished in industry pale by comparison. Considering himself a "high priest of civil religion," the agnostic Carnegie wanted to be "a leading player in civilization's progress at the dawn of the twentieth century." During his business career he had revolutionized manufacturing. "Carnegie was now determined to *improve mankind.*"[151] As a boy, Carnegie had saved his family. He now felt heroic enough to save the family of man. Mark Twain dubbed him "Saint Andrew." [152]

Once his Social Darwinism had made him insensitive to the human suffering he caused. Survival of the fittest was an immutable law. Why mourn the inevitability that life's competition must have losers when nothing could be done about it? Yet the problem dogged Carnegie's conscience, and he arrived at a satisfactory solution: he could alter the equation by *raising* the overall level of human fitness. He would lift up the masses so their hands could grasp that crucial first rung of the ladder. If he could move millions of tons of steel faster than anyone had ever imagined, he could elevate millions of people faster, too. He would speed up evolution!

An amazing autodidact who impressed even England's most noted men of letters with his ability to quote Shakespeare, Carnegie felt he owed his development as a human being in large part to books. He would always be grateful to Colonel Anderson, who had opened his library to working boys, allowing him to transcend the drudgery of mind-numbing manual labor with a book always in his pocket. There was no public library system then, and books were far too expensive for the average working man or boy. Colonel Anderson had shed a ray of hope in Carnegie's soul. What if that ray could be multiplied a million times over? The answer was *libraries*. "Libraries were his cathedrals, a holy place to worship knowledge, hallowed buildings where the sin of ignorance was washed away and individuals could improve their station in life. Libraries perpetuated social evolution." [153]

Before Carnegie retired, many asked him how he could square his "gospel of wealth" with his cruel wage cuts. Carnegie had donated a million-dollar library to the people of Pittsburgh with one hand, while lowering their pay below the poverty line with the other. As one steel worker put it, "We'd rather they hadn't cut our wages and let us spend the money for ourselves. What use has a man who works twelve hours a day for a library anyway?" [154] No doubt that argument made sense to most of Carnegie's workers, but not to Carnegie. He had worked twelve hours a day, and a library had been invaluable to his rise. It was precisely the men with evolutionary potential who would transcend their circumstances, if just given a chance. Carnegie believed he knew better than his workers what they needed. Had the money been paid to the workers directly, he reasoned, they would only have squandered it "in the indulgence of appetite." Merely "adding to the comforts of the home," Carnegie wrote, would accomplish little for "the [human] race as a race." In contrast, "wealth passing through the hands of a few, can be made a much more potent force for the elevation of our race than if distributed in small sums to the people themselves." [155] The flaw in his reasoning was that Carnegie could easily have afforded to pay the workers a few pennies more per hour while still practicing his philanthropy.

Nonetheless, Carnegie's impact on literacy was so immense that it is difficult to calculate. Carnegie spent more than $50 million to open 2,811 libraries in eleven countries and every state in the union but Rhode Island. Collectively, these institutions lent tens of millions of volumes each year to people who would not otherwise have had access to books. It was a famous expression that the sun never set on the British Empire. Carnegie liked to say that the sun never set on his libraries. Some derided him as a modern Ramses II, immortalizing his name in stone. In fairness, Carnegie never *required* that his name be attached to his libraries, though he always appreciated it and was ever ready to supply a photo of himself for the lobby. But he did require each building to be inscribed with these words from Genesis: "Let there be light." It showed the spiritual reverence Carnegie had for books and their capacity to enlighten. It also put Carnegie in the role of God—issuing forth intelligent life on Earth.

With $10 million, he more than doubled the endowment of Scotland's entire university system, marking most of the money for scholarships. The ultra-abolitionist also gave large sums to small black colleges. He helped start Spellman College and supported Booker T. Washington's Tuskegee Institute. Washington was a true evolutionary hero in Carnegie's eyes because he had not only raised himself from slavery but had also "helped raise millions of his race to a higher stage of civilization." [156] But Carnegie was tightfisted with his money when elite colleges asked him for funds. Why did they need his help? When Princeton president Woodrow Wilson showed Carnegie around the campus, hoping for a large donation, Carnegie noticed a spot where a little lake might be picturesque. "We asked for bread and you gave us cake," Wilson said

167

graciously at the very small dedication ceremony for Lake Carnegie.[157] Carnegie wanted to spread his seed where it was needed most. Always a fanatic about efficiency, he wanted to get the best evolutionary value for his dollar.

Similarly, Carnegie resisted the invitation to start a national university in Washington, D.C., hating duplication of effort in any form. It was a project that would have brought him considerable glory. George Washington himself had called for such a university, and Carnegie could have been its founder. But why start a new college when there were already fine institutions in the area, such as Johns Hopkins? Instead, he established a large endowment to support scientific research at existing American universities, and he created one for Scotland as well. Nothing like it had existed before. President Theodore Roosevelt was proud to be a member of its board. At the board's first meeting, Carnegie once again issued forth light: "Gentlemen, your work begins. Your aims are high; you seek to extend known forces, and to discover and utilize new forces for the benefit of man." [158] Carnegie also made large personal gifts to individual scientists such as Madame Curie. Sometimes he would read about a scientist in the newspaper and just send him or her a check.

Among Carnegie's more unusual charities were his "Hero Funds," which he established with $10 million in eleven countries. They were meant to recognize and reward acts of heroism, as an inspiration to young people. Considering what William Wallace had done for him, Carnegie thought that providing youths with heroes would raise their aspirations. Recipients—or more often their families if the heroes were killed performing their act of courage—were awarded a cash gift and a gold medal with the profile of none other than Andrew Carnegie.

Carnegie ultimately craved redemption for all he had denied his workers. By any accounting, he owed them, and he knew it. His first philanthropic act upon retirement was to use $4 million to create the Carnegie Relief Fund "to provide pensions for the retired, as well as aid for the injured and families of those who died in his mill." [159] He also gave $15 million to "aged university professors" to form what became TIAA, the retirement system that covers almost every professor in America today. Carnegie pursued his pension penchant in hypomanic fashion, giving away an additional $4 million in pensions to more than four hundred people chosen almost at random, from his childhood mailman to total strangers. He gave a pension to one woman he did not know, whom he passed on the street, because she physically resembled his deceased mother.

Speeding up evolution was a grandiose mission, but who can say that Andrew Carnegie didn't nudge humanity just a bit higher? How can one measure the impact of such a massive "democratization of knowledge"? We will never know how many Andrew Carnegies lit the lamp of the mind with one of his library books in their pocket.

Literary Men

When Carnegie heard the news that his guru Herbert Spencer was sailing from England to America on the steamer *Servia* in August 1882, he could hardly contain his excitement. He immediately booked passage on the *Servia*, thrilled at the chance to commune with the man whose writings on Social Darwinism had changed his life. Unfortunately, the feeling was not mutual. Spencer was an irritable sixty-two-year-old man, bald, with tufts of gray hair above his ears, long scraggy sideburns wrapped under his chin, and facial features, ironically enough for an evolutionist, that are described as "chimplike." He was "visibly grumpy" and "quickly wearied of Carnegie's frenetic character." [160] Carnegie arranged to be assigned to Spencer's table for the entire nine-day journey, enthusiastically anticipating a passionate Platonic dialogue with his intellectual hero. Spencer wanted only to eat in peace, but Carnegie would not shut up. When the waiter brought Spencer the wrong kind of cheese, he exploded, "Cheddar! I said cheddar, not Cheshire!

Bring me cheddar!" Carnegie was taken aback and a bit disillusioned about his great man by this incident: "I had imagined you, the great philosopher, brooding over all things. Never did I dream you could become so excited over the question of cheese." [161] Nor did he dream Spencer might be irritated at *him*.

But nothing could discourage Carnegie in the pursuit of his hero. Despite this poor start, Carnegie convinced Spencer to visit Pittsburgh. It was Carnegie's intention to show him the city as shining proof that America was the next step in social evolution that Spencer himself had written about. Unfortunately, the sage "did not recognize utopia when it was shown to him." "Six months here would justify suicide," he proclaimed. [162] The belching smoke and black soot of Pittsburgh were revolting to him. A man would be "fortunate to recognize his own hand held close to his face." [163] During his 1884 trip to England, Carnegie invited Spencer to lunch. He declined in a note that read, "You must excuse me from coming to lunch with you, for it would involve more talking than I just now wish to undertake." [164] Not taking the hint, Carnegie would continue to pursue Spencer, who repeatedly found himself the unwilling victim of Carnegie's hospitality.

Carnegie had better luck with other members of the British literati, such as Matthew Arnold, widely regarded as England's most prominent man of letters. Arnold and his family had extensive contact with Carnegie over the years, including shared vacations. Perpetually strapped for money, Arnold certainly didn't mind that Carnegie picked up the tab for their lavish hotels and restaurants. But Carnegie was more than a free lunch. He was a curious phenomenon to Arnold and the rest of their literary coterie. Never had any of them seen such "rapidity, energy, and confident enthusiasm," wrote their mutual friend John Morley. Of course he was rough around the edges, but Carnegie's "freshness of spirit" more than compensated for the "occasional crudity or haste in judgment as befalls the best of us in ardent hours." And with his "quick, racy, superabundant sense of humor," he was fun. [165]

Carnegie was also a "strenuous disputant," Morley noted.[166] He never stopped trying to convert his new intellectual friends to the cause of American-style democracy for Britain. William Black, another prominent writer who spent time with Carnegie, nicknamed him the "Star-Spangled Scotchman." (The press picked up on the nickname, and it stuck.) Black claimed that all in their circle grew weary of listening to Carnegie tirelessly "proclaiming the glories of the United States."[167]

Arnold was more favorably impressed with America than Spencer had been, particularly its Constitution and its egalitarian loosening of class boundaries. In the tone of a true member of the British elite he wrote, "What I like is the way in which people far lower down than us, live with something of the life and enjoyment of the cultivated classes." But like Spencer, Arnold was appalled by America's provincial culture. "Say what Carnegie will," he wrote, "this is the civilization of the Australian colonies and not of Europe."[168]

Newspapers and Public Matters

Carnegie had said he would buy a newspaper to advocate liberal reform, like Grandpa Morrison's *Precursor*. In fact, he bought an entire collection of left-leaning and radical English papers, forming his own syndicate. "Merged into one," he said, they could "strike like a thunderbolt." His syndicate helped elect his friend John Morley to Parliament, where he became an influential government player in the liberal cause. Carnegie's papers also successfully advocated for the 1884 Reform Act, which doubled the size of the electorate by enfranchising most agricultural workers and miners.

Between the influence of his newspapers and the enormous size of his personal campaign contributions, Carnegie entered "the inner sanctum of British politics."[169] Prime Minister Gladstone, for one, truly appreciated Carnegie. "The man is like a fresh breeze," he said.[170] In 1885, he even suggested that Carnegie run for Parliament. Gladstone was also a grateful recipient of Carnegie's financial and political support. Whether he was equally grateful for the harangues that came attached is open to question:

> Carnegie spoke to Gladstone brazenly—"breezy talk," he called it—about America's superior democratic system and Britain's troubles. Economic statistics spilled from his mouth, offered as proof of America's superiority while he argued Britain was to the United States what Greece had been to Rome—the headquarters of its culture but unimportant materially. The Crown and the House of Lords had to go, he would repeat at each meeting with the prime minister, and Ireland, Wales, and Scotland should be treated as independent states within a larger federal system, like New York, Virginia ... and so on and on. Gladstone could hardly get a word in, only able to exclaim, "Oh—Ah—How Extraordinary—Wonderful—Incredible—Astounding!" Mrs. Gladstone would remark to the audacious Carnegie, "William tells me he has the most extraordinary conversations with you." [171]

Carnegie's economic statistics showed that America's factory output now exceeded that of Britain, which came as a revelation to Gladstone. "Why does not some writer take up this subject and present the facts to the world—in a simple and direct way?" Gladstone asked. [172] That's exactly what Carnegie was planning to do.

Triumphant Democracy

Carnegie wrote eight books in his lifetime, and his magnum opus was *Triumphant Democracy*. In this book, Carnegie makes a serious attempt to prove to "the good people of Britain" that American-style democracy is a superior form of government. [173] The flaming red cover, decorated with a broken scepter and an upside-down crown, hints at its antiroyal contents. Carnegie dedicates the book to America, "the beloved Republic under whose equal laws I am made the peer of any man, although denied political equality by my native land." [174] Though "born a subject of monarchy" and stamped with "the stigma of inferiority" in Scotland, as an American he was "the peer of any human being who draws the breath of life, be he pope, Kaiser, priest or king." [175]

Carnegie argued that America—a more vigorous, flexible, fit, and *prosperous* society—was proof of democracy's triumph. "The old nations of the world creep on at a snail's pace; the republic thunders past with the rush of an express," trumpets the book's first line.[176] That was more than bluster coming from a man who had personally blown past the British steel aristocracy like a thundering train.

Carnegie presented a staggering array of statistics—a level of social science writing unusual for its time—that demonstrated a simple fact that most people on both sides of the Atlantic were unaware of: America was now the "wealthiest nation in the world." And that, Carnegie predicted, was just the beginning. The pace of America's economic growth was accelerating, and the gap was widening. Carnegie paired the geographic reality of America's immensity with its staggering rise in population growth. "The state of New York is almost as large as England, while Texas is larger than France . . . the miniature States of Europe can have no conception of distance as understood by Americans." [177] How big would the American economy be when Texas is as densely settled as France? he asked. The "petty states of Europe" had better take note, Carnegie warned; America was "building up a power none can hope to rival." [178]

Beyond these raw numbers, Carnegie argued that the democratic system was intrinsically more economically efficient. It allowed talent to find its own level, maximizing the use of human ability. "There is but one rule among Americans—the tools to those who can use them," Carnegie proclaimed. Carnegie was once again his own best example, because he ran his mills according to that philosophy. Partner or the cart, the decision was based entirely on performance, not pedigree. Carnegie teasingly mused that if a thousand Americans and a thousand Brits were suddenly dropped on a desert island, the Americans would "go ahead developing their country before an equal number of British would have discovered who among them was the highest in hereditary rank and had the best claim to leadership owing to their grandfather." [179]

Finally, Carnegie argued that the lure of freedom was not just drawing a large *quantity* of immigrants. It was selectively attracting Europe's highest-*quality* men and women. It was "well grounded knowledge among Europeans," he stated, that immigration "takes away the best of the population." As long as America offered political freedom and economic opportunity, "so long will the best workers seek its shores." [180] The conclusion was only logical. Immigrants were, by nature, "capable, energetic, ambitious" people of "superior character." That's *why* they were immigrants. The most capable were that segment of the population most likely to be "discontented" with artificial barriers to their advancement. "The old and the destitute, the idle and the contented do not brave the waves of the stormy Atlantic, but sit helplessly at home, perhaps bewailing their hard fate, or, what is still more sad to see, aimlessly contented with it." [181] This process of self-selection was making America stronger and wealthier. The flow of immigrants into the United States was a "golden stream" which contributed more to her national wealth than "all the gold mines in the world." Immigrants were America's economic secret weapon.

Carnegie had once experienced a revelation in which he had seen the truth of evolution: man ascending higher and higher, his face turned toward the sun. Now he saw America leading that glorious procession:

We have not traveled far yet, with all our progress on the upward path, but we will still go marching on. That which is, is better than that which has been. It is the mission of Democracy to lead in this triumphant march and improve step by step the conditions under which the masses live; to ring out the Old, and to ring in the New; and in this great work the Republic [America] rightly leads the van.[182]

Carnegie's book was immensely popular in both the United States and Europe. U.S. sales hit fifteen thousand in the first few months, and a cheaper paperback version sold forty thousand copies in Britain. The critical reviews were mixed, the most common criticism being that Carnegie's vision was so black and white, which is how hypomanics typically see the world. Carnegie had so idealized America that he glossed over all its faults, even making up outrageous claims, such as that, among Americans, "wife beating is scarcely ever heard of and drunkenness is quite rare."[183] Carnegie could see only utopia. "Where are the shadows?" one critic rightly asked. "The book was written at high noon when the sun casts no shadows" was Carnegie's self-righteous reply.[184]

The reaction of Carnegie's British intellectual friends mirrored the range of responses. Morley, the liberal reformer, excused Carnegie's excesses. "Some passages were a trifle too aggressively republican," he admitted. "But that does not matter. The book is a solid contribution on the right side. And it is written in high spirits which give it an attractive literary vivacity."[185] Matthew Arnold, whose daughter married an American, was visiting her in the United States when the book came out. "You should read Carnegie's book *Triumphant Democracy,*" he wrote a friend back home. "The facts he has collected as to the material progress of this country are remarkable, and I am told the book is having great sales, being translated into French, German, etc." But Arnold could still not ignore America's provincialism. "He and most Americans are simply unaware that nothing in the book touched the capital defect of life over here; namely compared with life in England it is so uninteresting, so without savor and without depth."[186] Spencer also granted that Carnegie had shown that the United States was an economic triumph, but he refused to call it evolution. He wrote, "Spurred on by his unrestricted ambitions, the American is, to my thinking, a less happy being than the inhabitant of a country where the possibilities of success are much smaller; and where, in the immense majority of cases, each has to be content with the hum-drum career in which circumstances have placed him." [187] How such resignation would make Europeans any more fit for survival, Spencer never explained.

After writing *Triumphant Democracy,* Carnegie hatched an even more ambitious plan to bring America's freedom back home. He proposed that England and the United States reunify as one happy English-speaking family. In 1893, he added a chapter to *Triumphant Democracy* promoting his reunification scheme. The capital of this new supercountry would be Washington, D.C. Its political foundation would be the U.S. Constitution. And it would use the American flag. It sounded as if Britain would become America's colony. The plan was mad, of course, but Carnegie pursued it with his usual energy. The first step, he reasoned, was the annexation of Canada. To achieve this aim, he formed the National Continental Union League with the support of many luminaries, including Theodore Roosevelt. "When the foreign colony of Canada recognizes its destiny and becomes part of the American union," Carnegie proclaimed, it "would double the value of everything in Canada, including its men." [188] Carnegie seemed personally hurt when both England and Canada rejected his plan.

Behind this scheme was an idea Carnegie himself named "race imperialism." It was Carnegie's view that the "English-speaking race" was destined to benevolently guide humanity upward. Its inevitable benign rule would bestow on humanity "that which it had been yearning for since its dawn—Liberty, Justice, Peace." [189] He was soon shocked and outraged, however, when American imperialism didn't conform to his idealized view of racial beneficence.

Anti-Imperialist Crusader

Historians agree that the Spanish-American War marks America's arrival as a world power. The United States kicked Spain out of its hemisphere and did so with élan, as epitomized by Theodore Roosevelt and his Rough Riders dashing up San Juan Hill. Americans were feeling virile. The war was the beginning of an American "empire," as America prepared to annex the Philippines as a spoil of war.

Carnegie was horrified. This was utterly undemocratic, contrary to the high-minded principles he had been publicly preaching and bragging about. The Filipino people were being offered neither the right to self-government nor the rights of U.S. citizens. President William McKinley was leaning toward making the Philippines a U.S. *possession*. That was how *old* Europe behaved, not the beloved Republic.

In an essay in the *North American Review,* Carnegie challenged those who argued that America had a "white man's burden" to civilize the Philippines. He quoted Lincoln: "When the white man governs himself, that is self-government; but when he governs another man, that is more than self-government, that is despotism." [190]

Suing for peace, the Spanish agreed to sell the Philippines to the United States for $20 million. Carnegie publicly offered to pay McKinley $20 million from his own pocket to set them free.

Meanwhile, American troops sank into the mire of a guerrilla war against Filipino nationalists. One Colorado regiment complained that it was sick with yellow fever, low on rations, perpetually ambushed, and wanted to come home. Thinking this one letter of protest would, at last, unleash a massive public outcry against the occupation, Carnegie wrote a letter in the *New York Tribune:* "It is glorious. The light has broken. Imperialism had received its first blow—I think its death wound; the Republic may yet be saved." [191] He encouraged soldiers to continue protesting.

But contrary to Carnegie's contention, the Colorado regiment's complaint was hardly the beginning of a grassroots groundswell for freeing the Philippines.

In a letter to Secretary of State John Hay, Carnegie lambasted McKinley for holding the Philippines, calling the president a "blubbering jellyfish" who should be renamed "Mr. Face both ways." More ominously, Carnegie seriously suggested to Hay that the president had gone mad.[192] "I am so sorry for the president— I do not think he is well."[193] He signed the letter, "Bitterly opposed to you yet always your friend Andrew Carnegie." The only person whose sanity Secretary Hay questioned was Andrew Carnegie's. He wrote to a colleague, "Carnegie really seems to be off his head. He writes me frantic letters signing them 'Your Bitterest Opponent.' He threatens the President, not only with the vengeance of the voters but with practical punishment at the hands of a mob."[194]

Carnegie also wrote McKinley directly, oblivious of his outrageously presumptuous tone:

> The true friend not only warns a friend of what he sees to be dangers that surround him, but he ventures to counsel him as to what he should do in the crisis.
>
> *Were I President of the United States* I should announce in my message to Congress that I demanded the Philippines from Spain, that I might give to them Independence which every people can claim as a God-given right [emphasis added].[195]

Failing to convince McKinley by letter, Carnegie stormed the White House to argue face to face with "Mr. Face both ways." McKinley received him politely on several occasions, as Carnegie, not one to take no for an answer, kept returning. McKinley couldn't afford to be rude to Carnegie. He was a major Republican campaign donor, after all. Moreover, some people credited

Carnegie with McKinley's having won the presidency. He had run against the silver-tongued William Jennings Bryan on the restoration of the gold standard, a topic the public didn't understand. Carnegie had explained why he thought the United States needed the gold standard in an easy-to-read essay entitled "The A-B-C's of Money." The McKinley campaign had printed and distributed 5 million copies. But McKinley was not so grateful that he would contemplate changing his decision about the Philippines.

Carnegie felt this left him no choice but to mount yet another campaign. In the *New York Journal* he wrote, "President McKinley, our 'War Lord,' is beginning to see that he can agree to pay twenty million for an opportunity to shoot down people only guilty of the crime of desiring to govern themselves." [196] Though a lifelong Republican stalwart, Carnegie reached out to Democratic presidential candidate William Jennings Bryan, also an anti-imperialist, to suggest they join forces. After meeting with Bryan, Carnegie prepared to publicly endorse him for the 1900 election. But Bryan panicked and got cold feet. He sent Carnegie an urgent note telling him to call off the endorsement because it "might embarrass me." [197] How would it look, after all, for a populist crusader against big business to be in league with a robber baron?

Even without his help, Carnegie predicted a big Bryan victory. "I am certain. Our party is doomed in the next election," Carnegie wrote to a friend serving as ambassador to Germany. In fact, McKinley won in a landslide. The more messianic Carnegie became, the more blatant his errors in judgment, especially his judgment of character, as he came to see the world's leaders as mere actors in his fantasy world.

A Mania for Peace

Carnegie's most messianic undertaking was his attempt to bring world peace. The policies Carnegie advocated were idealistic but not crazy: world disarmament, adjudication of international disputes through a world court, and enforcement of the world court's decisions by an international police force. What was insane about his plan was that Carnegie, "empowered by a sense of destiny," believed emphatically that he could personally make these things happen, and quickly.* "Desperate to become mankind's savior," Carnegie developed a "Christ-like complex," what biographer Peter Krass called "a mania for peace." [198]

"I have tried to like Carnegie," wrote America's next president, Theodore Roosevelt, "but it is pretty difficult." [199] "There is no type of man for whom I feel more contemptuous abhorrence than one who makes a God of mere money-making. And at the same time is yelling out that kind of utterly stupid condemnation of war." [200] Though TR won the Nobel Peace Prize, he was no dove. He believed in "carrying a big stick" and accordingly tripled American naval power. He believed that America was destined to become the preeminent military power of the twentieth century and that a war now and then wasn't such a bad

---

* Henry Ford also developed the messianic notion that he could personally bring world peace in a hurry. In December 1915, he set sail for Europe on a luxury steamer, dubbed the "Peace Ship," to stop World War I. "I'll bet this ship against a penny," he boasted from the rail of the ship before he shoved off, "that we'll have the boys out of the trenches by Christmas." The mission was launched on impulse. Two days after the idea was suggested to him, Ford ended up draped over a chair in the Oval Office lecturing President Wilson. "Bunk!" said Ford when the "small man" didn't endorse his plan for the Peace Ship. "If you can't act, I will." Ford called a press conference the next day from the Biltmore Hotel in New York. He invited every college president, governor, and officer of the government to join him in sailing to "some central point to be determined later." Not a single prominent man accepted Ford's invitation. "What is right cannot fail," Ford proclaimed, but of course it did fail. Ford sailed off "on a vast wave of ridicule," and historians treat the Peace Ship as a joke. But it is more than an oddity. It is a vivid demonstration of the messianism of the hypomanic. Later, Ford would pronounce mass production the "new Messiah."

thing.* He thought the "peace-at-any-price men" were "rarely bet-ter than silly." Their only saving grace was that they were "well-nigh impotent for good or evil."[201]

During TR's presidency, Carnegie was presumptuous and intru-sive as usual, barraging TR with "a flood of correspondence" that often began with phrases such as, "If I were you." As usual, Carnegie followed up on his letters with his one-man marches on Washington, subjecting TR to his hyperactive lobbying. Carnegie had no clue that TR disliked him. Being an astute politician, TR rose above his feelings and cleverly co-opted Carnegie for his own agenda. The capitalist's money was not too tainted for TR to accept his campaign contributions. Moreover, he convinced Carnegie to endorse many items on his environmental and progressive agenda.

---

* Theodore Roosevelt was arguably America's most hypomanic president. One British diplomat said the two most impressive natural phenomena in America were Niagara Falls and TR. "A steam engine in pants," Theodore Roosevelt defined hypomanic energy. As a crusad-ing New York legislator, the "cyclone assemblyman" entered the chamber each morning "as if ejected by a catapult" and submitted as many as twenty bills a day to the legislature (Ed-mund Morris, *The Rise of Theodore Roosevelt* [New York: Ballantine Books, 1979], p. 165). The world's fastest hand shaker (fifty grips a minute), he broke the world record on New Year's Day 1907 at the White House, shaking the hand of every man, woman, and child who wanted to wish their newly reelected president happy new year. He had little need for sleep: "Four or five hours a night was all he could stand before the motor inside him made him jump up and start moving again" (H. W. Brands, *TR: The Last Romantic* [New York: Basic Books, 1997], p. vii). Like Hamilton, he had an explosively prolific mind, "the most vigorous brain in a re-sponsible position in all the world," according to H. G. Wells (Morris, p. 23). He wrote twenty-three volumes of history, natural science, biography, and political thought, numerous articles, and more than fifty thousand letters. Afflicted with what he called "reading disease," TR stayed up into the wee hours reading at least one book a night and read with such energy that he felt obliged to tear out each page of a periodical after he finished it, hurling it to the ground with relish. His mood was peculiarly exuberant. His favorite expression was "dee-lighted," which he said so often and with such silly gusto that no one ever doubted his sincerity. I asked Pulitzer Prize–winning Roosevelt biographer Edmund Morris if he thought TR might have been manic-depressive. "He was definitely manic, but I don't think he was ever depressed," said Morris. I think what Morris meant, had he known the term, was that TR was intensely hypomanic.

TR even asked Carnegie to write an introduction to one of his books, flattering him no end, only because he thought it would help him sell more copies to libraries. Even after he left office, Roosevelt didn't hesitate to ask Carnegie for a personal gift of $30,000 when he ran short of funds on his African safari (which Carnegie sent gladly).

Less harmless was the way Carnegie allowed himself to be manipulated by the German kaiser. It was apparent to most contemporaries that the kaiser was a bellicose megalomaniac. He loved nothing better than marching around in full military regalia and had built up a huge military with the intention of using it. Carnegie was eager to intervene with the kaiser to preserve world peace. By giving Carnegie the impression that his efforts were working, the kaiser easily duped him into becoming his international apologist. "I believe the peace of the world has little to fear from Germany," he wrote.[202] The kaiser was "a wonderful man, so bright, humorous, and with a *sweet smile.*"[203] In 1912, in a ceremony at the Grand Palace in Berlin celebrating the twenty-fifth anniversary of the kaiser's reign, Carnegie presented him with a gold casket engraved with the message "We thank your Imperial majesty as the foremost apostle of peace."[204] When Carnegie looked at the kaiser, he saw a projection of his own grandiose self-image. Carnegie would ultimately be embarrassed by this passage from his *Autobiography:*

He is not only an Emperor, but something much higher. . . . I have for some time been haunted with the feeling that the Emperor was indeed a Man of Destiny. My interviews with him have strengthened that feeling. I have great hopes for him in the future doing something really great and good. He may yet have a part to play that will give him a place among the immortals. . . . Whether he is to pass into history as only the preserver of internal peace at home or is to rise to his appointed mission as the Apostle of Peace among leading civilized nations, the future has still to reveal.[205]

Carnegie had a plan: if he could just get TR and the kaiser together, he was sure that they would iron out the world's differences. He lobbied for this meeting furiously and to his credit actually made it happen, albeit after Roosevelt left the presidency. "Roosevelt eventually cracked and agreed to a summit with the Kaiser."[206] To TR, Carnegie wrote, "You will not fail. Let me assure you, dear Mr. Roosevelt, that the Emperor can be trusted. I believe in him." Carnegie wrote one friend exuberantly, "What a pair TR and HM [the kaiser] to hob-knob—well they will love each other like vera brithers and I have faith in both."[207] His faith was misplaced.

Roosevelt ridiculed Carnegie behind his back. To Carnegie he wrote, "When I see the Kaiser, I will go over the whole matter at length with him, telling him I wish to repeat our whole conversation to you."[208] But in fact, the only thing TR and the kaiser agreed on was that Carnegie was a fool. Roosevelt reflected, "There were many points of international morality where he and I were completely asunder. But at least we agreed in a cordial dislike of shams and pretense, and therefore in a cordial dislike of the kind of washy movement for international peace with which Carnegie's name has been so closely associated."[209]

The TR-kaiser summit did not usher in a new social order after all. Yet for Carnegie, another president meant another chance. Howard Taft wanted a legacy to distinguish himself from his wildly popular predecessor. A peace platform might be just the thing. Taft hosted the Carnegies at the White House for an overnight stay. The two men agreed to help each other. Taft promised to vigorously pursue treaties with other nations, agreeing to settle their differences by arbitration. Carnegie, in turn, would support Taft with money and public endorsements. Carnegie contributed a whopping $100,000 to Taft's campaign war chest.

But he didn't stop there. Carnegie donated a breathtaking $10 million to establish a "peace fund." Even a public now used to Carnegie's splashy gestures was taken aback. What *was* a peace fund, and what would it do with $10 million? It initially funded a blitz of publicity for the Taft treaties. But Carnegie had far grander long-term plans. Science was finding cures to human illnesses. Through "scientific investigation and study of the causes of war," the fund could provide "practical methods to prevent and avoid it." Carnegie was so confident of success that he directed future trustees, after curing war, to "consider what is the next degrading evil of evils whose banishment . . . would most advance the progress, elevation, and happiness of man, and so on, from century to century without end." [210]

Taft's one misgiving about his alliance with Carnegie was that "He might be a hard man to be responsible for because he talked so much." [211] His concern proved prescient. Carnegie "wrongly came to believe that the deal with Taft entitled him to speak for the country." Telling reporters that he was in "almost daily communication with Taft," he made pronouncements as if he were secretary of state. Statesmanship, Carnegie declared, was "like all great things extremely easy." When the real secretary of state, Henry Knox, was sent by Taft to tell Carnegie to *stop* talking, Carnegie was utterly baffled at their offense.

It seemed that all of Carnegie's work had finally come to fruition at last when, after protracted negotiations, the British agreed to an arbitration treaty with the United States. *The New York Times* called it Taft's "crowning achievement." The *Los Angeles Times* likened it to the Emancipation Proclamation. The pope issued a statement of praise to be read at Mass by every priest in the world. Carnegie was beyond ecstatic: "I am the happiest mortal alive," he telegrammed Morley. This was nothing less than "the greatest step upward ever taken by any race since history began." [212]

Unfortunately, it was a false step. The treaty died in the Senate, and the defeat knocked the wind out of Carnegie. In the middle of a speech in Edinburgh, soon after Carnegie heard the news, he paused, broke from his prepared text, and said sadly, "Millionaires who laugh are rare, very rare, indeed." [213]

Christopher Columbus.

John Winthrop (*top*), Roger Williams (*middle*), and William Penn (*bottom*).

2

3

4

The three faces of Hamilton (*clockwise, from top left*): a young-looking Hamilton dreams of glory; a confident Hamilton at the peak of his powers looks us in the eye; Hamilton, depressed after the death of his son, looks away.

5

6

7

The young immigrant Andrew Carnegie at sixteen with his younger brother, Tom. The mature Andrew Carnegie, captain of industry.

8

9

The older Andrew Carnegie, messianic philanthropist.

The grandfathers: Lewis Selznick (*left*) and Louis B. Mayer (*right*).

11

12

The children (*clockwise, from top left*): Myron Selznick, David O. Selznick, and Irene Mayer. The grandchild: Daniel Mayer Selznick.

13

14

16

15

Craig Venter (*clockwise, from top left*): staying alive in Vietnam's Da Nang field hospital; the Henry Ford of gene sequencing in front of his array of machines; "a day for the ages" at the White House with President Clinton and Francis Collins; the gene business: Venter in *Time* magazine.

17

18

20

19

But Carnegie had not given up. His greatest act for peace—the culmination of all his work, he believed—would be the multimillion-dollar "Peace Palace" that he proposed to build at The Hague. This would be home to the new world court. From this time forward, international conflict would be resolved in these hallowed halls instead of on the battlefield. When some bureaucrats proposed to name it the Library and Court of Arbitration, Carnegie erupted. How could they even consider such a "pathetic" name? he wrote back. "This is to me shocking. I am positively wounded . . . when a Temple of Peace is erected it will in my opinion be the holiest structure in the world."[214] Carnegie gave millions more for peace temples to be built around the world. The Peace Palace, as it was ultimately called, was built at The Hague. A dedication ceremony, in which a bust of Carnegie was to be unveiled, was scheduled for mid-August 1914.

But on August 4, 1914, World War I was declared. The news struck Carnegie like a blow: "It can't be true. Are you sure it's true? . . . Can't America do something to stop it?" Carnegie dropped limply into his chair. "All my air castles have collapsed around me like a house of cards," he said.[215] His guiding vision— humanity rising higher and higher—suddenly seemed a mirage. "Mankind's 'spiritual progress' became a tragic joke" and "Carnegie's ideological world was gone."[216]

Carnegie fell into a bottomless pit of depression, saying that he was just "waiting for his turn" to die. In her preface to his *Autobiography,* his widow wrote that the "fateful news of the 4th of August" had destroyed him:

Henceforth he was never able to interest himself in private affairs. Many times he made the attempt to continue writing, but found it useless. Until then he had lived the life of a man in middle age—and a young one at that—golfing, fishing, swimming each day, sometimes doing all three in one day. Optimist as he always was, and tried to be in the face of the failure of all his

185

hopes, the world disaster was too much. His heart was broken. A severe attack of influenza followed by two serious attacks of pneumonia precipitated old age upon him.[217]

The last passage in his *Autobiography* was, ironically enough, the description of the great twenty-fifth anniversary celebration with the kaiser. After World War I was declared, Carnegie could not write another word. "[Here the manuscript ends abruptly]" are the final words of his *Autobiography*.[218]

Bad news kept coming. His family could not shield him from the newspapers. Nightmare images: 15,000 French soldiers dying in a cloud of green German gas; a brave British attack that killed 60,000 British lads in one day, without gaining an inch of ground. Thirteen million soldiers died in all. Carnegie must have felt he had already died and descended into Hell. "At times, Carnegie found himself weeping uncontrollably."[219]

Having never seen him like this before, his friends were alarmed and tried to lift his spirits. Morley was shocked that Carnegie—"of all men"—had written, "Happiness is all over."[220] When Carnegie told his Scottish friend John Ross that he had no plans to return to his castle in Scotland, because his presence would only depress everyone around him, Ross wrote back:

> On the contrary, I feel sure that the very fact that you abstain from coming here will increase the sadness. . . . You are so much committed to the "Peace Crusade," and you have been so often the exponent of the belief that amidst all the contradictions in this world, the world grows better, that if you now make a public announcement that your sadness has altered your life, it would be accepted as a confession that your faith has been shattered.[221]

His faith had been shattered. Man was not ascending higher and higher. In fact, just the opposite was happening. He had sunk to new depths of depravity. Carnegie lost his faith in Saint Andrew.

However, if only for a few more breaths, the flame of William Wallace still flickered within Carnegie's soul. For the last time, Carnegie grasped his pen to write to another American president. To Woodrow Wilson he wrote:

Dear Mr. President:

Sometime ago I wrote you "Germany is beyond reason." She has ever since become more and more so until today she shows herself completely insane. . . . *Were I in your place* there would soon be an end to this. There is only one straight way of settlement. You should *proclaim war* against her, however reluctantly, and then settlement would soon come [emphasis added].[222]

A few months later, Wilson, "the man who kept us out of war," did reluctantly declare it. The precipitant was not Carnegie's letter. America discovered a secret German plot to invade the southwestern United States through a proposed alliance with Mexico, and an irrepressible war fever erupted across the nation.

It never occurred to Carnegie that he couldn't order around heads of state as he had his managers or single-handedly reengineer society as he had his mills. Human nature is harder to bend than steel, and evolution doesn't hurry easily. We can both laugh at his naive hubris and still hope some future generation will establish peace. If that were ever to happen, our descendants might proclaim Andrew Carnegie a prophet, a man ahead of his time and ours. Let us pray our children do rise higher and higher, with their faces turned toward the sun.

V The Selznicks and the Mayers

A Hollywood Family

When a generation of Jews fled eastern Europe at the turn of the century, the history of the Jews and America became intertwined forever. Among other things, the Jews in America created a new industry: mass media. Both commercial radio and television were launched almost single-handedly by David Sarnoff, a Russian Jewish immigrant. His chief rival, William Paley, the founder of CBS, was also Jewish. The nation's two most respected newspapers, *The New York Times* and *The Washington Post*, both rose from obscurity under Jewish ownership. Most of the large book-publishing houses were founded by Jews, including Simon & Schuster, Random House, Viking, Bantam, Alfred A. Knopf, and Farrar, Straus & Giroux. Most famously, this first generation of Eastern European Jews invented Hollywood.

Many of these enterprises began as family businesses. In the Jewish families that built the movie business, virtually every member was bipolar to one degree or another. This should not surprise us. Highly creative people are often bipolar, as Kay Jamison showed in her classic study of writers, *Touched with Fire*. And more than any other, media is the *business of creativity*.

When you examine the lives of these early pioneers, you see that they were as dramatic in the expression of their moods off the screen as they were on it.

RUSSIAN EXODUS

The nightmare for Russia's Jews began on March 1, 1881, when revolutionary terrorists assassinated Tsar Alexander II. The Jews were blamed, for reasons that appear mutually contradictory: the

191

socialists who hatched the plot were assumed to be Jewish; at the same time, Jews were considered to be the underlying cause of the social unrest that had led to the assassination because they were such exploitative capitalists.

Pogroms spread across Russia and Poland. They were "orgies of destruction." Drunken mobs burned, looted, raped, and murdered. The Cossacks and local police, who often had advance notice of a pogrom, did little to stop the violence and often joined in. When the Jews organized self-defense forces, they were arrested. When they pressed charges in court, the rioters were rarely convicted. When they appealed to the government for help, commissions were established to investigate. The national commission investigating the pogroms deemed the "disturbances" to be a "popular judgment," a spontaneous outpouring of well-deserved righteous indignation.[1] "The Jews, as a pre-eminently mercantile class, engage in 'unproductive' labor, and thereby 'exploit' the productive classes of the Christian population."[2] It was the Jews who should be punished, on grounds of their "economic injuriousness," not their killers.

During the next forty years, almost a third of Russia's Jews emigrated. Many of them fled to Palestine ("Zionism came into being after the pogroms of 1881–82").[3] However, 80 percent of the Jews who emigrated from eastern Europe came to a new promised land: America. As Russia pushed its Jews out, America seemed to magnetically pull them in. Letters from friends and relatives were the most powerful inducement to emigrate. "We eat meat every day like millionaires and there is no Czar in America," one man wrote.[4] Entire villages passed around such handwritten notes.

> America had been in everybody's mouth. Businessmen talked it over with their accounts; the market women made up their quarrels that they might discuss it from stall to stall; people who had relatives in the famous land went around reading their letters for the enlightenment of less fortunate folk . . . children played at

emigrating; old folks shook sage heads over the evening fire, and prophesied no good for those who braved the terrors of the sea and the foreign goal beyond it; all talked of it, but scarcely anyone knew one true fact about this magic land.[5]

Sometimes, in their exuberance, these recent immigrants exaggerated a little. For example, Ben Warner, a cobbler who lived in a small shtetl in Poland, received a letter in 1890 from a man he had previously known as the "village idiot." It was Warner who had to be the idiot to believe the outrageous lies Waleski told him about streets paved with gold, but Warner desperately wanted to believe. Since the pogroms began he had been tortured by mental images of his pubescent daughter being raped. When Warner arrived in Baltimore he hugged Waleski: "You lied. But I'm glad you did. If you told me it would be like this, I would never have come."[6] Warner came up with an idea that appealed to his impatient American customers: "Shoes repaired while you wait."[7] His four sons founded Warner Brothers studio, which gave the world its first "talkie" in 1928. *The Jazz Singer,* starring Jewish singer Al Jolson, was about an American Jew caught between his desire to be a secular entertainer and his father's demand that he be a cantor.

Between 1880 and 1920 more than 2 million Jews from eastern Europe emigrated to the United States. In 1880, there were 250,000 Jews in America, mostly of German origin. A mere 3 percent of the world's Jewish population called America home, while 75 percent lived in eastern Europe. By 1920, there were 3,600,000 Jews in America, 23 percent of the world's Jewish population. It was the greatest exodus since Moses led the Jews out of Egypt. "Every emigrating Jew realized he was involved in something more than a personal expedition," wrote one immigrant. "He was part of a historical event in the life of the Jewish people."[8] It was also a historical event in the life of America.

THE GRANDFATHERS

Lewis Selznick: The Boy Who Walked out of Russia

When Lewis Zeleznick ran away from home, he was only twelve years old. How a penniless young boy from Kiev made his way to America is a mystery. "Pop walked out of Russia," his son David O. Selznick said with awe. What kind of person walks out of Russia at twelve? In a word, someone with a triple helping of chutzpah. Lewis Selznick, as he came to be called in America, was chutzpah incarnate. While Selznick's seventeen siblings played it safe and stayed in Kiev, only he had the temperament to take this audacious gamble, believing against all odds that he would make it and make it big.

After making it as far as England, Lewis labored in a British factory for five years to earn his fare to America. In 1889, when he was seventeen, he landed in Pittsburgh, became a jeweler's apprentice, and by the time he was twenty owned his own jewelry store. At twenty-four, he had three stores. In 1910, he moved his wife and sons to New York to take the capital of the jewelry industry by storm. He opened a shop on Sixth Avenue and Fourteenth Street—Diamond Row—that grandiosely advertised itself as "the world's largest jewelry store." His favorite expression was "You can't keep a good idea down," but this one sank. The world's largest jewelry store collapsed under its own weight. Like many hypomanic entrepreneurs, Lewis Selznick's problem was that "he always went too far too fast," according to his grandson Daniel Selznick.[9] Selznick was forced to auction off his merchandise, but he didn't sell it all. For the rest of his life he would jingle a few hundred thousand dollars' worth of diamonds in his pants pocket. They made him feel lucky.

The week Selznick auctioned off his store, he ran into an old friend on the sidewalk. Mark Dintenfass had been a salesman in his father's salt herring business when Selznick knew him. But the now well-dressed Dintenfass bragged that he was making a fortune in the movie theater business. That night over dinner Selznick an-

nounced to his wife and sons: "I am going into the picture business
... Dintenfass is the dumbest man I ever knew. If he can make
money in pictures, anybody can." [10]*

Selznick was lucky to be in the right place at the right time. The
film business was born in New York in the first decade of the twentieth century. Thomas Edison claimed to have invented the movie,
though in fact he only improved on a projector developed by the
French Lumière brothers in 1895. In 1903, Edison produced the
classic ten-minute silent film *The Great Train Robbery*.† These early
movies were shown in a new venue called "nickelodeons," so
named because admission was 5 cents.

For eastern European Jewish immigrants such as Selznick, who
were desperately searching for *any* business that could keep them
alive, movies were a logical choice. The market for movies was
growing—nickelodeons were said to be proliferating "faster than
guinea pigs"—and there were few barriers to entry. No Gentile es-
tablishment blocked their path, as the industry was too new, and,
more important, it didn't take much capital to get started. Rent a
room, a machine, and a movie, and you were in business. Movies
were most popular in immigrant neighborhoods, particularly Jewish ones. In 1908, one third of Manhattan's 120 nickelodeons were
found on the predominantly Jewish Lower East Side. Most of the
movie moguls were Jewish immigrants who began their career as

---

* The idea that any idiot could make money in pictures was an opinion Selznick maintained. When testifying before a congressional committee investigating the film industry in
1917, he said, "Less brains are necessary in the motion picture business than any other." As
proof, he bragged that he had turned a $1,000 investment into $105,000 in ten weeks. His
fellow moguls were not amused.

† Edison was another great hypomanic American. Both an inventor and an entrepreneur,
he was an inexhaustible furnace of ideas, and still holds the world record for number of
patents (1,093). He often didn't sleep until he passed out on the floor after working forty-eight
hours straight. One of his assistants, Francis Upton, said, "His own physical and mental
strength have always seemed to be without limit. He could work continuously as long as he
wished, and he had sleep at his command" (Robert Conot, *Thomas Edison: A Streak of Luck*
[New York: Da Capo Press, 1979], p. 127).

theater owners in their own neighborhood and later expanded into production. The only one who stood in their way was Thomas Edison, who held all the patents. These entrepreneurs were confident that they could make better movies than Edison, who had proclaimed that the public would never have the patience to watch films longer than ten minutes. Edison sued the Jewish filmmakers, who defied him by making movies illegally. Eventually they won in court the right to make movies.

When Dintenfass met Selznick, he mentioned that he was trying to sell his private stock in Universal Pictures. A feud had developed between Universal's two partners, Carl Laemmle and Pat Powers, and neither was willing to buy out Dintenfass's share. Selznick said to let him take care of it. He went to Universal's office on Broadway to sell the stock. After Powers turned him down, Selznick met with Laemmle and convinced the German Jewish immigrant to buy.

The next day, Selznick showed up at Universal in an expensive suit, walked into an unoccupied office, hung up his hat, and began demanding files from the secretaries. Laemmle and Powers successively asked him what he was doing there. He told each of them that the other had hired him. Since the two partners weren't talking, Selznick gambled that his blatant lie wouldn't be discovered. Next, he had the nerve to appoint himself general manager. He had the title painted on his door, put himself on the payroll with a big salary, and started acting as if he ran the place. Laemmle finally figured out what was going on and demanded Selznick's "resignation." By then, with his on-the-job experience, Selznick figured he had learned the picture business and was ready to take on its king.

In photographs, Adolph Zukor is an elegantly dressed short bald man with a killer stare. The Hungarian Jewish immigrant had found a way to dominate the movie market by making theater owners his subscribers. He reliably delivered a movie every week, and theater owners had no choice but to take what he gave them. It was a package deal. Take all of Zukor's films or get none of them. In a market starved for new movies, most took the package.

The motto of Zukor's Famous Players Company was "Famous Players in Famous Plays." In 1914, Selznick launched the World Film Corporation, boasting "Features Made from Well Known Plays by Well Known Players." In fact, he had only one well-known player. Selznick had seduced movie star Clara Kimball Young (his reputation as a lothario was well earned), ripped up her contract with another studio, and organized a separate company dedicated exclusively to the production and distribution of Clara Kimball Young films. It was a big hit with theater owners, who were happy to pay four times what they paid Zukor for a guaranteed hit with a franchise star. They were even willing to pay in advance, which is how Selznick financed the production of his films.

Zukor complained that Selznick's move "disrupted the industry." Zukor's biggest star, Mary Pickford, was now demanding *her* own company. As he couldn't afford to lose her, Zukor was forced to comply. Quietly, he created Artcraft Pictures, intentionally omitting both Pickford's name and his own from the company's title. Zukor didn't want to advertise that he was competing with his own distribution monopoly. He wanted it kept quiet, so naturally Selznick announced it loudly in the local trade journal, where he published an open letter to Mary Pickford:

> I congratulate you, Mary. You are a pretty shrewd, as well as a pretty *little* girl.
>
> What stronger evidence could there be that the Clara Kimball Young Corporation is organized on the most progressive basis than your adoption of the Mary Pickford Film Corporation and of the idea and ideal that I myself have originated?
>
> Will you please express to my friend, Mr. Adolph Zukor, my deep sense of obligation? It is indeed delightful to encounter among one's co-workers a man so broad gauged that neither fake pride nor short sightedness can deter him from the adoption of an excellent plan, even though conceived by another.[11]

"Selznick is a menace!" Zukor raged.[12] From then on, "his vow to destroy Lewis Selznick became common knowledge."[13] B. P. Schulberg, director of production for Famous Players, recalled, "Zukor despised him." Schulberg had to admit, "I always had a sneaking admiration for him. He wasn't a good gambler because he liked to bluff all the time, in business and at cards, but at least he did it in a big way. . . . That gall was as big and durable as Gibraltar. The sharpest knives in the industry, including my own, couldn't make a dent in it."[14]

Selznick was the first person to display electrically lit signs in the theater district now called Times Square. He soon had six pictures opening on Broadway at once and a dozen signs with his new logo, "Selznick Pictures Make Happy Hours." He used these signs to maximum effect, both to advertise to the public and to irritate Adolph Zukor. His electric signs were strategically placed outside every window of Zukor's office. Enraged, Zukor marched over to Selznick's place. "Lewie, I will pay you five thousand dollars a week for life if you will go to China and stay there."[15]

Later, Zukor figured that if he could steal Clara Kimball Young, Selznick's biggest asset, he could crush Selznick. He offered Young a fortune, and she quickly broke with Selznick for having made "representations he didn't live up to."[16] But Selznick unleashed a pack of lawyers on them both and quickly won in court.

Finally Zukor suggested a truce and a partnership. He offered Selznick a package that was hard to refuse: Selznick would receive $250,000 in desperately needed cash for 50 percent of his company; he could use Zukor's studio in Hollywood to make films; and, to top it off, his eighteen-year-old son, Myron, would be apprenticed to none other than the great Cecil B. De Mille. Zukor just had one request: Please, no more flashing Selznick signs. They agreed on Select Pictures as the company's new name. Selznick had to promise, in writing, "I will not be or become interested in or engaged directly or indirectly in any other motion picture or theatrical enterprises."[17] Some film historians say Zukor did all this just to take the name Selznick off Broadway. One can imagine his reaction when he saw new electric signs advertising "Selznick Pictures." He confronted Selznick, charging him with breaching their contract. Lewis responded innocently that there was nothing he could do. His headstrong son Myron had incorporated his own production company, using the family name. It was a transparent ruse, but Myron and his fifteen-year-old brother, David, really *did* produce films. His father put them in charge and gave them huge salaries, limousines, and charge accounts. Zukor then tried to force Selznick out of Select, and when that proved impossible, he allowed Selznick to buy him out.

Everything Zukor had done to destroy Selznick had failed. But Zukor needn't have bothered. Selznick obliged him by self-destructing. He overspent himself into bankruptcy: buying twenty-page ads in *The Saturday Evening Post;* living like a king in a twenty-two-room apartment on Park Avenue decorated with Ming vases and attended by an army of servants; and, worst of all, losing a million dollars a year at poker. This hypomanic lifestyle seemed so normal to Selznick that he encouraged his boys to be as irresponsible with money as he was: "Spend it all. Give it away. Throw it away, but get rid of it. Live expensively. If you have confidence in yourself, live above your means. Then you'll have to work hard to catch up. . . . Never try to save money." [18] Though his company was valued at $23 million, it was a mere $3,000 debt that pushed him into bankruptcy in 1922. "Everything we owned personally was taken from us," wrote his son David. [19] Selznick tried half a dozen other business ventures, from radio to Florida real estate, but he never rose again. Not a single Lewis Selznick film has survived to the current day.

Louis B. Mayer, a fellow Russian Jewish immigrant, worked with Selznick for just a few months. But, like Zukor, Mayer had found Selznick intolerable. Mayer used Selznick's name as an "epithet," according to his daughter Irene. "Watch what I say, watch and see what happens to him. There is no firm foundation," he told

199

her.[20] And when Mayer saw how Selznick spoiled his sons, he said, "Mark my words, no good will ever come of those boys."[21]

He never imagined that one of them would marry his daughter.

Louis B. Mayer: The Histrionic Patriarch

In 1907, the first movie was shot in Los Angeles, and a gold rush soon began. Southern California was the ideal place to make movies. The warm weather allowed movies to be shot year-round. Its proximity to ocean, mountains, deserts, and cities meant that there was a location for any conceivable scene. And land was dirt cheap. Before the movie people arrived, Hollywood had been only a spot on a road that ran through the desert, with a drugstore, a gas station, and not much more.

Instinctively, the Jewish moguls created the only form of social organization any of them had ever known: a shtetl. On one half mile of beach stood the mansions of all the major moguls and their senior executives—a golden ghetto. It was an extended dysfunctional family. "We had no family tree [all the relatives were in Europe], yet ours was another kind of family, stretching horizontally, composed of motion picture pioneers," wrote Budd Schulberg, son of B. P. Schulberg, the director of production at Adolph Zukor's new company, Paramount.[22] Fierce rivals trying to screw one another in business were attending each other's weddings, bar mitzvahs, and funerals. Because Louis B. Mayer became the most powerful of all the moguls, they hated him the most. B. P. Schulberg told his son that "his final wish was that his ashes be blown in L. B. Mayer's face."[23] Samuel Goldwyn once said that the only reason so many people had showed up at Mayer's funeral was that "they wanted to make sure he was dead."[24] But meanwhile, Mayer's two lovely daughters, Irene and Edith, were frequent guests at the Schulberg and Goldwyn homes and counted them as surrogate parents all their lives.

When Mayer arrived in Hollywood in 1918, Zukor's Paramount

and Laemmle's Universal were on top. Fox and Goldwyn studios (both started by eastern European Jewish immigrants) were up-and-comers. Mayer was a mere wannabe. He rented the oldest and most run-down lot in Hollywood and built an elaborate façade that mimicked a Renaissance French château to inject a note of grandeur. The studio may have been small and gritty, but Mayer's ambitions were not. One day Mayer drove his wife and daughters past the state-of-the-art Goldwyn studio. "I'll bet you'd be surprised if I became head of a studio like this someday," he said.[25]

Mayer's first major California film was *Old Kentucky*. A plucky young girl disguises herself as a male jockey to win the Derby on her beloved horse. Mayer kept his publicists "working round the clock" to carry out his inspired publicity campaign. He redecorated movie theaters to look like racetracks. Orchestra seats were renamed "grandstands," and the ushers dressed as jockeys. The movie was a smash hit.

Mayer had "mammoth energy."[26] "He never sleeps," one of his old partners said. Often he was too anxious to sleep; he would call his secretary at two or three in the morning, insisting she sit with him while he drove around all night talking nonstop. He was both terrified of failure—he once said he would commit suicide before facing the shame of bankruptcy—and spurred on by fantasies of triumph. Alternately, he would "plunge into depression or become overexcited."[27]

Even in his leisure Mayer was hypomanic. As he got older, his doctor suggested he relieve his stress by taking up golf. Mayer took his advice but implemented it hypomanically, hitting five balls down the fairway at a time and exhausting three or four caddies. When his doctor said that this was not what he'd had in mind, Mayer told him, "To heck with one-ball golf."[28] The doctor had another idea: Why not raise racehorses? The "sport of kings" had become quite popular in Hollywood. The moguls even organized a polo club—"from Poland to polo in one generation" was the inside joke. Once again, Mayer followed the advice the only way he knew how: he built one of the largest horse breeding farms in the country. This Russian immigrant and former junk dealer, who didn't know a horse from a donkey, pursued the sport with his typical fierce competitive energy. His stable became the second-highest money winner in the country, and he was named trainer of the year in 1945 by the New York Turf Writers Association.

More Stars Than There Are in Heaven Marcus Loew, a son of Jewish immigrants, owned a chain of theaters and wanted to expand into production. He bought two California studios, Metro and Goldwyn. Loew, who was based in New York, needed a manager for his new west coast production facility, and a mutual business associate suggested Mayer. Loew put Mayer in charge, gave him a cut of the profits, and added his name to the new conglomerate: Metro-Goldwyn-Mayer (MGM). Mayer had once bragged to his family that he would run a studio like Goldwyn someday. He was now running Goldwyn and more.

The 1924 opening ceremony for MGM was quite a production. Mayer sat up on a wooden dais covered with stars and stripes and fronted by a massive picture of Marcus Loew. Twenty military airplanes flew overhead in formation, dropping roses. An admiral and three hundred sailors in dress whites stood at attention while a navy brass band played. Congratulatory telegrams from President Calvin Coolidge and Secretary of Commerce Herbert Hoover were read aloud. From the beginning, Mayer planned to make MGM big. "From a production standpoint Metro-Goldwyn-Mayer will reach a point of perfection never approached by any other company. If there is one thing I insist on it's quality," Mayer pledged from the dais.[29] As Mayer wrote to one young producer, "My unchanging policy will be great star, great director, great play, great cast. You are authorized to get these without stint or limit. Spare nothing, neither expense, time nor effort. Simply send me the bill and I will O.K."[30] MGM became the biggest and most glamorous studio of Hollywood's Golden Age, boasting "more stars than there are in heaven," and Mayer was its undisputed king. "For more than three decades Mayer was the most powerful man in the film industry."[31] And for much of that period, he was the highest-paid man in America, with a salary topping a million dollars a year.

Mayer was really more of a patriarch than a king. It was said jokingly that MGM stood for Mayer's-*Ganz-Mispochen,* the Yiddish equivalent of "Mayer's whole family." His thousands of employees were like his children, and in turn he was their father, due all the respect, love, obedience, gratitude, and loyalty that implied. Once the actor Robert Taylor stormed into Mayer's office, demanding a raise. After several moments of shouting, Taylor emerged misty-eyed.

"Did you get the raise?" asked a secretary.

"No, but I gained a father."[32]

His grandson Daniel Selznick remembered walking the MGM lot with Mayer. "He would look up fifty feet in the air on a scaffold and ask, 'Rudy, how's your daughter? Did she recover from that bicycle accident?' He knew the details of the private lives of hundreds of people."[33] And he would protect his people. "He could keep a murder out of the papers," said Daniel, or get a starlet an abortion from the doctor he kept on retainer (Greta Garbo alone had eight). "Oh, Mr. Mayer could really come to your protection. He could solve all problems in two minutes," recalled child star Margaret O'Brien.[34] And he was vindictive toward those who were insufficiently grateful for his beneficence.

Mayer's extreme emotional reactions were legendary, even by Hollywood standards. "The scenes in Mayer's office would win Academy Awards. He'd cry, he'd weep, he'd beg, he'd kiss, he'd love, he'd hate, he'd scream—he'd do anything!" one writer recalled.[35] Sometimes he would even faint. According to Budd Schulberg, there was an ongoing debate in their family about Mayer: Were his fainting fits and hysterics manifestations of a psychiatric abnormality or just a manipulative act?[36] Budd's mother believed that Mayer was genuinely a little crazy: "He was a very emotional man, so intense that he might be described as on the borderline of insanity." She noticed that Mayer swung wildly between grandiosity and panic: "He was always an extremist. One moment he could be so cocksure of himself that he was positively obnoxious. But the very next moment, facing a situation for which he was not prepared, or for which he knew he didn't have the resources, he could break out into a cold sweat, lose his voice and actually lose his ability to function."[37] Daniel Selznick believes that Mayer both had genuine emotional extremes and that he learned to use them to his advantage. When renegotiating a contract with a reluctant star, "he would work himself up into a temper tantrum: 'What, goddammit! We're paying you how much? You have a hell of a nerve. After all we've done for you. Goddammit!' "

Mayer used his emotionalism for more than financial negotiations. It was the lens through which he viewed potential movies. "If a story makes me cry, it's good" was his motto.[38] The first generation of moguls who came from eastern Europe didn't speak English as their first language, were not educated, and didn't read much. Mayer rarely read scripts. A "storyteller" would describe the scenes of any proposed movie for him. Mayer would demonstrate what he wanted. One producer recalled, "It was always an experience. He was a ham. He would get down on the floor and pray and sing and illustrate the kind of pictures he would like to see you make, which were cornball pictures."[39] But cornball pictures sold. The audience was not made up of "sophisticates," a term Mayer used with derision. It was composed of millions of poor, uneducated immigrants like himself. Studies from the 1920s showed that the less money one earned and the more hours one worked for it, the more movies one watched. Movies were the only industry to see an increase in business during the Depression.

Mayer inherited his emotional intensity from his mother. "He felt everything good in him came from his mother," his daughter Irene wrote.[40] Like Andrew Carnegie's, much of his sense of personal destiny came from his internalization of her devotion. When she was dying in 1912, she reassured him, "I wish I could have stayed a little longer, so I could see the things I know you are capable of doing. But I will watch over you. I will know all about you and your work."[41] Mayer always believed that she was literally watching. "She became his totem, his personal divinity. He became her devoted celebrant, determined to justify her love and faith in him."[42] As long as he lived, a giant picture of her hung over his bed.

Preserving the sacred image of motherhood and the family was imperative to Mayer. The wholesome Andy Hardy series was his personal favorite. At one preview, Mayer watched a scene in which Mickey Rooney is so preoccupied by problems with his sweetheart, Polly, that he pushes his mother's dinner aside. Mayer yelled at the producer. "Don't you realize that no decent American boy would treat his mother in such a way?"[43] The scene was reshot. Mayer was beyond mortified when John Gilbert, his biggest star at the time, proposed making a film based on the long poem *The Widow in the Bye Street* by British poet laureate John Masefield. The plot involved a working-class widow and her son; the boy loses his virginity to a prostitute, falls in love with her, kills her lover, and goes to the gallows. Mayer exploded:

> "Only you, you bastard would allow a whore to enter a story about a beloved mother and her young boy!"
>
> "What's wrong with that? My mother was a whore!" Gilbert replied.
>
> "You should have your balls cut off for making such a remark!" Mayer screamed and punched him in the jaw.[44]

When the great director Erich von Stroheim called "all women whores," Mayer beat him, dragged him out of his office, and threw his cane out after him. "If seventy-five percent of the American public didn't feel as I do about the American family, we wouldn't be here," Mayer declared.[45] Once again, Mayer was in tune with the masses. For the immigrants who poured into America, before anyone thought of a social safety net, family was all they had. If anyone presented a movie to Mayer that deviated from his idealized view of the American family, he would give that person a cold stare and ask, "Aren't you ashamed to tell me a story like that?"[46]

Yankee Doodle Dandy   Above all, Louis B. Mayer believed in America. Irene recalled, "He saluted the flag with such fervor. He was so proud to be an American. America the beautiful! He said Americans took it for granted. You had to be a newly naturalized citizen to appreciate the glories of the USA."[47] Louis B. Mayer didn't know his birth date, so he appropriated America's. Each Independence Day, he threw a joint birthday party for the United States and himself—a colossal affair with thousands of MGM's employees. They would "get together to pay homage to the king—literally," said Daniel Selznick. Movie stars serenaded him with "well-known songs, each with the lyrics written to pay homage to L.B." Tears streaming, Mayer would say, "Thank you, thank you, thank you. I love you all."[48] Attendance at John Philip Sousa night was also a command performance for MGM staff. Each year an elated Mayer led a parade out of the Hollywood Bowl as everyone marched behind him to the tune of "Stars and Stripes Forever."

Mayer believed that he was playing a unique role in America's messianic destiny. "Because of the wonderful USA the whole world was moving forward. He became evangelistic about show business, most particularly the movies. . . . They were a potent force and an important weapon. He believed that they would have a profound influence on the public, on the country and on the world," wrote Irene.[49] According to his grandson, "He felt he had a prophetic role in the spread of democracy. He absolutely felt he had a unique role in that destiny. It was important to import American values overseas, especially when Hitler started conquering Europe. He believed that the value of those humanitarian ideals would spread and that democracy would spring up all over the world, and that MGM films were partly responsible."

From the 1920s to the present day America has had an over-whelming international market share in the movie industry—"a near-monopoly unprecedented in American overseas commerce." [50] At a strictly commercial level, it was observed that these films served as advertisements for American products. An early dictum of the 1920s was "Trade follows film." Louis B. Mayer saw that the real product he was selling was America, and it was the most successful advertising job in history. In 1923, the London *Morning Post* noted with some alarm, "The film is to the American what the flag was once to Britain. By its means Uncle Sam may hope some day, if he is not checked in time, to Americanize the world." [51] That was precisely Mayer's plan. Movies offered a vision of a better world: "Girls could get their boys, and boys their girls, no matter what their income or social station; right could triumph over wrong no matter what forces of power or privilege stood in its way." [52] It was a world where the little guy won—whether it was Mr. Smith going to Washington, the Marx brothers making fools of rich aristocrats, or Gary Cooper standing alone against evildoers in *High Noon*. Movies such as these were like letters home to potential immigrants, much like the one Ben Warner received, singing the praises of America but exaggerating a little. The biggest impact of the movies was the increased demand they created for an American life.

The movies seduced the world with something more intangible: an *American temperament*. These optimistic fearless Americans cheered people up. "What attracted foreign audiences to American movies on an everyday basis was their speed, humor, brashness and glamour." [53] The world fell in love with the United States then. You could say they fell in love with our chutzpah.

THE PARENTS

Myron Selznick: The Tough Guy

Myron was aggressive. His grade school teacher from P.S. 94 in Brooklyn could still recall years later that he was a "dominant and manipulative young man."[54] He got into fights—over being Jewish, protecting his younger brother, David (when he wasn't beating up the "chump" himself), and just for the hell of it. He *liked* to fight. As an adult, at Hollywood parties, a drunken Myron would jump at the chance to punch anyone over anything. He was a "magnificent brute," according to David.[55]

Like his father, he liked to thumb his nose at those in authority. David recalled:

> His tendency to become a perfectly legal outlaw was early demonstrated at school, where it was his habit to refuse to join the school teams—despite a natural athletic tendency—and to organize rival teams within the school, with no rules for training, for the purpose of challenging and defeating the school team.[56]

One consequence of Lewis Selznick's bankruptcy was that his junior mogul sons had to get jobs, and Selznicks didn't work well for others. To stay in the movie business, Myron had to go hat in hand to the moguls he blamed for his father's downfall. When Myron and David arrived in Hollywood, they hardly received red-carpet treatment. First, Myron went to Carl Laemmle, the man who had once "fired" Lewis Selznick for impersonating his general manager. "Myron, my boy, let me give you some good advice. Get out of the picture business. You don't know anything about it, and you'll never get anywhere in it."[57]

Fortunately, the Selznicks had two powerful allies in Hollywood, Joe and Nicholas Schenck, Russian-born Jewish brothers who had been friends of their father. Joe Schenck, chairman of United

Artists, gave Myron a job working as an assistant producer, but Myron "clashed violently" with his boss.[58] When he was fired, Schenck gave him another chance with a different producer, and he was fired again.

Myron was incapable of working for anyone, and he couldn't quell his rage at the moguls. He didn't want to enter their world; he wanted to destroy it. He had sworn that he would make the bastards pay—and he did, quite literally. Myron created a new profession: the talent agent.

The studios had a system. To avoid bidding wars, the moguls did not try to steal one another's stars. Instead, they rented out their talent to one another. Myron busted this trust. He found out whose contracts were expiring and, one by one, convinced actors, directors, and writers to let him negotiate for them, setting off one of the biggest salary escalations in history. "Myron, Myron, be reasonable," Zukor demanded. "You have cost the industry fifty million dollars this year." Myron smiled. "I haven't started yet. . . . I'll break them all! I'll send all those thieves and four-flushers crawling to the poorhouse. Before I'm done the artists in this town will have all the money."[59] "Remember what those bastards did to my father," he said to one writer after a successful day of negotiations. "They paid more than a million dollars for it today."[60]

One of his clients, the writer Ben Hecht, said:

> His work of vengeance changed the Hollywood climate. It doubled, tripled, and quadrupled the salaries of writers, actors and directors, myself among them. Myron making a deal with a studio head was a scene out of Robin Hood. He was not only dedicated to his task of bankrupting the studio but ready to back up his sales talk with fisticuffs.[61]

He called the all-powerful Louis B. Mayer "a bastard and a sonofabitch" to his face. Mayer became so incensed that he barred Myron from the MGM lot. Myron retaliated by barring his client William Powell from completing an important movie that was in production at MGM. Mayer rescinded his ban. When it was time to renew Powell's contract, Mayer's right-hand man, Eddie Mannix, invited Myron to MGM. Myron crowed, "No, I've barred *M-G-M*. Come to my office."[62] He did, and Myron let him cool his heels in the waiting room for half an hour, while he and his staff had a few well-chilled martinis.

By 1937, Myron Selznick's agency was grossing $15 million a year. His client list was a *Who's Who:* Frances Dee, Kay Francis, Helen Hayes, Katharine Hepburn, Carole Lombard, Myrna Loy, Ida Lupino, Ginger Rogers, Fred Astaire, Charles Bickford, Gary Cooper, Jackie Cooper, Henry Fonda, Boris Karloff, Charles Laughton, Fredric March, Raymond Massey, Laurence Olivier, William Powell, and George Raft, to name only some. "Everybody needed Myron."

Myron's behavior after work was no less colorful. His hypomanic brawling, bragging, boozing, womanizing, and gambling were the stuff of Hollywood legend. He was almost guaranteed to disrupt any social function. He showed up to one formal dinner party underdressed, drunk, and two hours late, loudly demanding to be fed. "Were you invited?" his embarrassed brother, David, asked him. "Not only was I invited," Myron replied indignantly, "I declined."[63]

Myron had an innovative idea to build a competing studio: directors and actors would participate in the profits. This is the way most movies are funded today, but in 1938 it was a revolutionary idea. *The New York Times* called it "one of the most startling developments in the picture industry in years."[64] The moguls came together to crush this threat to their system by ensuring that no theater they did business with would ever show a Myron Selznick film. Myron acknowledged defeat by sending the moguls a sarcastic congratulatory letter entitled "Open letter to the Dictators."[65]

Another attempt to put the Selznick name up in lights failed. After that, Myron's drinking escalated. Increasingly bitter, he stopped coming into the office and returning clients' phone calls.

Staff and clients drifted away. He had always battled hidden bouts of depression, confessing once to Loretta Young that he inexplicably cried himself to sleep many nights: "Me, a grown man!"[66] The hard-boiled, cynical Myron suffered from a secret "self-loathing."[67] After 1938, his "suicidal alcoholism" spiralled out of control—and in 1944 it killed him.

David O. Selznick: The Prodigy

David's genius for the film business manifested itself early. When he was ten years old, his father would take him to Broadway plays to discuss whether they would make good films. When he was twelve, Lewis took David along to meetings to negotiate the start of World Films and directed questions his way. When David was fourteen, Lewis made his youngest son an executive, paying him $750 a week. David and his father were extraordinarily close. Until David left home for his honeymoon, Pop undressed him and tucked him into bed almost every night. He may have been a prodigy, but emotionally he was a little boy.

By seventeen, David already looked like a manic mogul. The novelist and screenwriter Niven Busch, who attended parties at the Selznick home, recalled, "I was rather in awe of David. David was a ceaseless stream of animal energy. We'd be up all night, and I'd have to go sleep. But when I awoke there was David ordering in a catered breakfast."[68]

In 1926, at age twenty-four, David went to MGM looking for a job. Harry Rapf, who had once worked for Lewis Selznick, offered to give him a chance. When Mayer found out, he decreed, "No one named Selznick will ever work here!"[69] Regretfully, Rapf had to rescind his job offer. Nicholas Schenck had once told David when he was a child, "Look me up if there is ever anything I can do for you." As president of Loew's, MGM's parent company, there was something he could do. Selznick camped outside his hotel for two days to find him, and Schenck forced Mayer to take on David.

David was apprenticed to Rapf, reading scripts for $100 a week. Selznick announced, "I'll do more than that. I'll help you fix them. I'll write titles. I'll do everything that has to be done on them."[70] He read every script the studio had on file. Soon he was submitting story idea after story idea. He "overwhelmed Harry with memos" and "stuffed the suggestion box at the commissary so full it had to be emptied daily instead of weekly." Rapf pleaded, "Enough, enough!" but rewarded his initiative by doubling David's salary and making him a story editor.[71] A month later his salary was doubled again, and he began producing B pictures. Even Mayer was impressed when David was given a budget to make one Western and came back with two. "How did you do it?" Mayer asked. "Easy, I took along two scripts and two supporting casts. I moved McCoy [the star] back and forth between the two plots."[72] Mayer began to think that maybe it wasn't so bad to have a Selznick around after all.

Irene Mayer: The Stuttering Princess

That Irene Mayer had a stuttering problem seemed to say it all. Her whole life she lived with voluble men who could not shut up, while she struggled to speak up. Finding her voice would take a lifetime. From birth, Irene was trained to respond to the moods of a hypomanic man who was brilliant, exciting, self-centered, and unstable:

> My father was not only omnipotent but also omniscient. In a curious way I got him mixed up with God, because of the word 'Almighty!' If ever there was a master in his own home, Dad was it. Our day was geared to his homecoming. Excitement, eagerness, usually accompanied by a bit of suspense. What was his mood? Whatever it was, we met it. If he was upset, we girls made ourselves scarce. . . . If he had a good day his high spirits would animate our evening meal. He could be spellbinding and made the great world outside seem fascinating. We shared the excitement of his life.[73]

Irene had a longing to be closer to her father: "I had a secret desire to become his secretary, be where the action was, anticipate him at every turn. But then didn't every girl want the same?"[74] L.B., as he was sometimes called, would serve as a template for Irene's future attractions. She would not marry a normal or boring man. She was destined to be drawn to the bipolar flame.

L.B. was intensely conservative, controlling, and overprotective, and the effect was to stunt Irene's emotional and intellectual growth. He told his daughters to "never trust anyone except the family." He wanted to keep them away from Hollywood people because they were a bad influence, but those were the only people they knew. He didn't want them to skate, bike, or drive. Worst of all, he prevented Irene from going to college even after she was accepted to the highly selective Wellesley.

Irene lived like the fabled Arabian princess in the tale of Aladdin, pampered, but a prisoner in her own palace, longing desperately to see life outside the walls. Soon, her prince would come.

David and Irene

In 1926, Irene and her sister, Edith, went on strike. They demanded dates for the annual Hollywood ball at the Mayfair Hotel. If they couldn't have dates, they weren't going. Mayer relented, but *he* would choose the young men. Harry Rapf volunteered the services of his wonder boy David. Despite his being the son of Lewis Selznick, Mayer reassured Irene, "This one got saved, the old man didn't have time to ruin him. Harry says he's a clean boy, has a good character."[75]

The date was a disaster. Selznick had no stomach for dating the boss's daughter and loudly said so. He was angry at having allowed himself to be pressured into this "fucking thing." When Irene accused him of being drunk, he replied, "Not drunk enough." Irene changed her seat to escape, but he chased after her. "Listen, Miss Mayer, I have something to say to you. Once I was a much bigger prince than you are a princess. I know all about it, and let me tell you, there's nothing to it. Don't take it too seriously."[76]

They met again at a party two months later. Irene was walking down a circular staircase when out of nowhere David came swinging toward her "like the man on the flying trapeze" and tried to kiss her. No one had ever tried to kiss her before. She repulsed his advance but was intrigued when he invited her to join him, Myron, and their friends at their weekly Sunday tennis match at a private court by the beach. Just being in such a social setting was liberation. "I thought myself quite daring in this fast company." Irene inhaled the up-tempo atmosphere and irreverent banter and became fascinated by David. He spoke "with such zest and crackle."[77]

When Selznick asked her out on a real date, only her mother's persistent intercession convinced Mayer to let her go. On the way to dinner, Selznick stopped the car in front of a building with tall white colonial columns, once the studio of Thomas Ince, believed to have been the first person to shoot a movie in California. "That's the kind of place I'd like to have," he told her. A lot sooner than anyone thought, he was going to have his own studio, he swore. He took Irene to the expensive Cocoanut Grove restaurant. Sensitive to the steep prices, she ordered a small meal. David ordered half the menu, including lobster and steak. He couldn't eat a fraction of it, and it cost a fortune. Such irrational excess should have been a warning to her, but what most impressed her was how he talked: "The words poured out: anecdotes, reminiscences, opinions, fresh ideas, punctuated by witticisms and some fairly profound observations. Marvelous talk for an audience of one. I was overawed."[78]

The way David talked got him fired from MGM. He "engaged in violent arguments" with senior MGM producer Hunt Stromberg, who refused to incorporate aspects of Polynesian culture into *White Shadows of the South Seas*. Selznick demanded a meeting with their boss, the legendary Irving Thalberg. When Thalberg sided with Stromberg, Selznick shouted insults at both of them in front of the entire staff in the commissary. Thalberg ordered Selznick to apologize or consider himself fired. "I've already cleaned out my desk," said David defiantly.[79]

Selznick strode over to Paramount, the studio headed by his father's *other* old enemy, Adolph Zukor. Producer Bernard Fineman convinced B. P. Schulberg to give him a chance. Schulberg and Fineman were viewing a film in the projection room when they were interrupted by a call from Schulberg's secretary:

"I said I didn't want to be disturbed," Schulberg snapped.

"I'm sorry, Mr. Schulberg, but Mr. David Selznick is here to see you."

"Tell him to wait."

"He says he doesn't want to wait. He wants to know what his salary is going to be."

"Why, that goddam—" Schulberg stormed out and yelled at Selznick, "You are the most arrogant young man I have ever met."[80]

Schulberg gave Selznick a two-week trial "against my better judgment." Selznick realized he was in trouble when his two weeks were almost up. He had annoyed the boss and done nothing to distinguish himself. Selznick seized on a memo announcing a contest to title seventeen new films. Selznick read all seventeen scripts and submitted suggestions under pseudonyms. All seventeen of his suggestions won. Schulberg got the point: Selznick may have been the most arrogant young man he had ever met, but he was also among the most brilliant. Schulberg made Selznick his executive assistant.

Now that Irene was not the boss's daughter, David felt less conflicted about pursuing her. Mayer reluctantly allowed it—on one condition: she could date David only every other night. Mayer was hoping that Irene would meet someone more suitable on the alternate evenings. Ironically, the plan was best suited for their developing relationship. It gave Irene room to breathe and allowed David to carry on with starlets and secretaries on their nights off.

215

Tacit rules were established. When he blabbed about the girls, Irene stopped him. She didn't want to hear about them.

Irene should have suspected that David's mood swings went to pathological extremes the day she came to his house to help him set up for his annual Christmas party:

> When we arrived we were dismayed. At the end of the big story-and-a-half living room stood the biggest tree I had ever seen in a private house. The room was awash with ornaments, tinsel, strings of lights, and presents, scores of them. They were all unwrapped because he had not yet decided to whom they were going. . . . His enthusiasm for the gifts he was giving was enormous, and their number was enormous, many of them bought because he thought they would suit people not even on his list. . . . He alternated between panic that no one was coming and the realization that there were some friends he hadn't yet asked, so he started making telephone calls, stalling some guests and inviting others. Dusk came on and the mess was bad as ever . . . the magnitude of his undertaking accentuated its doom.
>
> Suddenly he was not to be found. . . . I rapped on his study door . . . I rapped again, and heard muffled sounds. "Give me a few minutes." Then the door opened a couple of inches. He stood there without his glasses, tears streaming, eight years old. He said, "I can't stand it, forgive me, I'm so depressed. Christmas is almost over. Holidays are terrible, worse than Sundays, and Christmas is the worst of all. I get melancholia." [81]

But she ignored these warning signs and agreed to marry him.

Even David's method of proposing marriage revealed his extreme hypomania: "Once he started proposing he never stopped. . . . No evening was complete without still another proposal, more original, more devastating than the one before." David had just one condition: "I will never take anything from your father." [82]

216

Lewis Selznick was delighted to hear of the engagement, but he too had one condition: "When you are married to David, you will give me a grandson. . . . There's just one thing that worries me: will he be a Mayer or a Selznick? Tell me. Will you let my grandson dance on top of the piano if he wants to? I never said no to a child of mine. You shouldn't either. I want him to be a Selznick." [83] This was a serious matter. Selznick men acted out their hypomanic impulses without limits.

Mayer was surprisingly agreeable to Irene and David's plans. He declared that Lewis Selznick had "mellowed." And David was making good at Paramount. The bone of contention—and of course there had to be one—was the date of the wedding. Mayer wanted them to delay. The idea of waiting made David irate, especially since he and Irene had agreed to postpone sex till marriage. "You cannot do this to me, Mr. Mayer. I cannot wait any longer. You're a man. What kind of hell do you think I go through?" Walking out in a rage, David turned to his fiancée: "Irene, are you coming?" Caught in a tug-of-war between the two men she loved, Irene "was momentarily paralyzed." She stayed, and stood up to her father for the first time: "No man has ever had a more obedient and loving daughter. But when I tell a man I will marry him, in spirit I am his. . . . I cannot fly two flags. His flag must come first." [84] (At this point in her development, Irene couldn't even conceive of flying her *own* flag.) After her speech, she fainted.

Even though the ceremony was in his own home, Mayer threatened to boycott it. But as the processional was playing, he dramatically emerged from his study at the last moment and announced, "You may start the wedding." [85]

David was a rising star at Paramount. Adolph Zukor told him that he might soon be chosen to replace his boss, B. P. Schulberg, who had not effectively managed the transition to talking pictures. But Selznick and Schulberg began "disagreeing violently," and Selznick quit.[86] Mayer was horrified. He told Selznick he couldn't do that after marrying his daughter. He had a family to support now, and it was the middle of the Depression. "A young man in 1931 had to be either optimistic, courageous or foolhardy to walk out on $2,000 a week. He was all three," wrote Irene.[87] But she backed his gamble. David wanted to launch his own production company.

The Selznicks moved to New York to negotiate financing for the venture. To project the right image, they stayed in an opulent four-room suite at the Pierre Hotel, which they couldn't afford. David made phone calls so hypomanically that the hotel staff was "astonished by David's monopoly of their switchboard."[88] Every day Selznick went looking for backing. And every day all doors seemed closed. Irene wrote, "David shook off rejection like a spaniel out of water and regrouped his forces. No two days were alike except for the degree of optimism, very little of which was warranted. . . . We were always 'on the verge.' "[89] What neither Irene nor David knew was that the moguls, led by her father, had conspired to stop him. They had decided that Selznick's proposed company "was not in the best interest of the picture business," Irene later heard through a third party.

Fortunately, Selznick met David Sarnoff. A short, hyperactive man who liked to be called "the General," this Russian Jewish immigrant had hypomanically hustled his way from messenger boy to president of NBC, becoming the father of radio—America's first mass medium. Irene recalled the effect Sarnoff had on David: "Sarnoff, with his expansive personality and tremendous vision, completely bowled David Selznick over, the only person, I believe, who ever did. David found him a giant."[90] Sarnoff threw him the keys to RKO, a small, struggling movie studio owned by NBC, and said, in effect: Do what you want—just win. David O. Selznick returned to Hollywood, a mogul at last.

Manic Mogul Louis B. Mayer had been messianic about the pro-American, profamily, and prodemocracy message his movies conveyed. David O. Selznick was equally idealistic about making pictures, though for different reasons. "Movies were like a great cause to us; to be pretentious, you could call it a sense of mission," wrote Irene.[91] In David's mind, he too would change the world—by making movies so great that they would elevate the art form forever.

In the excitement of finally being able to make movies his way, without interference, his brain exploded with ideas, recalled Irene:

Ideas were hatched at an incredible speed, yet they tumbled out so wonderfully structured. He had such a fertile brain the alternatives were endless. He just emptied his mind as he went.... He left for the studio, his pockets jammed with endless bits of paper.[92]

One sleepless night, David couldn't find any writing paper. The next morning he brought memos to department heads written on a roll of toilet paper. This led to a new idea. "He found a gadget that held a huge roll of paper," wrote Irene. Keeping it next to his bed "enabled him to start his day with a single piece of paper from six to sixty inches long. And from it memos flowed." Selznick's memos were sprees of free association. If you wanted to illustrate what flight of ideas means, you would be hard-pressed to find a better example than the memos of David O. Selznick. "He realized how illogical he really was," wrote Irene. "Sometimes in a memo to me he would recognize that the memo itself was preposterous and dictate his own reaction, in fact tell me to forget the whole thing, but send it anyhow so I would acknowledge that he was also reasonable."[93] His son Daniel recognized the same flight of ideas when he spoke: "He would have a second idea, and a third idea and a fourth, and he wouldn't wait for a response. He would keep going."

David was at RKO just over a year, and it is amazing what he accomplished to further the state of the art in that short time. He promoted or discovered such talents as George Cukor, Fred Astaire, and Katharine Hepburn. He advanced special effects with the legendary *King Kong,* spending a fortune on elaborate miniatures. He took on taboo topics, such as a critique of Hollywood itself, with *What Price Hollywood?* He hired Viennese composer Max Steiner to write large-scale scores that contributed to the mood of the pictures, which "established a role for musical scores that has hardly changed in sixty years," wrote David Thomson in *Showman.*[94] Most of all, David represented a new generation of moguls who appreciated words. Unlike the immigrant moguls who rose with the silent picture, David O. Selznick came to the height of his creative powers in the age of the talking movie and wanted to make films out of great books. He began doing this at RKO, casting Katharine Hepburn in *Little Women.*

Unfortunately, it was not only David's creative energies that went into hypomanic overdrive. David's sexual behavior, his spending, and his gambling spun out of control. "At the studio he was trying to screw every secretary who was willing. It was not serious, he told himself, no threat to Irene. He was only getting rid of his great energy."[95] Every female who entered his office received at least an "obligatory" advance. He was usually gracious in accepting a no, but many said yes.

No matter how much David earned, he spent more. "David was a poor man with a big salary," wrote Irene. "He didn't believe in saving pennies; pennies were chicken feed and there were millions on the horizon. . . . David spent himself and his money with equal abandon."[96] He had a particular passion for impulsive and extravagant gifts. "He was crazy about last-minute shopping; he made his secretary call stores and ask them to keep open."[97] Christmas, anniversaries, and birthdays were marked by a staggering array of gifts organized in increasing splendor. "As I opened each gift, I was moved, delighted, excited. It was intoxicating. But when the height of luxury and expense has been reached on the twentieth gift and there are five more to go, panic sets in."[98] Irene was struggling to keep the family books balanced, which insulted David. "Coming home one evening, David found me at my desk, bent over my checkbook. The image of his wife poring over figures offended him; it was depressing. He accused me of economizing. It showed a lack of faith. . . . If I would learn to be extravagant, even go into debt, it would prove my confidence in him."[99] He wanted her to be a Selznick, but she couldn't change who she was.

Gambling was his most addictive and self-destructive habit. At times, he irritably defended his behavior: "When you married me you knew I was a gambler. I'm gambling right now as a filmmaker, and it's my gambling instinct that's going to help me make some of the best pictures this country has ever seen. . . . I can't turn it off at the end of the day."[100] He would talk exuberantly about "going gloriously broke."[101] But alternately, he was flooded with remorse and shame and begged Irene for forgiveness, as in this note:

Darling:

It is after 5:30 in the morning, and one of the most miserable hours of my life . . . sleep is unthinkable and I shall not try to achieve it.

I have lost a large amount of money—four thousand dollars. No loss of money could seriously upset me: this you know. But I have broken my most devout word to you, and I cannot tell you the torture of self-disgust I feel. . . . I don't mean to be dramatic, but I feel so desperate and futile about it. "For each man kills the thing he loves." And I love you as I hate myself.

Your wretched David[102]

He repeatedly promised Irene he would quit, offering "vows so sincere that one couldn't doubt him, until the next time."[103]

In 1932, Irene gave birth to their first son, Jeffrey. David became delusional, claiming that their baby had been stolen by the hospital staff and replaced with another. He showed up at the hospital unshaven and "in terrible shape" after being up all night. "Our baby is gone," he told Irene. "This was no mix up, it was a plot! Ours was a prize baby." [104] Irene tried to reason with him. They had both seen the ID bracelet put on Jeffrey. A delusion, however, is impervious to any amount of evidence or rational argument. "He wanted no part of my logic—there are ways around such precautions." [105] By the time they left the hospital the delusion had cleared. It simply went away, but it had been there. Diagnostically, this unmistakable evidence of psychosis means that David must be considered a bipolar type I, a manic-depressive in the classical sense.

On the way home from the hospital, they stopped at David's parents'. David put Jeffrey proudly at the end of Lewis Selznick's bed and announced: "Pop's eternity." [106]

Redeeming the Selznick Name   It is hard to imagine the grief that struck David when his father died suddenly. Irene described the moment when the doctor told him it was "all over":

> David screamed, "No!" Sam [the doctor] grappled with him as he rushed forward but he couldn't hold him. The three of us watched stunned, as David, totally out of control, stood at the foot of the bed, arms outstretched, beseeching his father to hear him. "Pop, it's David. Speak to me! It's David asking you. Do it for me, Pop." . . . It was the most dramatic scene I have ever witnessed. [107]

At the funeral David collapsed. His secretary, Marcella, had "never seen such a manifestation of grief as David's. It was hard for anyone to take. He was being held up, by Irene on one side and someone else on the other . . . his crying was so intense that the mucus from his nose just fell and drained right to the ground." [108] "For two years afterward he cried out in his sleep for him. He was raw! And he *never* got over it," wrote Irene. [109] David was plagued by what he called "mercurial moods of indifference and depression that have made me damned impossible to live with." [110]

Lewis Selznick's last words to his younger son were "Blood is

222

thicker than water." He wanted David to rejoin MGM, where he would be working for family. "The Son-in-Law Also Rises," jibed the *Hollywood Spectator* when announcing David's appointment. But the son-in-law jokes stopped when the Oscars started rolling in. David made a number of memorable movies at MGM, including *David Copperfield* (with the unforgettable performance of W. C. Fields), *A Tale of Two Cities, Anna Karenina,* and *Viva Villa,* about the life of Mexican revolutionary Pancho Villa.

Soon David was talking again about starting his own company, but his father-in-law was determined to do whatever it took to keep him. He offered David a full partnership in MGM. David waffled back and forth until L.B. began to suspect that his own daughter was working against him. He showed up unexpectedly at Irene's door in a rage. Irene "took a deep breath" and explained, "He's still young enough to try and fail." To her amazement, Mayer said, "I understand," turned on his heel, and walked out.[111]

David formed Selznick International Pictures (SIP) in 1935. It looked as if the third Selznick would be the charm. The Selznick name was up in lights again. David took possession of the Thomas Ince studio, the one he had shown Irene on their first date. Just as her father had bragged that he would have a studio like Goldwyn's someday and then had taken it over, David had claimed he would have a studio like Ince's one day and now had that very one. SIP was a critical success. *A Star Is Born,* Hollywood's first hit in color, was a strong start. David also produced a string of well-regarded movies from classic novels: *Little Lord Fauntleroy, The Adventures of Tom Sawyer,* and *The Prisoner of Zenda.* David was suddenly the king of high-end cinema, his films nominated for the Oscar for best picture four years in a row.

But SIP was not a financial success. It was a boutique operation in an industry where studios functioned as glorified factories. With their high overhead, they needed to make movies in volume to be cost-effective. David's financial backers were increasingly nervous, but he dismissed their concerns, writing them, "Contrary to any other opinion that may be held by anyone, I think I am a superb executive (sounds of mixed laughter and cheers). . . . I flatter myself that practically single-handed I have built a company that in its first year and a half of existence has a better record than any other company that has started in the history of the business."[112] To stay solvent, David needed a blockbuster, and miraculously he found one. He bought the rights to a yet-unpublished, thousand-page first novel on a topic that had always been taboo in Hollywood: the Civil War. David could not have predicted that *Gone With the Wind* would become a runaway best seller and a national phenomenon. Once the book became so well known, all eyes turned to Selznick. America was desperate to see this movie, but it would have to wait three years.

The Greatest Film Ever Made   In the spring of 1937, David asked his doctor for something to help him work through the night. He was prescribed benzedrine, which he used more or less continuously from 1937 to 1950. Unintentionally, the doctor wrote a prescription that made his patient much sicker. Amphetamine abuse produces symptoms very much like those of mania: psychomotor acceleration, diminished need for sleep, feelings of grandeur, impulsivity, poor judgment, paranoid thinking, and psychosis. The symptoms are so similar that Dr. Robert Post, chief of biological psychiatry at the National Institute of Mental Health, has argued that they must operate using the same neural pathways.[113] Benzedrine pushed David from hypomania into mania. "I think the benzedrine was the worst thing," Irene said fifty years later. When David made *Gone With the Wind*, he was in a full-blown manic episode.

David prepared Irene. Until the picture was done, the family was under siege. "We were in a war and we were in it together," she wrote.[114] David was on a round-the-clock schedule, often going for two or three days without sleep. He would work until 3 A.M., play roulette until dawn, lose a fortune, and go barreling back into the office. Irene kept two full-time cooks on staff to feed him any time, twenty-four hours a day. He might fail to show up for days or bring thirty people over for dinner unannounced at 2 A.M. The agencies couldn't find any more cooks willing to work for him. Irene went to one agency and noticed a box of cards marked "Cooks." What about these people? Then she turned one card over. On the back of all the cards was written, "Anyone but Selznick." To accommodate his round-the-clock habits, Selznick employed three shifts of secretaries. One team would begin in the morning, a second would start at four and the anchor shift came in at night. Some collapsed under the strain, requiring medical or psychiatric hospitalization.

David's "memo mania" went into high gear. He dictated a million and a half words during the production of *Gone With the Wind*. Teams of messengers delivered his memos to cast and crew, often in the middle of the night. Only a cast rebellion established a 9 P.M. curfew. Vivien Leigh received one memo that weighed more than a pound. In his career, David O. Selznick would write a quarter of a million memos.

All of this activity seemed to be going nowhere. Selznick kept postponing production, and people began calling the film "Selznick's folly." David's search for the perfect Scarlett O'Hara was one example. Every actress in Hollywood wanted the part. Bette Davis wrote bitterly in her memoirs that it had been made for her. Katharine Hepburn, Paulette Goddard, Jean Arthur, Susan Hayward, and Lana Turner were angling for it. But David made the startling announcement that he would choose an unknown, setting off the biggest casting call in history. SIP spent $100,000 on hundreds of screen tests with women from around the nation. But when it came time to shoot the movie, after two years of looking, David had still not found his Scarlett. Filming began with the burning of Atlanta on the night of December 11, 1938. David created Hollywood's biggest bonfire, burning the old sets of an entire studio. As he lit the match, Myron arrived with a new client on his arm, British actress Vivien Leigh. "I want you to meet Scarlett O'Hara," Myron said." [115] David quickly agreed.

It was a huge challenge to turn a sprawling thousand-page epic novel into a movie while remaining faithful to a book America loved. The author, Margaret Mitchell, refused to consult on the script. She thought the task impossible. David turned to Pulitzer Prize–winning author Sidney Howard. A highly disciplined, productive writer, he wrestled with the assignment and produced an excellent script on time. This was the beginning of the most insane bout of rewriting anyone had ever seen. "David, himself, thinks HE is writing the script," one member of the *Gone With the Wind* production staff complained, and he never stopped writing it. [116] As work ended in the evening, the cast would frequently get a rewritten scene to be shot the next day. Then a revised version would appear in the morning, after Selznick had been up all night, chain-smoking (five packs a day) and scratching on his yellow legal pad. Often cast and crew sat idle while David continued to write. Director George Cukor told David that "he would not work any longer if the script was not better and he wanted the Howard script back." David said, "OK, get out!" [117] Cukor, one of the greatest directors of all time, as well as one of David's best friends, had been involved in the preproduction of the movie for two years, but David impulsively fired him after only three weeks of shooting.

David hired a new director, Victor Fleming, who immediately saw the problem. "David, you haven't got a fucking script." [118] Selznick drafted veteran writer Ben Hecht, who recalled that Selznick and Fleming appeared at his bedside one Sunday morning at dawn. [119] Hecht was amazed: "David had done a hundred million things preparing for this movie. The only thing he overlooked in his perfection mania was a script." [120] It wasn't that he had overlooked it; rather, it was precisely his "perfection mania" that wouldn't let him finish it. Hecht, Fleming, and Selznick worked on the script for a week, eighteen hours a day, living "on peanuts and bananas," until a blood vessel in Fleming's eye exploded, David collapsed, and Hecht claimed he was physically unable to move off the couch.

David then brought back Sidney Howard, the original screenwriter, who wrote his wife, "How really astonishing, that a man can spend the time and money he has spent and find himself so unready at the end. And he is completely unready, as though he had barely started." One day, David gave Howard a scene that was to be shot in two hours and asked for changes. "Rewrite it for me," he said. Howard asked, "What do you want, David?" and concluded that "David has not the faintest idea."[121] Between the fall of 1936 and the summer of 1939, David hired and fired eleven writers, including F. Scott Fitzgerald, "sometimes hiring a new writer almost before he bothered to read what the previous writer had written."[122] Even his loyal secretary, Marcella, had to admit that her boss was out of control: "It was a case of utter chaos. Everybody hated David. He interfered in everything. . . . Everything had to be done and redone. He was despised."[123]

To make up for lost time, Selznick had the cast and crew shoot twelve hours a day, six days a week, in a heat of up to 120 degrees. Howard wrote, "Half of the staff look, talk and behave as though they were on the verge of breakdowns."[124] Fleming went over the verge. "Driving home one night, he contemplated heading his car over the edge of a cliff. He was hospitalized with a nervous breakdown."[125] Selznick hired a third director, Sam Wood, and when Fleming got out of the hospital he retained them both in order to run double shifts, Fleming directing in the morning and Wood at night.

Some of Selznick's demands for perfection were irrational. For example, he spent tens of thousands of dollars on historically authentic handmade lace underwear no viewer would ever see, just to help the actresses get into character. In other respects, it was precisely that obsessive perfectionism that made *Gone With the Wind* a classic. In one of the film's most powerful shots, a camera pans upward to reveal thousands of wounded Confederate soldiers sprawled out in front of a train station waiting to be evacuated. Despite the cliché "a cast of thousands," Hollywood rarely used so many live actors. But David insisted on thousands of extras because it was historically accurate. That one breathtaking silent shot, as the field of wounded becomes larger and larger and larger, communicated more about the scale of the Civil War's carnage than anything anyone had ever seen. David may have been going mad, but he was a mad genius.

Gone With the Wind was hailed by critics as "the greatest film ever made." It swept the 1939 Oscars, establishing a record for the most Oscars ever won by a single movie. Never had a studio had such a brilliant launch as that of Selznick International Pictures. And SIP was no one-hit wonder. For a second act, David had waiting in the wings two talents he had discovered on his travels in Europe: Alfred Hitchcock and Ingrid Bergman.

Then he destroyed it all.

The Breakdown　In his state of "extreme exhaustion," everything celluloid suddenly seemed toxic to David. He wanted to be "shut of the whole thing" and impulsively decided to disband Selznick International Pictures and sell his interest in *Gone With the Wind*. Irene called it "madness" and "begged him to reconsider." She predicted that he would once again ask her, "How could you let me do it?" [126] She was right. "He confessed some years later that he should have listened to me; he considered it the greatest error he ever made, and regretted it increasingly through the rest of his life." [127] David owned a quarter of the film, and after five years MGM's 50 percent would have reverted to him (L.B. got his hands on a piece of *Gone With the Wind* in exchange for Clark Gable and $1.5 million). Instead, Selznick sold his interest to his partner, Jock Whitney, for $400,000, and Whitney quickly resold Selznick's share to MGM for $2 million. Since 1939, *Gone With the Wind* has grossed almost a *billion* dollars for MGM. Selznick had to spend the rest of his life watching his movie make money for other people. "As I grew up, I would ask Dad about *Gone With the Wind,* but he never seemed to want to talk about it," wrote Daniel Selznick.[128] Later he understood why.

Selznick even threw away the $400,000—gambling, of course.

Things got worse for David and Irene. Endeavoring to retire in splendor, they had bought a mansion in Connecticut, where David was going nuts. "It depressed him there was nothing to do. . . . Nothing stimulating! . . . Not working gave him no outlet for his drives." More ominously, "I found that when I left him alone, he brooded about Hollywood. Mild paranoia set in." [129] It began with "little scenes in other people's houses." He would get into arguments and challenge people to fights. "Everyone in Hollywood was his enemy."

Only to Irene did David confess the shape he was in:

Most Wonderful of Women:
    This letter will, I fear have little form. I'm scribbling madly because I must talk to you—to you, and only you.
    I've been depressed, as I've told you and wired you: depressions such as I haven't known in a long time, such as I didn't know in my most confused Hollywood hours. . . . The boil is coming to a head. I know I can't go on much longer, without making any sense, without going mad. So *please* don't be upset by this outburst: the thought of that possibility tempts me not to mail this—but I shall, I know, because in my egotism I'm sure that *you* at least want all my moods—and for that, and for ten thousand other reasons, I am
                    Yours-at-the-pedestal's base,
                    David[130]

Irene later described those harrowing days:

He could no longer drown his depression with drink or outrace it with Benzedrine. Now and then I got out for an hour or so, and when I returned he would look at me as if I were his savior. His mood deepened and he became really scared. So did I. He confessed he was afraid he was going insane, and told me I'd better get him some help.[131]

Irene was referred to a "top man," but David wouldn't go to the psychiatrist's office. In his manic entitlement, the unemployed mogul insisted that "the analyst come to him."[132] Instead, Dr. Rado met with Irene to tell her that David was "having a breakdown."[133] Rado referred David to "a wise little motherly" Russian Jewish immigrant psychiatrist-psychoanalyst, Dr. May Romm, who arranged to see David every day on an emergency basis. Irene was relieved to see him in treatment. "Once I got him there I felt a burst of freedom; I was out from under!" Or so she thought.

After a few weeks of sessions, Selznick said he felt better and denied that therapy had had anything to do with his sudden recovery. He began to miss more sessions than he made—or worse, show up late and refuse to leave when his time was up because he was "just getting started." He rang the doorbell at Dr. Romm's home at midnight and "demanded to be heard." In his conversations with Irene, "he recounted these antics as though they were amusing." She "implored him" not to sabotage his treatment. He knew more than Dr. Romm, he told her. *"He* could analyze *her."* Furthermore, he bragged that "Dr. Romm was in love with him." In David's grandiose fantasy world, he was the center of everyone's admiration. Selznick dramatized his transference to Dr. Romm in *Spellbound,* the Hitchcock classic in which beautiful European analyst Ingrid Bergman falls in love with one of her patients, Gregory Peck. After close to a year, Dr. Romm announced that David was simply incapable of continuing their work "in any way acceptable to her."[134] Instead, Irene became her patient.

David needed to be obsessed about something to discharge his prodigious energy, so it is not surprising that an erotic obsession arose to fill this vacuum. He fell in love with an unknown actress,

Jennifer Jones, and became committed to the idea that he would make her the biggest star in history. David's infidelities had been too numerous to count but had usually lasted only as long as one li-aison. Irene had been able to tolerate them because her dignity had remained intact. It was essentially the don't-ask-don't-tell system they had worked out when they were dating. But David went out with Jones publicly, making all the gossip columns. Just as he had expressed his erotic transference toward Dr. Romm in *Spellbound,* David acted out his erotic fantasies about Jennifer in a Western, *Duel in the Sun.* Jones is raped by Gregory Peck, with whom she falls in love, and exposes more breast than anyone had ever seen on film. Selznick was determined to push the edge of the sexual en-velope. He complained to the man writing the musical score, "It isn't orgasm music. It's not *shtup.* It's not the way I fuck." [135]

David was manic during the filming of *Duel in the Sun.* He slept even less than he had during *Gone With the Wind.* His gambling losses went into the hundreds of thousands of dollars. He sent the cast and crew more than ten thousand memos. The movie was over budget and over schedule. The cast had to wait as he continued to rewrite the script. Jones had a breakdown: she emptied a bottle of pills, had to have her stomach pumped, and almost died. It was an-other hurricane like *Gone With the Wind,* and David claimed that *Duel* would be an even bigger success. Unlike the siege Irene had endured for *Gone With the Wind,* it was hard to tolerate all this chaos a second time for a Western meant to glorify her husband's mis-tress.

In the summer of 1945, she packed his bags.

1947 The year 1947 was a bad one for the careers of both David O. Selznick and Louis B. Mayer. David produced *The Paradine Case,* "his first complete failure since going independent," a really bad film that both Alfred Hitchcock and Gregory Peck would try to forget. [136] It was the last movie David ever produced in Hollywood. David tried frantically to keep Irene, plying her with diamonds, charm, and promises, but she would not revoke her decision. David eventually married Jennifer Jones. But David, Irene, and the boys religiously spent every Christmas together until his death in 1965.

As for Mayer, 1947 was also the beginning of his end. David Sarnoff had introduced America to something new: television. In 1947, sales of TVs rocketed and movie ticket sales dropped like rocks. The movies' monopoly on America's attention was over. All the studios experienced steep declines in revenue, but MGM's declined by a staggering 75 percent. And MGM films weren't winning Oscars anymore either. At sixty, Mayer wasn't in tune with his audience as he once had been. "His taste didn't continue to be the taste of America. He couldn't accept that America's taste was changing," said Daniel Selznick. When people tried to explain this to him, he wouldn't believe it. "What do you mean? My taste is America's taste. Their taste is my taste . . . Are you saying people don't love Lassie?"

Nicholas Schenck fired King Louis in 1950.

Mayer had thought he was building a dynasty. But it was the end of the House of Mayer. Mayer had once told Irene that she could have run a studio if she'd been a boy. He was too blind to see that the heir he needed so desperately had been there in front of him all along.

In 1947, Irene moved to New York, where she produced one of the most famous shows in the history of Broadway: *A Streetcar Named Desire,* written by Tennessee Williams, directed by Elia Kazan, and starring Marlon Brando. The play is still referred to in *The New York Times* as "Elia Kazan's *Streetcar Named Desire,*" but it was Irene who recruited Kazan. She went on to produce other classics, including *The Chalk Garden.*

Because she lived in the shadow of titanic male egos her whole life, no one had noticed, including her, that *she* had a gift too.

THE BABY

Daniel Mayer Selznick

Daniel Mayer Selznick lives in a brownstone in Greenwich Village. Meeting Selznick, it seemed as if an apparition of Louis B. Mayer had suddenly appeared before me. He was not displeased that I noticed the family resemblance. Danny was Mayer's favorite grandchild: "I don't think he ever said one harsh word to me." A glamorous black-and-white 1940s-style studio photo of Louis B. Mayer, smiling resolutely, hangs over Daniel Selznick's desk. On the adjacent wall is an Al Hirschfeld caricature of David O. Selznick, a tidal wave of hair spewing forth. You can still recognize the cherubic smile of sixty-seven-year-old Daniel Selznick from his baby pictures, but that smile expressed an ironic sadness as he described the decline of his grandfather and father in response to my questions about affective disorder in the family.

As long as Daniel had known him, his grandfather had been "extremely elated, supremely elated." After he was fired, Mayer was crushed. "He thought, 'They can't take this away from me. I'm a kind of god. I'm an emperor. I'm Louis B. Mayer.' "[137] From Daniel's description, it sounds as if Mayer was in a mixed state after he was fired—simultaneously hypomanic and depressed. "He'd get up in the morning, and there was no place to go. There was no staff, no one to give orders to. He had all that energy and drive and ideas for films, and now he couldn't get anyone on the phone." One morning Daniel heard the secretary making calls and getting the same response: "He'll have to call you back, Mr. Mayer. He'll have to call you back, Mr. Mayer." Daniel said, "You can't imagine the humiliation. He'd start grumbling, 'They have to call me back? When the hell are they calling me back!?' " He began yelling at the servants. "He was troubled, just troubled. And he was brooding: 'What have I done wrong? What have I done wrong? What have I done wrong?' He was like a building when the façade was there,

233

but behind it was crumbling. I was weeping inside for him." Mayer was humiliated by the idea that his depression might show. "He said to me a few times, 'Do I seem different?' I said, 'No, no, Grandpa, you seem fine.' He was very concerned that other people might notice it."

By the late 1950s, when Daniel was a Harvard undergraduate, he observed that his dad was "pretty depressed and anxious" and that whatever was wrong with him was interfering with his ability to earn a living. David came to Daniel desperate one night:

"No one wants to make a picture with me."

"Dad, that's ridiculous."

"No, no, I can't set up a deal anywhere."

"People wanted the skills but not if it came with the personality," Daniel told me. The "final insult" was when Fox optioned his script for *Tender Is the Night,* on the sole condition that David O. Selznick *not* produce it.

"I'm of no value to anyone," David told his younger son.

"That was pretty hard to hear," Daniel said to me, fighting back tears.

Daniel has tried to preserve the memories of his famous progenitors. He hired Rudy Behlmer to edit his father's memos and worked alongside him on the classic *Memo from David O. Selznick.* That project gave Daniel a real window into his father's disordered mind. "We really, really, really edited them down. I saw how long-winded and pompous and offensive they were, how insulting they were. I realized how many people he had antagonized and why he had antagonized them. His personality was out of control."

Irene had made sure all his memos went out on stationery printed with the warning "Dictated but not read by David O. Selznick." If the recipients knew these were unedited thoughts off the top of David's head, she hoped, it would minimize their relational damage. Even in retrospect, with the benefit of hindsight, it never occurred to David Selznick that his memos had been destructive to his professional relationships. Bipolar denial can be as impervious to the light of insight as a black hole, as Daniel learned one day when he confronted his father about the memos:

"Dad, why didn't you read those memos before they went out?"

"Danny, I never had time to read them."

"Don't you realize how damaging it was not to read things before they came out?"

"I would have had to spend hours rereading them."

"But didn't you stop to think what it meant not to reread them before they came out?"

"Why should I read them before they came out?"

After her work with Dr. Romm, Irene hoped that psychology would help her to protect her sons. A vast array of child psychology books filled her shelves, and "they were all heavily underlined." Irene introduced Daniel to the idea of his father's mental illness gradually. "She began saying things like 'Your dad is more emotionally unbalanced than you realize.' She only told me he was manic-depressive when I was old enough to know what the term meant, around twelve or fourteen." But even the levelheaded Irene suffered from "mood swings." She took psychiatric medication every day. When Daniel asked her what the pills were for, she snapped at him, "They keep me stable. That's all you need to know." At the end of her life, Irene became severely depressed; she said it was because neither Jeffrey nor Daniel had ever had children.

I asked Daniel how the family genes had manifested in his life. "A lot of psychiatry and three marriages have taught me to live the good in your genes and control the bad. When the right hand reaches out to do something destructive," he said, "I grab it with the left," which he did in a gesture reminiscent of the famous scene from *Dr. Strangelove*. The greatest challenge was to overcome the family grandiosity. When Daniel was ten, he wrote a play. His father copyrighted it, distributed it to his colleagues, and declared

Daniel a genius. Louis B. Mayer used to tour Daniel around MGM and whisper, "Someday this will all be yours." Daniel Mayer Selznick's show business career has not lived up to that star billing. He has been active for many years directing and producing theater, television, and movies, as well as publishing drama criticism in *The New York Times,* but his work is not widely known. Nonetheless, he seems at peace with his place in the Hollywood firmament. "For myself, I've decided I'd rather be a modest success in a nondestructive way than a big success, scorching the earth around me. I can't complain. I had a balcony seat to the greatest show on earth." It was clear to me that Daniel Selznick had done "the work," as psychotherapists like to call it, of analyzing himself.

After the interview, I stepped onto Bank Street on an unseasonably cold and windy November day. I was gripped by a feeling of sadness, realizing that I had probably just said good-bye to the last of the Mayer-Selznicks. With no descendant, their family saga had come to an end. A winter gust seemed to blow right through me, and I was struck by the thought: A hundred years ago, Lewis Selznick walked out of Russia, and now it's all gone with the wind.

But the industry the Mayers and Selznicks helped create is alive and well. American movies still account for 83 percent of world box-office revenue.[138] While we frantically search for ways to improve our sagging image abroad, there is still no better advertisement for America than its movies. John Winthrop predicted that America's light would shine to all the nations of the world. He never could have imagined that it would shine through the lens of a projector.

Nor could he have guessed that the good news about his new Israel would be carried by the sons of the old. The Jews who fled the tsar, as their ancestors had escaped Pharaoh, found sanctuary in Winthrop's new promised land and sang its praises to the world. Could Hollywood have written a better ending?

VI Craig Venter

Playing God

In the hundreds of newspaper and magazine articles about Craig Venter, he is most often described as a genetic pioneer and maverick. But there are many other colorful titles: gene master, gene tycoon, the selfish geneticist. *Time* magazine called him "the bad boy of science," and a senior colleague at the National Institutes of Health told *The New Yorker* that Venter was "an asshole" and an "egomaniac," a view shared by many of his colleagues.[1] Venter is often described as "playing God" for having helped unlock the code to create a human being. When asked "What's the role of God in all this?" Venter replied, "He's been a big help so far," as if to suggest that we'll take it from here.[2]

Nowhere among the millions of words written about Craig Venter does the word "hypomanic" appear. Yet in many interviews, when I described the traits of hypomania to people who knew Venter well, all agreed that it sounded like Craig. Venter himself told me: "My self-diagnosis: I probably have a very mild case of manic depression." He was certain that he had never been fully manic, but he "oscillated" between "very big energy, for long periods of time," and "low energy." When I recited for him the symptoms that constitute the diagnostic criteria for bipolar type II, a term he had not heard before, he said, "That characterizes some pretty big stretches of my life. . . . It's bumming me out to be so textbook."[3]

"We are now starting the century of biology," Venter has declared.[4] To understand how he helped usher in that century, it helps to have insight into *his* biology. Without his hypomanic temperament, Craig Venter wouldn't have pushed the fields to new heights or pushed his colleagues' buttons.

BORN TO CHANGE HISTORY

Craig Venter grew up in the 1950s, a blond-haired rebel with an irritating smirk. As a child, he felt compelled to challenge anyone or anything bigger and more powerful than himself. For example, "My friends and I, out of boredom, would pedal our bikes over to the airport. I got the idea one day to take the bikes out to the runway. I said, 'Why don't we race the airplanes?' I bet I could get a hundred yards before a plane passed me." By the time the plane sped past him and he heard the sirens of the airport police cars chasing him, he escaped into the reeds and thickets. "I never got caught, and I did that quite frequently. Then one day I came back, and there was a fence around the airport. I like to think I did my part to improve airport security." What Venter could not have known was that someday he would race an entity far larger than any plane and set off alarms louder than any police car.

In seventh grade, Craig began boycotting spelling tests. In high school, he organized a student action that shut the school down for two days to protest the firing of a teacher (one he knew was giving him a well-deserved F). Though his older brother excelled academically, Craig's grades were abysmal. He "didn't give a shit about going to college."[5] His parents were stymied. "My parents drove me up to the juvenile detention center as a warning. They talked about military school."

Yet despite this poor start, Venter told me that he always felt that he was "destined to do something great":

> I can only call it delusions of grandeur. Throughout my life I had this sense that I was going to accomplish something greater than normal—a feeling that was separate from self-esteem. It was always an unusual feeling. I knew I would be in a powerful historic position. I had no objective basis for that as a kid. None. I was a kid from a lower-middle-class home who was flunking out of

school. There was certainly no feedback telling me I would be great. It's a definite feeling that has sustained me throughout a lot of things and led to specific decisions and plans at various stages. . . . It wasn't an out-of-body experience, but it was a feeling that sounds like what I've heard described as religious experience. It was an unusual feeling, contradicting everything else in my life.

With the exception of a reference to God, this sounds much like a religious calling. "I'm descended from strongly evangelical Mormons on my father's side," Venter explained. Though his father was thrown out of the church—"for drinking, smoking, and getting an education"—Venter feels a connection with his Mormon roots.[6] "One of them got murdered somewhere in the South for his preaching." That's the occupational hazard of being a firebrand. "My ancestors date back to the 1600s in Virginia and Pennsylvania. One of my relatives was the first person kicked out of Virginia. They sent him down to prison in Barbados, but he came back again," Venter said with a grin.

Only once can anyone remember the young Craig laboring patiently toward a long-term goal. When he was fourteen, he saw a picture of a hydroplane boat in *Popular Science* and decided to build it with only a schematic set of plans to guide him. He got a paper route to pay for the materials and worked on it in the garage for months. "Get that shit out of my garage," his father said one day. "Like it was some religious ritual to park his car every night." It was then that Craig first showed his great talent for creative problem solving under pressure. He built a pulley system that allowed him to ingeniously raise the hydroplane parts above the car when his father came home and lower them again after he left—a mobile laboratory. When Craig finished his hydroplane, "his family watched from the shore, while Craig zipped around and around with his face drawn up in adolescent ecstasy, half blind from the spray off the bow."[7]

After high school graduation, his older brother went to Berkeley to study math and physics and Craig moved into his grandmother's garage near Newport Beach, where he lived the idyllic Beach Boys Southern California surfer lifestyle.

Staying Alive

Venter's endless summer came to an abrupt end when he was drafted in 1964. He had no educational deferment. No connections to get him safely into the National Guard. The game now was to survive. Craig's first move was to strike a deal with the navy to be on its swim team in San Diego. Then President Lyndon Johnson disbanded military sports teams, needing all hands on the battlefield for the war he was escalating. Craig found himself behind a chain-link fence in boot camp, destined for Vietnam. But he wasn't going quietly.

He hatched a plan with a friend to swim out of boot camp through a drainage pipe. An officer got wind and told Venter that he knew "what you assholes have been planning," and reminded him that desertion in a time of war was punishable by death. What saved Venter from immediately being shipped to Vietnam was that he scored off the charts on the navy's intelligence test, which meant he was given a choice of assignments. He chose to be a medical assistant at Balboa Navy Hospital in Southern California, where the staff was free to surf after three o'clock and restrictions on hair length were minimal.

Venter began a romantic relationship with one of the nurses, who was also his superior officer—a violation of military rules. When he got orders to transfer to the emergency room in Long Beach, effectively ending their relationship, she became vindictive and ordered him to cut his long blond hair. "Fuck off!" was Venter's reply—a typical example of impulsive behavior with potentially painful consequences (one of the diagnostic criteria for hypomania). Hypomanics get themselves in trouble by speaking impulsively, probably more often than through any other type of acting out. Venter was court-martialed and ordered to report to the brig for six weeks of hard labor, after which, according to standard military procedure, he would lose his preferential posting and almost certainly be sent to Vietnam. He would most likely serve as a battlefield medic at a time when the Viet Cong had a bounty on medics, virtually painting targets on their backs. The new orders were a potential death sentence.

The orders to report to the brig were fastened outside an envelope containing his original orders. There were no computer records in those days, and soldiers carried their paperwork from place to place. Venter had been court-martialed on his last day at Balboa. "I started thinking, all this happened at the last minute. I wondered if they had time to change the records on the inside of the envelope." He steamed open the envelope. Sure enough, the original orders were unchanged.

"I decided to take a gamble. If I was going to the brig, what's another month, or year?" Venter rode his motorcycle up to Long Beach, a major transit point into and out of Vietnam, and presented himself to an intimidating sergeant behind a desk. "I'm checking in," he said. "Where are your orders?" he asked. "I told him I was driving my motorcycle up there, had the orders in my backpack and they flew off my motorcycle onto the highway, got shredded, and blew away." Craig handed him a damaged manila envelope with his original orders. "He looked at it. Then he looked at me. Looked at the envelope again, and looked me in the eyes. He went away for a few minutes and came back." The sergeant said: "Son, you're in really deep shit." Venter began freaking out. " 'Oh my God, there was a copy of the new orders and they sent them ahead,' I thought. My heart was below my gonads. It was the worst feeling in my life. Here was my grand experiment, and I was probably going to end up with life imprisonment for refusing to get a haircut." The sergeant looked at him sternly: "Okay, here's what's going to happen. You're confined to barracks for two weeks of cleanup detail. I hope this teaches you a lesson." The ruse had

worked after all! He was being disciplined only for "losing" his orders. "Those were the cleanest fucking barracks ever. I was happy
to do it! And the sergeant was right about one thing. It taught me a
lesson: Take command of my own life."

Six months later, when he received orders to ship out to Vietnam, he once again escaped service as a battlefield medic, this time
by getting a doctor to write a letter to the surgeon general saying
that Venter's emergency room skills were needed in the military
hospital. He was assigned to the Da Nang Field Hospital, a unit
much like that portrayed in the movie *M*A*S*H*. There he was
briefly thrown in the brig for once again telling a superior officer
"Go fuck yourself!" [8]

The carnage Venter faced at Da Nang was overwhelming. Thousands of mangled and destroyed boys sometimes arrived in a single
day, especially during the Tet offensive, when the hospital itself was
also under attack. He was surrounded by pointless gore, suffering,
and death. "It was sheer hopelessness." Venter decided to kill himself. He swam a mile out to sea, so far he thought he would be too
exhausted to make it back. When he could no longer see the shore
and it was getting dark, suddenly a thought burst into his mind:
"What the fuck am I doing?" [9] The former competitive swimmer
turned around and made it back to the beach.

That experience changed his life. Venter describes this brush
with suicide in the opening scene of the autobiography he is
preparing, because that day he felt born again. "It was an energiz-
ing experience." He vowed that if he made it out of Vietnam alive,
he would do something great with his life, maybe even great
enough to change history.

The Cocky Professor

Venter entered college at the University of California at San Diego.
While earning a bachelor's degree in two years, he began work as a
research assistant in the lab of famed biochemist Nathan Kaplan.

Kaplan was endeavoring to prove that the receptor in the brain for the neurotransmitter adrenaline was located outside the nerve cell. A rival British team was claiming the opposite. Venter, a mere undergraduate, devised an ingenious experiment to settle the matter. He attached adrenaline to glass beads too big to enter the cell and found that they bonded to the receptor, proving his professor right. The neurotransmitter receptor was outside the cell. The work was published in *Proceedings of the National Academy of Science*. When he had entered college, Venter had been planning to become a doctor. But this changed his mind. He told his brother, Keith, "A doctor can save maybe a few hundred lives in a lifetime. A researcher can save the whole world." [10] His role in history was getting clearer.

Venter accumulated a dozen such prestigious publications while completing his Ph.D. in three years. "I was a local folk hero." Though some of the graduate students in his lab sent out hundreds of résumés and didn't even get an interview, Venter was offered two faculty positions without even applying. He accepted a position as an assistant professor of pharmacology at the State University of New York at Buffalo, bought a new baby blue Mercedes, and drove across the country to New York.

The move proved a disaster. "I should have known this was a mistake. Instead of being in sunny La Jolla, California, I was in Buffalo in the middle of winter. Buffalo is appropriately called 'the asshole of the country.' I saw *Chorus Line* the night before we left. One character said, 'Committing suicide in Buffalo is redundant.' He was right." Whereas Venter had been surfing, swimming, and getting "lots of fame and attention" at the University of California, Buffalo was cold and dark, and much of the attention he got was negative.

The morning he arrived, a high-ranking professor invited him to attend the Ph.D. oral defense of one of his prize students. "What did you think?" he asked Venter. "That was the most mediocre load of shit I've ever heard," he told his senior colleague. [11] With hindsight, Venter can now see that "I offended them extremely from day one. My first day there, I killed any chance of long-term survival there." It did not increase his popularity with his colleagues that he boasted about his successes, such as getting more grant money than they did. "I thought I was hot shit at the time," and he made no secret of it. "He would go to meetings with these distinguished professor types, and pretty much tell them they were stupid. That's not the way to make friends," recalled his second wife, Claire Fraser, then a graduate student with whom Venter was having an affair.[12] He was "painfully clueless as to why he was not being accepted by the others," wrote James Shreeve in *The Genome War*—a typical dilemma faced by the hypomanic.[13] "I'm the greatest" is the message they send out loud and clear, yet they are mystified that some people take offense.

Even Venter's appearance was offensive. His clothes were outlandish even by the standards of the 1970s: white polyester bell-bottoms with red roses, a neon green shirt decorated with Disney characters, and a bright yellow fringed suede vest were typical examples of his standard attire.

Craig actually believed that he was doing great at Buffalo and should be promoted early. After only four years, instead of the normal seven, "I requested early tenure—well, actually, I demanded early tenure." To no one's surprise, except Venter's, his senior colleagues elected not to give him a lifetime berth in their department.

At the same time as Venter's colleagues were rejecting him, his first marriage, to a woman he had wed in graduate school, was breaking up. "This was the first time I realized that I was truly depressed, in the midst and after I was getting divorced in Buffalo." It became the beginning of a lifetime pattern. "As I got older, things oscillated, especially when goals were not going well. Some years I would cycle in and out of clinical depression ten or twenty times." But Venter became expert at hiding his psychic pain. "I don't think there was anyone in my life who was ever aware of these depressive periods. My wife had no clue. Fellow workers had no clue. They might have thought I was in a bad mood, but I was able to function. I describe it as a numbness that takes over my head. I just feel numb. It's a terrible feeling. I'm a relatively high-energy person and the high energy always feels good."

Venter's description is more typical than many realize: clinical depression does *not* mean being unable to function, except in a small percentage of the most serious cases. Being able to hide psychic pain is not unique to Venter. When you are hypomanic, everyone knows it, because they must suffer your arrogant, erratic behavior. When you are depressed, quite often you suffer alone.

THE RACE

The Nobel Prize

In 1984, after Craig and Claire wed, they both won research positions at the prestigious National Institutes of Health (NIH), the large federal research organization in Rockville, Maryland, that controls most of America's biological research dollars. Craig knew that in this environment there was a chance he could do something really great. He would free-associate out loud with Claire, dreaming up one grand plan after another:

> He used her as a sounding board for his big future-sized ideas. A lot of them were less than brilliant, and some were downright stupid. Early in their marriage, she would tell him so. He would get angry. They would fight, and she'd end up in tears. She soon decided that when Craig asked her for an opinion on some brainstorm, she would tell him it was terrific. If it wasn't he'd figure that out later for himself.[14]

"Craig has a new grandiose idea every day," his longtime colleague Hamilton Smith told me. "Claire helps keep his energies focused."[15]

Though never boring, Craig was not the easiest person to be married to, according to Shreeve. He "made a mess of their finances," especially on a "speedy little catamaran they couldn't afford." Even later, when his income rose into the millions, he perpetually overspent them into insolvency. The boats, cars, and houses got bigger and more numerous.

When Venter first went to NIH, there was only one man he really wanted to impress: James Watson. Watson shared the Nobel Prize in 1962 with Francis Crick for their discovery of the shape of DNA—a double helix that resembles a twisted ladder. Each rung of that ladder, they found, was composed of a pair of *nucleotides,* of which there were four: adenine, guanine, thiamine, and cytosine, abbreviated A, G, T, and C. The pairing rule they discovered was that A always combines with T and C always with G, leaving four possibilities: A-T, T-A, C-G, or G-C. All our genetic information is written in this four-letter alphabet. Many rank Watson in the same circle as Charles Darwin, and Watson would be the first to agree. He takes pains to point out that "There are Nobels, and there are *Nobels.*"[16] When one colleague at a meeting mentioned that he had won a Nobel, Watson corrected him: "I did not win *a* Nobel Prize, I won *the* Nobel Prize."

Watson was the impresario of genetics at NIH, where he was orchestrating another breakthrough. In 1977, the English biologist Frederick Sanger developed a technique for decoding DNA, winning the 1980 Nobel. In 1987, Watson convinced Congress to take on a massive project to sequence the entire human genome and commit $3 billion over a fifteen-year period. In 1990, the Human Genome Project (HGP) was formed by the NIH under Watson's direction.

Venter was also interested in genetic sequencing. A perpetually impatient person, he kept thinking about how to do it faster. It had taken Venter a year to sequence one gene for his own research— after it had taken him ten years to find it. To sequence the DNA of the human genome by hand, as Sanger had done, would take

100,000 years. When Venter heard that there was a prototype of a machine that could sequence DNA, he leaped at the chance to buy it in February 1987. Watson was delighted to discover Craig Venter, whose lab became the official NIH test site for the new machine. The machines had problems, but Venter got them to run and became the first person to sequence an entire gene with a machine. "The Human Genome Project is going to succeed because I've got this guy who can get automated sequencers to work," Watson exuberantly told fellow HGP scientist Gerald Rubin.[17] But that didn't mean he thought of Venter as a peer or protégé, as Venter had secretly hoped. To the imperious Watson, Venter was just a technician.

By 1990, Venter had four machines running and strutted around "like a teenager showing off the latest loudest stereo equipment."[18] He applied to NIH for a large intramural grant to sequence the *entire* X chromosome. The review committee thought the project preposterously grandiose and turned it down. The collective efforts of the entire scientific community had mapped only one thousandth of a chromosome to that point (there are twenty-three chromosomes in the human genome). Who did this guy think he was?

It is unfortunate that Watson could not see Venter's talent. He should have been tipped off when Venter made a huge scientific leap. Only 3 percent of human DNA is made up of genes. The rest, called "junk DNA," has a function we don't understand, if it has any function at all. Venter's idea was to pan for the 3 percent guaranteed gold: the genes. Rather than sequencing the genome line by line, as the HGP was doing, Venter developed a way to separate the genes from the junk to sequence them first. Genes contain the DNA blueprints for the manufacture of the body's proteins. But DNA itself does no work. Messenger RNA copies the code and transports it to the ribosome, the cell's protein factory. Venter extracted this RNA and used it as a template to make a DNA copy. He knew these pieces of genetic code were genes because junk DNA isn't copied by RNA.

Next he found another shortcut, a way to identify individual genes—to "tag" them without fully decoding them. Each gene has a unique beginning and end, about 150 to 400 base pairs long. Venter called these Expressed Sequence Tags (ESTs), because he was just tagging the genes, locating them for future decoding. Like a librarian, he was organizing a bookshelf so each reader could find the book he wanted. Venter published his EST data in *Science* in June 1991.

To this day, Venter cannot understand why Watson turned against him. "The easiest thing for Watson to have done would have been to say, 'This is a good advance or a great advance. Let's incorporate it and move on.' Instead, he actively tried to destroy my career. To me that's a bizarre action." I spoke to Nicholas Wade, a science writer for *The New York Times,* who followed the Venter story for years in a series of articles and later wrote a book about the genome, *Life Script.* He agreed that Watson would have been well advised to ally with Venter: "Watson was stronger with Venter under his tent than outside it." [19] Yet Watson's animosity does not seem all that mysterious. Venter was publicly vaunting his new EST technique as far more efficient than the method Watson's HGP team was using. He wrote in *Science* that his approach "was a bargain by comparison to the human genome project. . . . We can do it for a few million dollars a year instead of hundreds of millions." [20] Typical of Venter, he had no clue that this might insult or threaten Watson, who later admitted that he had feared Venter's EST shortcut because it could produce a skeleton outline of the genome, and then "nobody will pay for us to do the genome." [21] The publicly funded HGP would often face this kind of perverse logic when presented with opportunities to speed up. If it looked as if it had accomplished its task, it would lose its funding.

A second reason that Watson went from patron to antagonist was that Venter got caught in a power struggle between Watson and NIH chief Bernadine Healy. Healy was patenting Venter's ESTs, and Watson was strongly opposed to the patenting of genes. Though he derisively called them "the Venter patents," the impetus was coming from Healy, not Venter, who was quite ambivalent

CRAIG VENTER

about the government patenting his work. In a Senate hearing in July 1991, Watson attacked them both. He said that Healy's idea of patenting Venter's ESTs was "sheer lunacy," because there was no intellectual property to patent. Venter's automated sequencing work "wasn't even science." His work was "brainless," and his machines "could be run by monkeys." [22] Venter, shocked by the attack, turned visibly pale. "Watson was the ideal father figure of genomics and he was attacking me in the Senate." [23] Venter now regards Watson as "the most Machiavellian person I have ever met in my life. Apparently Watson planned this. He had practiced these lines weeks ahead of time. I can't relate to someone who goes through life like that. My spontaneous outbursts are really spontaneous, which is probably why they always get me in trouble."

In response to his Senate sneak attack, Healy fired Watson as director of HGP—though he would continue as adviser to and spiritual leader of the effort. She replaced him with Francis Collins, a born-again Christian with a deceptively bland demeanor, who rode a motorcycle and played guitar in a rock band. Collins had discovered the genes for cystic fibrosis, Huntington's chorea, and other diseases. In every case, he had successfully raced a competing team of investigators to the wire, and he made a notch on his motorcycle helmet for every gene he found. "If you drew a circle around what God knows, it would be unimaginably huge. What I know is a teeny, teeny dot within that circle," he said humbly. "But every once in a while we humans get to sneak out of the little dot and find something that wasn't known before. That's the way it was with the cystic fibrosis gene. I felt I was getting a tiny glimpse into God's mind." [24] Collins might have appeared self-effacing, but he was a fierce competitor who always managed to slip past his mortal rivals. He would soon find Venter his most formidable rival of all.

Ironically, HGP researchers would later adopt Venter's EST method as standard procedure. HGP scientist John Sulston admitted that the EST technique proved "to be extremely useful in assisting the mapping effort." [25] Even Watson would grudgingly

251

admit that it "should have been encouraged."[26] HGP researchers would later look back on this row as a crucial Watson mistake, one that sent Venter over to the dark side of the private sector.

In 1992, Venter received a $10 million NIH grant to sequence DNA; however, it stipulated that he could *not* use any of the funds on his newly discovered EST method. Venter returned the $10 million and quit NIH. Ever since Venter had published his paper on the EST technique in *Science,* entrepreneurs had been ringing his phone off the hook. He had resisted their offers because he saw himself as a scientist and not an entrepreneur. But in 1992, Venter met a health care venture capitalist named Wallace Steinberg, a poor kid from the Bronx who had worked his way up without a college degree. Steinberg made Venter an intriguing offer: he would give Venter $70 million to form a private *nonprofit* research institute, The Institute for Genomic Research (TIGR). As a nonprofit, it was eligible for government grants, and Venter could still feel like an academic scientist, not a corporate man. But TIGR was set up to work in partnership with a for-profit biotech company, Human Genome Sciences (HGS), simultaneously established by Steinberg. The deal was that HGS had exclusive first dibs on anything Venter found and that Venter got 10 percent ownership in HGS, so he could profit from his own discoveries. This arrangement seemed to offer the best of both worlds.

Catching the Flu

At the end of 1994, Venter met Hamilton Smith, a retiring Johns Hopkins biologist and Nobel Prize winner. Smith told me that before he met Venter, he had assumed, like everybody else, that Venter was "an asshole." "He had been demonized by the scientific community." But when he met Venter in person at a scientific meeting, he was impressed by his data, as well as by his personal energy and verve. "Where are your horns?" Smith asked him as a joke. That evening, when Venter saw Smith drinking alone at the bar, he invited him to join his dinner party. Smith found this rare social experience enlivening and merry. Venter would reenergize not just his evening but his career, which at that point was winding down. Venter invited Smith to join TIGR's advisory board the night he met him—typical impulsive Craig—and it was an inspired choice. Smith's work had revolutionized microbiology. He had discovered the first "restriction enzyme," a naturally occurring substance that cuts DNA into pieces, which is now used in the laboratory as a kind of microscopic scissors to isolate specific pieces of DNA. Smith had a Nobel but thought he didn't deserve it, while Venter thought he deserved a Nobel but didn't have one. They were truly an odd couple.

Though TIGR was busy mapping human genes, Smith had a modest proposal. At a board meeting he wondered if they would consider trying to map the genome of an *entire organism*. Smith suggested *Haemophilus influenzae,* which, despite its name, is not the flu virus, but a bacterium. They would be the first team to map the genome of a free-living organism (a virus had been mapped, but a virus needs a host in which to reproduce). Smith could provide the bench work expertise. He had worked with *H. flu.* DNA for years. Smith also suggested that they use a controversial new genome-sequencing technique: the "shotgun." Using this method, DNA is broken into millions of random 500-base-pair bits (a machine can sequence only 500 base pairs at a time). The random fragments are sequenced, and a computer puts the jigsaw puzzle back together. In stark contrast, HGP was methodically mapping DNA one line at a time. There was a long pause; then Venter said, "Let's do it."[27]

Venter did not personally conceive of many of his best ideas. "A genius," said Smith, "is someone who knows a good idea when he hears one."[28] In fact, a genius is someone who *acts* on a good idea when he hears one. What psychiatrists call "impulsivity," entrepreneurs call "seizing the moment." Venter has made some of his best, and some of his worst, decisions at this hurried pace. James Shreeve, author of *The Genome War,* who shadowed Venter during the race to map the human genome, told me he was amazed by Venter's rapid-fire decision making: "He would make decisions quickly, and they were often wrong, but that didn't seem to matter. If it turned out they were wrong, he would retroactively remake the decision in his own brain and set off on a different course."[29] Hypomanics think fast. They talk fast. They move fast. And they make decisions fast. When I asked Venter about his style of decision making, he wanted to clarify that it wasn't as impulsive as it might appear. In the case of *H. flu.*, for example, he had previously considered mapping the genome of an entire organism using the shotgun and been told it wasn't feasible. So the idea was not new to him. But taking on the *H. flu.*–shotgun project was a gut decision made in a moment: "When Ham suggested we do *H. flu.*, it was an instant acceptance on my part. It was clear to me that this was the opportunity I'd been looking for. It was the right solution with the right people. There was no hesitation whatsoever. I can be spontaneous and opportunistic."

Venter applied to the NIH for a grant to map the *H. flu.* genome using the shotgun. The NIH reviewers called the project "overly ambitious" and "ridiculous" and rejected his grant proposal.[30] "There were two reasons why those grants were rejected," said one of his assistants. "First, we were way ahead of everybody else, and nobody realized it. And second, Craig was an asshole and everybody realized it."[31] Venter went full speed ahead without any NIH funds, and in 1995 he succeeded. Ironically, *after* Venter had successfully sequenced the *Haemophilus influenzae* genome using the shotgun technique, he received a letter from the NIH appeals committee upholding the denial of his grant application on the grounds that "the experiment wasn't feasible."[32] Craig tacked that pink rejection letter on the wall above his desk as if it were a trophy.

Venter's paper describing the *H. flu.* experiment became the most frequently cited paper in the scientific literature. This breakthrough "revolutionized microbiology," according to Nicholas Wade. Genetic researcher Fred Blattner said it was "an incredible moment in history." Geneticist Martin Blaser said that TIGR had found "the Holy Grail." [33] When Venter presented his data in May 1995 to hundreds of microbiologists at a meeting in Washington, D.C., he received a standing ovation.

I'll Do It, Guys

Michael Hunkapiller was virtually unknown outside the biotech community, but "he was a legend within it." [34] When he was a graduate student in the 1980s, he invented the first machine that could automatically sequence DNA. Venter's original gene-sequencing machine had been one of Hunkapiller's prototypes. ABI, the company Hunkapiller and his professor cofounded, had the monopoly on gene sequencers for a decade. But in the late 1990s, competition from another company forced Hunkapiller to invent a faster machine. In the meantime, ABI had been bought by PerkinElmer, a scientific instruments company. One day in 1997, Hunkapiller was sitting in an executive meeting with Tony White, CEO of Perkin-Elmer. Someone at the meeting casually wondered aloud if its new machine could sequence the human genome faster than the timetable promised by the HGP. Hunkapiller grabbed a yellow pad and began scratching out numbers. His calculations showed it could be done. There was a pause in the room; then White said, "Let's get it over with. Let's just do it." The whole conversation took ten minutes, and they hadn't even discussed how they would make money sequencing the genome—just one more example of the rapid decision making of the American entrepreneur.

They called Venter to ask if he wanted to head the project. Venter said they were "crazy," and then said yes. Once again, Venter had the genius to act swiftly on a good idea when he heard it. The name of the new company would be Celera, the Latin word for "speed." And their motto would be "Speed counts. Discovery can't wait." Hamilton Smith laughed. "That's the perfect name for a company run by Craig Venter."

On May 10, 1998, Nicholas Wade wrote a front-page story in the Sunday *New York Times* in which Venter bragged that his company would single-handedly beat the HGP consortium by sequencing the entire human genome by 2001—four years ahead of the public target date, at one tenth the cost. The Human Genome Project should just forget about the human genome, said Venter. "They should do the mouse."

Any congressman reading the Sunday *Times* would have had to ask: Why are *we* funding this thing when a private company can do it faster, better, and cheaper without costing the taxpayers a dime? Even more alarming to HGP scientists who read their *New York Times* that Sunday was the fact that Francis Collins and the NIH had accepted Venter's terms: give up the human and take the mouse. "When Venter set up Celera and said 'I'll do it, guys,' for a few days they agreed," Wade told me. At the time, Wade wrote in the *Times,* "Both Dr. [Harold] Varmus [head of the NIH] and Dr. Collins expressed confidence that they could persuade Congress to accept the need for this change in focus, noting that sequencing the mouse and other genomes had always been included as a necessary part of the human genome project." [35]

A few days later, both Collins and Varmus denied having made such statements. Yet, it seems unlikely that Wade could have misquoted *two* people who had told him the exact same thing. Something else had changed, Wade told me: "It was just a tactical shift on their part." After a brief surrender, they decided to fight.

This Should Not Be Munich

Two days later, at the annual meeting of the genome project at Watson's Cold Spring Harbor Laboratory, the HGP scientists confronted Collins. They were shocked by what they had read in the *Times.* He was giving up? To make matters worse, Venter arrived uninvited at the meeting to tell them personally that they should leave the human genome to him. It was like telling the entire consortium of scientists to "walk into the sea and drown," Watson recalled, and "it would be an understatement to say it was done in an insulting fashion." [36] Collins recalled that Craig was "his usual supremely confident self, bombastic, dismissive of the efforts of everyone else." [37] One scientist recalled that Craig came up to him and said, " 'Ha, ha, I'm going to do the human genome. You should do the mouse.' I said to him, 'You bastard. You bastard.' And I almost slugged him." [38] Another scientist said he wanted to strangle him. "At each stage, it was as provocative and confrontational as Craig could make it," Wade told me.

Venter had one calm conversation. He privately pulled aside Gerald Rubin. Rubin was sequencing the genome of the fruit fly for HGP, and he was about 20 percent done. Venter said he wanted to test his new technology on the fruit fly and wanted to know if Rubin would collaborate. Venter said he expected Rubin to hit him. Instead, Rubin said "Sure." He had agreed to sequence the fruit fly in the first place only because he needed the genome to do his real research. He wasn't possessive about it.

Rubin may have been the only one who didn't feel threatened by Venter. His challenge was outrageous, insulting, and—what was worse—credible. As Venter put it, "I scared the shit out of them." Watson said, "I worried that there would be the perception that we couldn't win." [39] The worry was justified, according to Sir John Sulston, a Nobel Prize winner who headed the Sanger Center, the largest gene-sequencing facility in the world, which served as the British wing of the HGP coalition. In his memoir, *The Common Thread: A Story of Science, Politics, Ethics, and the Human Genome,* Sulston wrote:

On the face of it Craig's proposal looked pretty strong. He was a scientist with a proven track record in running high-throughput sequencing labs. His commercial partner was the head of the company that made the sequencing machines, ABI. The joint venture was funded to a degree that was beyond the wildest

257

dreams of any of the individual genome project labs. . . . There was absolutely no doubt that armed with these resources, Craig was capable of equaling or even exceeding the existing world output of raw genome sequence.[40]

A mood of "shock, anger and despair" fell over the scientists.[41] "Darth Venter," as they called him, looked as if he were riding his genomic sequencing machines down upon them, poised to destroy the civilized genomic world.

Watson paced the lobby frantically, saying "He's Hitler. He's Hitler. This should not be Munich." After that day, Watson got into a habit of calling Venter "Hitler." He confronted Francis Collins, asking him in front of the other senior scientists: "Are you going to be Churchill or Chamberlain?" When Watson heard that Rubin had made a deal with Venter, he confronted him, too: "So, I understand the fruit fly is going to be Poland."[42]

If there was a Churchillian figure rallying a dispirited HGP, it was Sir John Sulston. With his bushy gray hair and beard, the Birkenstocks-wearing Sulston looked an unlikely wartime leader, but the "old British lefty" and former hippie took a stand for civilization. "I don't want my genetic information under the control of one entity or corporation. We had to fight," wrote Sulston.[43]

Sulston met with governors of the Wellcome Trust, Sanger's sponsor and the world's largest private medical charity. After that meeting he flew to America. When he arrived at Cold Spring Harbor, everyone was "very down." The next morning, Sulston brightened their mood considerably when he announced that the Wellcome Trust was doubling Sanger's funding immediately, and Sanger was committing itself to mapping one third of the genome, double its previous one sixth. They would not give up! "The crowd in the packed hall rose to its feet in acclamation." It was "electric." Sulston vowed that "whatever happened," the genome would now be decoded in the lifetime of "a certain individual," meaning the grand old man standing in the back, Jim Watson. "The crowd erupted again, stamping their feet in approval."[44] It wasn't a matter of "racing for glory," Sulston wrote.[45] Celera was threatening to "establish a complete monopoly position on the human genome. Without us the human genome would be privatized."[46] They would fight Venter in the laboratories, in the halls of Congress, and in journals. And they would win, because they must. Francis Collins called the speech "a shot in the arm."[47] Watson said, "It was absolutely critical, psychologically."[48] One senior scientist said, "NIH could stand up a little straighter."[49] An approving editorial in *Nature* said, "The talk was of healthy competition rather than throwing in the towel."[50]

One of the mantras of the HGP program used to be "People will forgive you for being slow but they won't forgive you for being sloppy."[51] That work ethic had yielded the following: after eight years, HGP had mapped only 3 percent of the human genome. All that changed when Celera jumped into the race. The scientists had to readjust their biological clocks to the hypomanic tempo of Venter time. It would be survival of the fastest.

The G-5

The heads of the five largest gene-sequencing labs met with Collins at Baylor University. They called themselves the G-5 as a joke, but the name stuck. "The nickname had muscle and a whiff of militancy about it. It stuck, because it summed up how they felt about themselves. They considered themselves in a war, and they were meeting to decide how to deploy their forces."[52] The HGP had been an unwieldy battleship—"stunningly inefficient," admitted one of the principal HGP scientists.[53] "A Manhattan Project for sequencing it wasn't."[54] HGP's budget was spread over more than a dozen universities and medical schools, as well as half a dozen small labs around the world. It was not accidental that the money was dispersed to so many institutions of higher learning. When Watson first proposed the Human Genome Project in 1987, many prominent researchers had voiced strong objections. They could see this behemoth sucking money out of their grants. Spreading the HGP spoils around was a politically expedient way to overcome opposition, but it wasn't efficient.

Eric Lander, director of the Whitehead Institute/MIT Center for Genome Research (WICGR), was the chief architect of the aggressive war strategy. Lander argued that they should "speed up production of the sequence to beat Craig at his own game."[55] All resources must be diverted to the strongest, most modern large-scale sequencing centers (which happened to be the labs headed by the G-5), to reap the benefits of scale. And those centers had to be vastly upgraded. They needed *money*, a lot more money. Everybody would have to ante up. In 1998, Collins had spent only $60 million of the HGP budget on sequencing. He now committed $200 million to the three largest centers, Whitehead, St. Louis, and Baylor. The Department of Energy, which had its own genome-sequencing lab, added $85 million over two years. Wellcome Trust had already agreed to double funding for Sanger to $77 million.

Collins cautioned, "The private and public genome sequencing efforts should not be seen as engaged in a race."[56] Collins vigorously told reporters, "If anything, we're racing against ourselves." HGP also launched a public relations counteroffensive. On March 16, 1999, Wade reported in *The New York Times* that the consortium was moving its completion date to the end of 2000. "If met, the new date set by the consortium . . . could allow the public venture to claim some measure of victory over its commercial rival, Celera."[57] Wade later wrote in *Life Script,* "For someone not engaged in a race, Collins was not without guile in seizing the lead."[58]

If the HGP scientists were reluctant to admit that they were in a competition, Venter was at the opposite extreme. *Everything* was a competition to him. "They're trying to say it's not a race, right?" Venter scoffed. "If two sailboats are sailing near each other, then by definition it's a race. If one boat wins, then the winner says, 'We smoked them,' and the loser says, "We weren't racing—we were cruising.' "[59] Venter enjoyed racing sailboats, and the flag of his million-dollar yacht, the *Sorcerer,* seemed to illustrate his persona: "It bore the image of a sorcerer wearing a tall pointed hat, a full white beard, and a Cheshire cat smile."

Venter sounded confident, but privately the HGP's announcement that it would be done in 2000 worried him. And the public relations counteroffensive was personally hurtful to him. In Congress, Robert Waterston, head of the St. Louis HGP gene sequencing center, said that Venter's shotgun would produce a genome that looked "like an encyclopedia ripped to shreds and scattered on the floor." Collins told the congressmen it would be the *Reader's Digest,* CliffsNotes, or *Mad* magazine version of the human genome. Venter's approach would be "woefully inadequate," Sulston and Waterston wrote in *Science.*[60]

At the next annual gathering of the HGP in Cold Spring Harbor in 1999, "the mood was very different than the desolate affair the previous year. The decision to outrun Celera had galvanized the academics into a cheerful, righteous militancy."[61] They weren't scared of Venter anymore. "Craig should not be portrayed as a maverick," jeered one HGP scientist from Oklahoma. "He should be portrayed as an opportunistic maniac and a leech."[62] Jim Watson sat onstage, smiling. Collins stood at the podium and seemed almost to lead the packed meeting in prayer. "I hope this doesn't sound corny or grandiose, but I feel this is a historic moment. This is the most important scientific effort that humankind has ever mounted. This is far bigger than going to the moon. It will change biology for all time."[63]

By challenging this sleepy scientific bureaucracy, Venter had transformed it into an avenging army. This must be counted as among his most impressive achievements. To some, it was a mystery how Venter generated such explosive animus. None was more mystified than Venter himself. "I think I scare people through ideas and what they regard as unpredictable behavior. Why that should make a small group of people hate me, I don't understand it. I'm oblivious to it." Hypomanics usually are oblivious. When you threaten to invade another group's territory, strong reactions should not be unexpected. We know that charismatic leaders excite their followers, but to an equal degree they enrage their rivals. "You either love [Venter] or you hate him," Smith told me. Charismatic leaders polarize the human field around them into those who are for them or against them. Their followers idealize them, and their rivals demonize them. If the HGP hadn't transformed itself into a militant organization poised to oppose Celera, it would have become extinct. There is no more basic instinct than the fight to survive.

The Most Exciting Project on Planet Earth

Venter is a case study in the dynamics of charismatic leadership. He gathered around him an extraordinary team of top-rank scientists who left their secure tenured positions to follow him because they caught his enthusiasm for his grand vision. "Initially everyone was buoyant. It was like we were launching some spacecraft to the moon," said Shreeve. "We all want to believe in something bigger than ourselves," Venter told me, and Celera tapped into that idealism. "I'm able to articulate a vision. I try to inspire people to be driven by what is possible and do it." As one Celera employee told me, "He was a charismatic leader. We wanted to please him. We felt like we were part of something big." One scientist who left a lucrative corporate job to join Celera put it this way: "I thought about how I could keep on helping Ericsson make better phones, or I could come here and cure cancer. Which would you choose? This is the most exciting project on Planet Earth."[64]

Venter thinks charismatic leadership might be in his blood. "When I look at my genetic past, my father's parents were Mormons, not just Mormons but the strongest evangelical leaders. They were very fervent." If he had been less educated, he said, he might have put his energies into religion. "In Germany they wanted to know if I was going to start a religion around what I had accomplished. I thought they were kidding, but they were deadlv serious." His longtime personal assistant, Heather Kowalski, told me, "I've always thought that it would be easy for Craig to start a cult." She is reminded of it every time he gives a public lecture, which always includes what she calls "the moment": "There is a hush, the eyes go wide, and that sort of feeling comes over the crowd. It's a pretty universal thing that happens every lecture. Afterward they jump up to shake his hand and get his autograph."[65] As Shreeve described it to me, "Craig has radiant energy. He comes into a room, and it seems like the room has been empty until he got there. He's very uplifting to be with."

Just as the HGP feared, Venter was aiming to build the biggest gene-sequencing facility in the world—triple the size of any other. Celera took over twin five-story mirrored buildings in the heart of the "Biotechnology Corridor" along Route 270 in Rockville, Maryland. "They had nothing. Less than nothing. Their facility was an old, ripped-up defense contractor's office," said Wade. From a dead stop, it was trying to overtake a public program that had been up and rolling for years. Worse yet, Mike Hunkapillar's new gene-sequencing machines were really untested prototypes that had been rushed into production. They had bugs, lots of them, and no one could figure out what was going wrong. Months after they had thought they would be sequencing genes, they were working round the clock trying to fix the damn machines. People at Celera began to think they might fail. "Things got pretty grim there," Shreeve told me. "People began to get down, close their doors, and snap at each other."

But Venter's optimism buoyed up the entire organization. "Time and again I saw him hold a meeting with a bunch of surly folks that ended with an up note," said Shreeve. "Obstinate optimism" is what Kowalski called it. "The more people were down, the more he was saying: 'No, it's okay, we're doing fine.' " For example, Venter had declared that they would begin sequencing the fruit fly in January. When they didn't begin until June, Craig told everyone,

"God, this is great." In his mind they were on schedule and every-thing was going exactly as planned. "He would say it in such a way that he didn't seem to be lying so much as glossing over the un-pleasant truth and rearranging the pattern in his brain so it fit a more optimistic scenario," said Shreeve.

Venter is hard-pressed to explain his confidence: "What we had was an extraordinary group of people with almost insurmountable odds against them. When I look back, there are a thousand reasons why we should have failed." In fact, the worse things got, the more ebullient he became. Paradoxically, the only times Kowalski re-called seeing Venter depressed were during comparatively peaceful periods. "I've often been surprised at the times he's been depressed. They were lulls, when we weren't rallying against something. . . . He likes the challenge of a difficult situation. There is something about those sorts of moments that he derives energy from." This is not an uncommon pattern among hypomanics. Nicholas Wade thought that Venter needed his enemies "to get his juices going." Venter has noticed that "when everything is falling apart is sometimes when I have my greatest clarity. In Vietnam, I ran an ER. When everyone else was panicking, I functioned extremely well."

Craig's "manic pace" was a powerful factor in Celera's progress, according to Hamilton Smith, who told me, "Working with Craig is like being on a high-speed treadmill. He sets completely unrealistic deadlines, announces them to the press, and forces us to scurry like hell. Not everyone can take the pressure." One scientist in his six-ties told me that he had declined anything more than a part-time position with Venter because after one month working with him he needed six weeks' vacation to recuperate. "I guess you could say he is an adrenaline junkie," said Kowalski. People at Celera worked for Venter as they had never worked before. "Really smart, extra-ordinary people can work far beyond the level they are used to working at," said Venter. And indeed they did.

People who work with Craig have to cope with his rapid-fire brain and its flight of ideas, which stretches multitasking to the limit. "He likes to throw thirty or forty balls in the air and see which ones stick, which ideas work, which ones he can make happen. That's what it's like working for Craig," said Kowalski. "He jumps back and forth between a thousand things, from idea to idea. . . . He likes eighteen things happening at once. Otherwise he's bored." Like most hypomanics, Venter would be lost without a Kowalski in his life. A central part of her job is to make order of his chaos and explain it to everyone else. "I can put it all together, but I have to do it for other people. It confounds a lot of them."

What Makes a Charismatic Leader?

We should not be surprised that Venter is both hypomanic and a charismatic leader. If we look at the traits that empirical research has found to be characteristic of charismatic leaders, it looks like a list of hypomanic traits. University of Pennsylvania Wharton Business School professors Robert House and James Howell reviewed the empirical literature on charismatic leaders, searching for characteristics found *consistently* in multiple studies.[66] Jay Conger, professor of management at McGill University, has conducted the single most extensive empirical study of charismatic business leaders.[67] Independently, these two groups of investigators have come to similar conclusions.

The first factor mentioned by House and Howell was "high levels of energy." Charismatics work tirelessly with "enthusiasm." Conger, too, found them to be "full of energy." Charismatic leaders show superior "self-confidence," according to House and Howell, which could border on "grandiosity," according to Conger. House and Howell found them to be "creative" and "innovative." Conger wrote that they have a talent for synthesizing "multiple often unrelated sources of information." Conger also noted that charismatic business leaders are quick, restless, impatient, and impulsive—all traits of hypomania.

House and Howell wrote that charismatic leaders are "vision-ary" and "inspirational." Conger found the same and examined how these leaders evangelize for their vision. They communicate the feeling that their mission is urgent, momentous, and achievable. Often it takes on mythic proportions and is described in the language of an epic struggle. As an example, he offers Steve Jobs, who evoked the David-and-Goliath metaphor in Apple's competition against "Big Brother" IBM. Conger's data showed that employees of charismatic leaders work longer hours and regard their bosses more highly.

I asked Conger what he thought about the astounding overlap between his empirically derived description of charismatic leaders and the symptoms of hypomania. He admitted honestly that the idea had never occurred to him and that he was unaware of any literature on it.[68] Instead, Conger has diagnosed these charismatic business leaders as having another psychiatric condition: *narcissistic personality disorder*.[69] It's true that charismatic leaders are narcissistic. *All* hypomanics are narcissistic. But diagnosing these leaders as narcissistic personalities does nothing to explain the other important traits Conger has identified: increased energy, creativity, restlessness, impulsivity, and risk taking. Hypomania explains them *all*.

The link between hypomania and charismatic leadership has not escaped some in the psychiatric field. Kay Jamison has written about hypomanic leaders in the fields of religion, politics, and the military, citing such examples as Alexander the Great, Martin Luther, Oliver Cromwell, Napoleon, Lord Nelson, Alexander Hamilton, Theodore Roosevelt, Winston Churchill, and Mussolini.[70] Ronald Fieve argued in *Moodswing* that hypomanic temperament is virtually required of political leaders:

> Hypomanic politicians are the tireless campaigners, the charismatic leaders, the indefatigable organizers. . . . In fact, anyone who has the drive and stamina to survive in American electoral politics has to be a little manic.[71]

Fieve devoted sections of his book to Abraham Lincoln, John Brown, Theodore Roosevelt, George Patton, Ralph Nader, Newt Gingrich, and Bill Clinton as examples of hypomanic American leaders.*

The importance of this point is hard to overstate. Virtually every new movement in human history—religious, political, intellectual, and economic—has been led by a charismatic leader. Hypomania is the common thread that connects these world changers, a thread as invisible, as powerful, and stretching back as far in time as a strand of DNA.

The Henry Ford of Gene Sequencing

When it was completed, Celera looked like "the command deck of a starship."[72] Some observers compared it to NASA. Its sequencing facility was by far the biggest in the world. In one building, Venter had the most powerful civilian computer in the world. In the other, there were rows and rows of gene-sequencing machines. Each machine was the size of a portable refrigerator and cost $300,000. DNA was treated with fluorescent dye, forced through hair-fine tubes, and read with lasers. "We operate twenty-four hours a day, seven days a week," said Venter. His monthly electricity bills came to $100,000. Venter was mapping as much each *day* as the entire consortium had collectively done in the previous two years. "This is the most futuristic manufacturing plant on the planet. You're seeing Henry Ford's first assembly plant," boasted Venter.[73]

---

* During the impeachment proceedings I was amazed that I could not find a single writer who linked Clinton's sexual indiscretions to hypomania. It was most often attributed to a defect in character, a "sexual addiction," or the trauma of growing up with an alcoholic stepfather. Clinton was extraordinarily charismatic, gregarious, creative, indefatigable (often needing little sleep), and evidenced other impulse control problems, such as overeating. Once again, hypomania explains not just one trait, but a whole constellation. Sexual indiscretions are very common among charismatic leaders precisely because they are virtually all hypomanic.

In March 2000, Venter announced that he had completed the sequencing of the fruit fly genome, by far the most complex organism to ever be mapped. It was also one of the most useful. Like the lab mouse, the fruit fly is an organism used frequently in laboratory science, especially by geneticists, because they breed once a week and don't take up much lab space. Venter made his announcement in his typical showmanlike fashion. At a meeting of a scientific society devoted to fly research, thirteen hundred scientists found a CD-ROM placed on their seats—the complete fruit fly genome. The president of the association proclaimed that they were being "handed an incredible tool that many of us have only dreamed about for many years."[74] Venter received a standing ovation. *Science,* where he published his findings with coauthor Gerald Rubin, called it "a monumental technical achievement."[75]

The fruit fly was "the first test of Venter's method. Everyone expected it to fail, and it was a spectacular success," said Wade. If the shotgun could do a fly, maybe it could do a human, too. Some HGP scientists in the audience at another meeting where Venter presented these findings looked at one another in consternation. "Those fuckers are actually going to do it," one of them said.[76] Celera's success with the fruit fly "changed the power balance between the two sides."[77]

On March 24, 2000, in the Celera cafeteria, Venter raised a bottle of beer in a toast: "This is *our* moment. We got our fly on the front page of the *New York Times.* Just like the president's fly. Only our fly will have a more lasting impact on history."[78]

A Day for the Ages

On June 26, 2000, Venter and Collins stood by President Clinton in the East Room of the White House. They were there to announce a "tie" in sequencing the human genome.

Clinton called it "a day for the ages":

Nearly two centuries ago, in this room, on this floor, Thomas Jefferson and a trusted aide spread out a magnificent map— a map Jefferson had long prayed he would see in his lifetime. The aide was Meriwether Lewis, and the map was the product of his courageous expedition across the American frontier, all the way to the Pacific. Today the world is joining us here to behold a map of even greater significance. . . . Without a doubt this is the most wondrous map ever produced by mankind.[79]

At Clinton's left hand was Francis Collins, who said, "It is humbling for me and awe-inspiring that we have caught the first glimpse of our own instruction book, previously known only to God." At Clinton's right hand was Venter, who said, "Today, June 26 in the year 2000, marks a historic point in the 100,000-year record of humanity. We're announcing today for the first time our species can read the chemical letters of its genetic code."[80] British prime minister Tony Blair, who joined the East Room ceremony by video link from London, concurred: "For let us be in no doubt about what we are witnessing today. A revolution in medical science whose implication far surpasses even the discovery of antibiotics, the first great scientific triumph of the twenty-first century."[81] When asked his feelings on that historic day, James Watson said, "It's a happy day," though he was said to have looked quite grumpy and refused to talk to reporters.[82]

Venter was on the covers of both *Time* and *Business Week*. "Could anything, even the human genome sequence, live up to such intense billing? A turning point in history, a divine revelation, a cure for cancer, all rolled into one?" Nicholas Wade asked in *Life Script*. The answer, he concluded, was yes. What did not live up to its billing was the story itself: that the two sides had supposedly joined forces in the final hours to complete the genome in a thrilling and heartwarming tie.

In fact, the task had not been completed—neither side had a

complete draft of the genome—and there was no tie. The rivalry "had become a political issue," with the Republican Congress backing Celera as a champion of private enterprise, while Democrats were more supportive of the public sector. Clinton had handed down an order: "Fix it . . . make these guys work together."[83] The tie was "pretense," according to *The Economist,* which likened it to the scene in *Alice's Adventures in Wonderland* where the judge, the Dodo, announces after a race, "Everyone has won and all must have prizes."[84] Celera was in fact way out in front. Venter told me it was "a charitable tie." What it actually represented was a deal, according to Wade: "Neither side would publicly criticize the quality of the other's work"—what HGP wanted, as its sequence was the inferior one. And in exchange, "Collins would extend to Venter the world's most prominent podium for his victory address. The White House."[85] It wasn't easy for Venter to declare a tie when he was winning. "It was a bittersweet moment because it was based on this truce, not the accomplishment I felt my team had actually made."

By agreement, the teams published their results simultaneously in February 2001. Venter's article appeared in the American journal *Science,* while the HGP's findings were published in the British journal *Nature.* Wade wrote that Venter's genome was in fact "more complete than the public consortium's."[86] And *The Washington Post* reported that even the "publicly funded scientists conceded this point."[87]

What enraged the HGP scientists was that Venter had leaped ahead of them in part by integrating *their* data with his own. The HGP had made it its policy to publish all genetic sequencing data online within twenty-four hours of their discovery. This was "unprecedented in science," according to Wade. The decision was an idealistic one, reflecting their belief that the genome belonged to all mankind. (Releasing the information into the public domain made it both freely available to all scientists and, equally important, legally unpatentable.) The problem was that mankind included Craig Venter. Venter didn't try to hide his strategy but rejoiced in hoisting HGP on its own high-minded petard. Venter told Lander, "Our business plan is to take your data, combine it with ours, and have the genome done on our own in a year." Lander's face reddened in rage: "What you just said proves you don't give a shit about us. All you're interested in is winning."[88] For the HGP scientists, that Venter could "scoop them with their own data" was nothing less than "insufferable," wrote Wade.[89]

And so the HGP scientists broke their agreement not to criticize Venter's data. They portrayed Venter as piggybacking on their findings in an unethical manner and announced that this proved his shotgun method was a failure. Collins, Waterston, and Varmus wrote a letter calling it a "breach of scientific ethics."[90] Sulston accused Venter of "hoovering" (vacuuming) their data and told the BBC it was a "con-job."[91] "It didn't work. Celera's shot gun was a flop. No ifs, ands or buts," Lander wrote in a broadcast email to the press.[92]

Venter told reporters it was a shame that his rivals "had got their panties in a gather."[93] Talking to me, he used a less benign metaphor: "That group pursued me like a pack of rabid dogs since the beginning of my career." Venter had indeed roused their primitive rage. "It frustrated them that I kept winning."

I'll Prove It with a Mouse

Under the radar, a second race to decode the mouse genome was taking place in parallel with the human project. "Race Is On to Decode the Genome of the Mouse" read a *New York Times* headline on October 6, 2000, in an article buried deep inside the paper.[94] Mice and humans had a common ancestor 100 million years ago and share an extraordinarily high number of genes, which are also conveniently the same size. Because scientists can conduct experiments on mice that would be unethical with people, the mouse genome is essential to laboratory research. Venter called it the "main annotation of the human genome."[95]

271

The triumvirate of Sulston, Lander, and Waterston, the directors of the three largest public gene-sequencing centers, formed the Mouse Sequencing Consortium in collaboration with corporations such as pharmaceutical giants SmithKline Beecham and Merck. The NIH committed $58 million. Venter told the *Times* he didn't know why they were forming a Mouse Consortium. "Instead of duplicating efforts again and wasting public money," they should leave it to Celera, he said. After the mouse story in the *Times,* no one heard about the mouse again. Everyone's attention was on the human race.

Venter took a "breathtaking gamble." [96] He "switched his DNA sequencing machines from human to mouse at a point when they had barely gathered enough human DNA for its assembly program." [97] Risk taking and split-second timing were part of Venter's hypomanic psychology. As one colleague put it, "Craig likes to do high dives into empty pools. He tries to time it so the water is there by the time he hits bottom." [98] Using HGP's human genome data allowed Venter to secretly accelerate the mouse race. Venter saw the strategy early on. In the summer of 1999, he told his senior staff, "The public program has played right into our hands. We can use their draft to finish our human genome sooner, then move on to sequencing the mouse by early next year, way ahead of everybody else. We'll be surfing into the beach while they're still getting their boards out." [99] "Craig outthought them in a lot of ways," Wade told me.

On February 12, 2001, at a carefully planned Washington news conference, Venter and the HGP were scheduled to jointly discuss the human genome data they had both published that month. It was meant to be another nonpartisan moment of shared celebration acknowledging the joint accomplishments of the two teams. Venter chose that moment to announce that he had beaten HGP again, this time definitively. Celera had completely assembled the mouse genome with his shotgun method, using no public data. Celera is "the only place to get the mouse genome," Venter crowed. "I certainly hope that this demonstration of the power of the whole genome shotgun technique will put to rest their griping about the human genome assemblies," he added, standing next to the men who had done the griping.[100] "Celera Has Mouse Map Monopoly" read the *Washington Post* headline.

Even more humiliating, the NIH became a Celera customer. On July 10, 2001, the *Times* reported that the National Cancer Institute, a division of the NIH, had signed an agreement to allow its researchers access to Celera's genome database at a cost of $10,000 for each Cancer Institute researcher who used it. Venter used the occasion to mock HGP once more, saying he was glad the NIH had been able to "get past petty politics." Wade reported in the *Times,* "Dr. Venter suggested that the NIH should cease its own efforts to sequence and assemble the mouse genome because the work duplicated what Celera had done. 'NIH could provide a subscription to every scientist in the U.S. to see the complete annotated genome for less than it costs them to sequence it'."[101] "He loves to needle his rivals," Smith told me.

On May 7, 2002, the Mouse Consortium announced that it had finally mapped *its* mouse but neglected to mention that Venter had already done it. "Scientists are usually scrupulous in acknowledging prior work lest they seem to claim credit for the achievements of others. But the consortium directors' news release neglects to mention their rival, Dr. J. Craig Venter, the former president of Celera Genomics, decoded the mouse genome more than a year ago," Wade wrote in the *Times*.[102] To those outside academia, this might not seem such a terrible oversight. When announcing a new product, corporations don't credit rival companies who might have given them the idea. However, by the rules of academia, failing to acknowledge the previous work of another was an appalling breach that bordered on the unethical. That Venter had provoked these high-minded scientists to behave in such an aberrant manner was another stunning illustration of his enormous power to annoy them. When the barbarian attacked their academic civilization, civility was abandoned, and more primitive instincts took hold. When asked about Venter's mouse genome, Collins said, "There is a rumor it exists."[103] A rumor? NIH, the organization that employed Collins, was paying hundreds of thousands of dollars in subscription fees to use Celera's mouse genome. Lander's reply to the charge that he had failed to reference Venter was: "We never claimed to be first."

Nor did the Mouse Consortium make any proud claims about *how* it had sequenced the mouse. It had used the *whole-genome shotgun*—the very Venter technique it had maligned so viciously. "It has become the universal technology for genome sequencing, though the more plodding public method is still used to fill in the inevitable small gaps the shotgun leaves behind. The shotgun assembly obviously worked, and that is the way genomes are now assembled," Wade told me.

Failing to mention Venter's name on this occasion was not a onetime event. Venter told me that the HGP is trying to "erase my existence." As a matter of unstated policy, his name is *never* mentioned at HGP meetings, according to Shreeve, who spoke to me after attending HGP's most recent annual meeting. He has virtually become "He-who-shall-not-be-named." When I emailed Watson in January 2004, seeking an interview, the director of public affairs at Cold Spring Laboratory replied, "In the last few years Dr. Watson has declined ALL requests that relate to Craig Venter." Francis Collins declined to be interviewed for this book. A representative for Eric Lander said he would consider my request but never approved an interview. Bob Waterston, Harold Varmus, and John Sulston never responded to my repeated requests for interviews.

Swedish Gold

Perhaps the most important reason that Venter and the HGP can't just get along is this: "A Nobel Prize is expected to be awarded for the work, and the prize can only be split three ways."[104] It's Swedish gold these men lust for, and there isn't room enough on that Stockholm podium for all of them. "My rivals may not be very smart, but they can all count to three," Venter told me. "It's like *Survivor.* They keep trying to vote me off the island. What happens in *Survivor*? The weak people get together and vote the strong one off every time."

A fundamental tenet of Nobel protocol and etiquette is that you never publicly suggest that you deserve the prize. You are not supposed to indicate that the thought has ever crossed your mind. But there is the normal way, and there is the Venter way. "If anyone deserves the Nobel, I do," Venter told Shreeve, who reported that Venter had taken the unprecedented step of going to Sweden personally to lobby members of the Royal Swedish Academy of Sciences on his own behalf. Shreeve told me:

> If Venter were to win, it would be in spite of his self-promotion, and Venter must know this but he can't help himself. He wants that sucker. He wants that little baby, and he's going after it. He's not obsequious about it. He's not going to kowtow to the members of the Swedish Academy. He's just going to be in their face and say, "This will probably affect the future of mankind for untold millennia. But be that as it may, you guys make up your own minds." People like Collins would be horrified, but I respect it. Everybody wants the fucking thing. Why not just say you want it?

Even his friend Hamilton Smith believed that Venter had "gotten in the faces" of a few Royal Academy members.

Venter denied to me that getting a Nobel Prize was a personal goal. "I already have a disproportionate number of scientific awards." Venter has already won Germany's, Japan's, and Canada's highest scientific honors, sometimes referred to as their Nobels. His large desk is surrounded by statuettes and medals representing these international prizes, as well as photos of him receiving these honors. But these prizes are not *the* Nobel. Venter said that the notion that he had lobbied for the Nobel was "bullshit," and he denounced Shreeve's account as "just a way to sell books." Venter claimed that his trips to Sweden were only to give scientific lectures. And though he might be friends with the head of the Swedish Royal Academy of Science, he claims he has never discussed the prize with him. Venter did tell me that he deserved the Nobel, certainly more than his rivals: "The only thing I would not want to see is other people get it in this field and be left out. That would not be a fun thing to go through. . . . If there's going to be a prize in genomics, I think my accomplishments rank up there with anybody."

It might be difficult for the academy to give the prize to a flamboyant controversial figure like Venter. "They're very concerned with the dignity of their damn prize, and they know if they try to give it to Venter there will be a firestorm of protest from senior academics in the U.S.," said Wade, who thinks Venter's original breakthrough with *H. flu.* would alone justify a Nobel. "He deserves the Nobel," Smith told me with feeling and conviction. "He's a genius. And he's revolutionized biology."

Venter has called himself "a super enzyme" because "I catalyze things." [105] That's probably a good description of the function hypomanics like Venter play in society. "If Craig hadn't jumped into the race they wouldn't be finished even now," Wade told me in January 2004. Everyone I talked to said the same thing. Even Watson grudgingly admitted that the genome sequencing had "occurred faster due to the fact that industry came in," though he could not bring himself actually to utter the words "Celera" or "Craig Venter." [106] But Venter must be given credit, whether or not he ever gets a Nobel. Thanks to him, the human genome was sequenced years sooner than planned—in no small part because he inspired both so much enthusiasm and so much hate. "At this point, the only judge will be the historians," said Venter.

A Map of All Humanity

From a scientific point of view, it didn't really matter who supplied the DNA for the mapping of the human genome. "But symbolically, it matters because the genome map stands for all humans," said Arthur Caplan, director of the Center for Bioethics at the University of Pennsylvania, who served on Celera's advisory panel.[107] At Caplan's suggestion, Celera had carefully picked "a cross section of individuals representing major ethnic and racial groups and touted the composite sequence as belonging to all of humanity."[108]

On April 17, 2002, on *60 Minutes II,* Venter announced that the human genome was a map of . . . Craig Venter. He had sequenced his own DNA. It confirmed what many geneticists had suspected for years. Arthur Caplan was understandably upset that Venter had violated the procedure that he and others had so thoughtfully put into place. He wrote an op-ed in *The New York Times:* "Starting with such a broad sample could teach an important lesson: Genetically, human beings have much, much more in common than not. . . . Now that Craig Venter has outed himself as not only a major contributor to the mapping of the human genome but also its major ingredient, these lessons are in jeopardy. It should be a map of all of us, not of one," complained Caplan.[109]

Venter just didn't get what all the fuss was about and was unfazed by the negative reaction. "What scientist wouldn't take this opportunity if he got the chance?" he asked me. I was shocked by his rhetorical question. Didn't Venter realize this was *not* what any scientist would do? Even Craig's friends and admirers have described this move as tacky, childish, over the top, obscenely egotistical, and grossly exhibitionistic. "It would be as if every computer came with a picture of Bill Gates's nose as the default screen saver," said

Shreeve. "It was as if one family claimed the bones from the Tomb of the Unknown Soldier," said Wade. "It *was* a universal genome—until we found out it was just Craig's." The world now has the genome not of our species but a specific variety: *Homo sapiens var. Venter.*[110] Some joked that perhaps Venter's body would become the subject of future experiments or be displayed in the Smithsonian. "That would be his wish, no doubt, to be prominently displayed in the Smithsonian," said Stephen Warren, editor of *The American Journal of Human Genetics.*[111]

Why did Venter choose that moment to reveal his secret? Hamilton Smith thinks that Venter felt as if he had been out of the news for too long. When Venter was asked by a reporter if he didn't think making the announcement had been egotistical, he replied jovially, "I've been accused of that so many times, I've got over it." [112] When I interviewed Venter, I pressed him on this point. Couldn't he at least *see* why other people, even those who liked him, viewed this as narcissistic behavior? He couldn't. "I know narcissistic people. I wouldn't describe myself as a narcissistic person. I don't even carry a mirror. I was curious about myself. Is that self-curiosity narcissism?" At that point, Venter mentioned casually that he is in fact a *case study* in a book about narcissists. Even that did not give him pause. "It's just the way that it was portrayed in the press" that made it look narcissistic, he maintained. "It had very little to do with reality."

Craig Venter *is* a genius, and like most people who answer to that description, he just doesn't get it.

THE GENE BUSINESS

He Could Have Been the Bill Gates of Biology

As much as his academic rivals hated him, Craig Venter's business partners hated him even more. "My greatest success was that I managed to get hated by both worlds," said Venter.[113] Venter's partners knew they had a gold mine on their hands with the human genome, but Craig kept insisting on publishing data for his own academic glory, giving away proprietary information they wanted to patent and exploit. The problem was that Venter was not in business to make money. He "had not gone into research to get rich—not that he was opposed to that development. He wanted to do recognizably great things." [114] The irony is that his academic rivals hated him because they thought Venter wanted to be the Bill Gates of biology. And his partners hated him because he chose *not* to be. "Craig wants to go down in the history books as the father of a biological revolution. He wants to be Charles Darwin," Smith told me. Venter admitted to me that his companies were mere stepping-stones to that larger ambition. "I've been driven by ideas and science. The biotechnology companies were a means to accomplish an end." *Their* capital was a means to *his* ends. As that began to dawn on his business partners it made them irate.

When venture capitalist Wallace Steinberg first set up the two twin companies—nonprofit TIGR and for-profit HGS—Venter was ecstatic. "It's every scientist's dream to have a benefactor invest in their ideas, dreams and capabilities," Venter told *The Washington Post*.[115] William Haseltine, CEO of HGS, didn't fancy himself a benefactor. Already notorious for his aggressiveness in both science and business, "Haseltine vaguely reminded Venter of Gordon Gecko, the high-powered speculator played by Michael Douglas in the 1987 film *Wall Street.*"[116] He wore dark expensive suits, his thinning hair was slicked back, and he traveled in chauffeur-driven limos and private planes. He was a true researcher-entrepreneur, a former Harvard Medical School professor who had already founded several biotech companies. "He had tycoon-sized objectives, and by some reports would use extraordinary tactics to achieve them." [117] As an AIDS researcher, when he was racing another team to understand the virus, "Haseltine would call up his competitors at three o'clock in the morning, just to throw them off balance," according to Shreeve.[118]

Venter's business plan was to charge companies for the use of the genetic information his research uncovered, earning a fee, but making the data widely available. Haseltine saw their findings as potentially valuable proprietary intellectual property. He envisioned HGS becoming a multibillion-dollar pharmaceutical company. When he met Venter for the first time in 1992, Haseltine realized that they had radically different visions for the company and were obviously working at cross-purposes. But that was okay. Privately, he declared that he didn't care what Craig's goals were. Venter was just a "booster rocket," an engine that would propel HGS and then fall away. "I knew we wouldn't need him for very long." [119] But in the meantime, he thought Venter's discoveries "were the key to the future of medicine." [120]

Contractually, HGS had six months to examine Venter's genetic findings exclusively before Venter could publish them. If there were any particularly promising results, HGS could invoke a special clause that gave it another year to explore a gene's commercial value. What Venter wasn't prepared for was that HGS invoked the clause automatically on every scrap of data he produced. He felt double-crossed. Haseltine replied unsympathetically, "We're damned if we were going to pay 10 million a year to somebody and not get to file a patent." [121] By the end of 1994, Venter collapsed with diverticulitis, an inflammation of the intestines caused largely by stress. The relationship with Haseltine, he said, was killing him.

Haseltine owned Venter's findings, but he couldn't control *what* findings he produced. It was at this time that Venter began working on the *H. flu.* genome, which had no commercial value for HGS but great value for the grand mission of Craig Venter. That the *Science* paper with the *H. flu.* genome was considered a major breakthrough and became the most cited work in biology did Haseltine no good. Haseltine would be damned, he said, before he would hand over millions to Venter to "sequence worms, bugs and so forth." [122] At a board meeting, Haseltine told Venter, "I'm going to get you." Venter took the threat so seriously that he became concerned that Haseltine might try to have him killed.[123] If Venter died, according to contract, HGS was released from its financial obligations to TIGR. On one occasion a business associate of Haseltine sent a private helicopter to pick up Venter and his wife. Recalling his Vietnam days, Venter hesitated to get in. "Do you know how easy it would be for somebody to push us out?" he asked Claire.[124] Like most hypomanics, "Craig definitely had a paranoid side," said Shreeve.

The conflict was resolved bloodlessly in 1997, when the two agreed to dissolve their partnership. HGS was relieved of having to pay the $37 million it owed TIGR, and Venter was free to publish. "Venter gave up over 30 million just for the pleasure of never having to see Haseltine's face," said Wade, who describes them as "enemies." William Haseltine declined my request to be interviewed. "He's probably jealous you're not writing about him as entrepreneur of the century," Venter said with a smirk.

When Tony White, the CEO of PerkinElmer, approached Venter about founding Celera, he knew he was taking a big risk. He sold the corporation's core business, a reliably profitable scientific instruments company, to finance this flyer. What made him come to hate Venter was the same thing that had enraged Haseltine: while Venter was using PE's money to grandstand all over the world (White detested the long wall of framed press clippings one must still pass to reach Venter's office), he seemed halfhearted about providing any return on PE's investment. Venter said he didn't rule out taking out "a few hundred patents," but he wasn't staking a claim to anywhere near the territory he could have. He was supposed to be mining for gold, but he didn't act as if he cared if he found it.

When patent attorney Robert Millman took a job at Celera, he called the company "a patent attorney's wet dream." Millman was excited by what he could accomplish there. "Nobody here understands the land grab like me," he boasted. "I'm going to be Francis Collins' worst nightmare." [125] But there was trouble in paradise for

Millman. Celera had agreed to release its data within twenty-four hours to its subscribers, mostly big drug companies, which would have no compunction about patenting everything they could. Every night before the clock struck twelve, Millman drove desperately to the patent office with hurriedly prepared documents claiming whatever Celera had discovered that day. When Venter wouldn't listen to Millman's broad patent strategy, Millman complained to White, "You've got to stop the bleed. You're giving away all your jewels. . . . Patent the hell out of everything you find." [126]

At one point, a merger with the biotechnology company Incyte was under discussion. Celera was the fastest gene-finding factory on Earth, and Incyte was the planet's most prolific gene patent holder. The only reason it didn't happen is that Venter craved fame more than money. "Craig was indeed giving it all away for his own academic glory," said Wade. If Venter's priorities had been the other way around, he might have become the owner of the human operating system. If he had never issued his public challenge to HGP, but instead stealthily mapped the genome without making a big display of it, the public project would have never sped up in response until it was too late and Celera had the whole genome mapped and patented. It could have been biology's Microsoft.

Ironically, as his business partners were tearing out their hair, Venter was a star in the business press, appearing on the cover of *Business Week* and in hundreds of economic and business articles. The story of the race between an entrepreneur and public-sector scientists to crack the human genetic code was irresistible. And there was no question who the capitalists were rooting for. But always Venter was bedeviled by the same question: Did his business plan make sense? Would this company make money? "It's like a private company in 1967 announcing that they are going to race NASA to the moon. And they did it. The next question is: What's the business plan?" [127]

"Our fundamental business model is like Bloomberg's," explained Venter over and over again. He saw himself as being in the genomic *information* business. Despite the fear that he would hoard the genome's secrets for himself, Venter's idea was to distribute them as widely as possible, providing genomic contents to researchers in a user-friendly form for a fee. Venter predicted that a day would soon come when there would be a retail market for individual genomes. He started by offering to provide personal genomes for a million dollars. Just as Henry Ford dreamed of a $250 car that any man with a job could afford, Venter imagined a $1,000 genome paid for by health insurance that would be integral to twenty-first-century health care. Venter predicted, "There will be an incredible demand for genomic information." [128] He claimed that one day Celera would have a hundred million customers. But that day was hardly around the corner. How would Celera make money in the meantime? Wall Street wanted to know.

In the go-go nineties, a good story was all that was needed to sell stock, and no one had a better story than Venter. Trading in Celera's stock was "violent," alternating between "panic buying and panic selling." [129] The entire biotech sector was even more volatile than tech stocks. On December 19, 1999, the Motley Fool, a widely read investing website, put a strong buy recommendation on Celera's stock with this comment: "We mean, come on! Celera has no profits, no real revenue and it has no clear business model, just a bunch of promises." On the other hand, "Celera may become one of the most important brand names in your life." [130] In December 1999, Celera's stock shot so high, so fast, that trading had to be halted several times. Everyone wanted to buy, and no one wanted to sell. Everyone at Celera (all employees owned Celera stock, even the secretaries) was checking the stock market online every few minutes.

When Celera hit its peak on February 25, 2000, at a presplit price of $550, it looked as if Venter, whose personal stock was worth $700 million that day, might become biotechnology's first billionaire. Shares in Celera had increased twenty-five-fold in less than a year. Comparisons to Bill Gates became frequent in the press. If Microsoft had made billions with its monopoly on the computer operating system, investors were imagining what Celera could do with its exclusive knowledge of the human operating system. Craig bought a bigger yacht and multimillion-dollar homes—as always, spending beyond his means.

On March 14, 2000, President Clinton and British prime minister Tony Blair issued a joint statement that all genes in the human body "should be made freely available to scientists everywhere," implying the announcement of a new government policy that would forbid the patenting of genes. Francis Collins and John Sulston were said to have lobbied for more than a year for such a statement. Celera's stock dropped 57 points in an hour, and once again trading had to be halted, now because it was falling so quickly. The whole biotech sector crashed in sympathy, losing $40 billion in market capitalization in one day. Nasdaq had its second biggest point loss in its history. "It's not every day you get attacked by the President and the Prime Minister. I'm expecting a call from the Pope any day asking me to recant the human genome. I feel like Galileo," said Venter, never one to think of himself in small terms.[131]

The day after the market crashed, a White House spokesman stated that the administration *supported* the patenting of genes. Clinton didn't want to appear to be personally responsible for destroying the budding biotech industry or wrecking the stock market. "I'm just grateful the whole market didn't crash because of something stupid I said," Venter told me. What no one could know at that time was that the March 14 decline was the beginning of the end for the entire bull market. Despite brief rallies, the market fell off a cliff in March 2000 and, five years later, it still hasn't recovered much of the ground it lost. "In hindsight, the boom was grotesquely overripe. Any number of things could have triggered its collapse. It just happened to be the human genome."[132]

In the euphoria of the White House ceremony in June 2000, few had noticed that Celera's stock had begun falling again. One person who noticed was Tony White. White was offended when he was literally pushed aside at the ceremony. Though he had bankrolled and helped conceive of the entire project, White sat in the audience, unacknowledged. To make matters worse, this ceremony was not good news from a business perspective. While HGP and Celera were celebrating their "tie" on Pennsylvania Avenue, Wall Street was left wondering: If it's a tie, then what unique intellectual property did Celera have to sell?

Another person who was unhappy at the White House was Robert Millman. "He [Venter] got what *he* wanted. It's great for *him*. But it's shit for the company," Millman complained at the party immediately following the White House ceremony.[133] And he was right. The patent attorney's wet dream had turned into a nightmare. "In this dream you roll over and discover that the beautiful young woman beneath you is your mother," said Millman about Celera. "If Dante created a hell for patent attorneys, this would be it." [134]

Despite the complaint that its business model made no sense, Celera signed up an impressive list of clients subscribing for genomic information, especially after they sequenced the mouse: government agencies, foreign governments, major universities, and large pharmaceutical companies, some of whom paid as much as $15 million a year. In 2001, Celera had revenues of $100 million.

But in January 2002, Venter was forced out of Celera. The Bloomberg model didn't make sense anymore, at least not to Tony White. As the public sector caught up, publishing more and more genomic data online for free, Celera's biggest asset appeared to be a highly perishable one. White wanted Celera to switch gears and become a drug company, because that's where the money was. Venter had no experience or interest in running a pharmaceutical company, and White had certainly had enough of him. After winning the race of the century, he was fired.

According to Venter, he became depressed for about a month afterward. "The most difficult thing was the totally crass way it was done. After working intimately with a team for three years, literally day and night, they wouldn't even allow me back into the building to say good-bye to my team. That was the social structure for my entire life for three years. It typified the petty vindictiveness of the people I had to put up with to sequence the human genome." "Just after he was fired, he was very depressed," Shreeve confirmed to me. The changes were physically palpable. "He didn't tell any jokes. He didn't have that radiance. He just faded into the crowd. . . . He was pulled inward. He seemed suddenly much shorter." Venter told Shreeve, "I still think there is at least as good a chance that I'll commit suicide as die from some disease." [135] Suicide, he confessed, was always an option in his mind. "I still think it might be the way I go." When we spoke in March 2004, Venter denied he ever really contemplated suicide, "but when you are depressed those thoughts cross your mind."

In many ways, President Clinton's comparison of Venter to Meriwether Lewis was an extremely apt one. Both of them drew maps that opened new territory to future generations. Lewis didn't make a dime, but the '49ers couldn't have panned for gold without him. Venter too was more of an explorer than a fortune hunter and drew a map that allowed a new gold rush to begin. But the comparison goes deeper than that. What many people do not know is that Meriwether Lewis was a manic-depressive, according to his biographer Stephen Ambrose, and he committed suicide. If you are Craig Venter or Meriwether Lewis, there are only two choices, glory or death. As the Marquis de Lafayette said when he first landed on American soil during the Revolution, he had come "to conquer or perish!" The hypomanic is wired this way: Give me greatness or give me death. When you are no longer changing the world, you might as well die. "I don't think Craig wants to get up in the morning if he's not doing something earth-shattering. What's the point?" asked Shreeve. Venter agreed with that statement: "Everything is goal-oriented. Throw away the goals, and I'd be depressed. I have to have a goal to exist. I look at the majority of civilization, and they just exist from day to day. Sometimes I'm envious of them. Sometimes I feel sorry for them." In fact, ordinary people do not "just exist." They have goals too—thank you very much—but not such astronomical ones. For the hypomanic, the only escape from a black hole is a big bang. For Venter to avoid Lewis's fate, he had to take on an even more ambitious project. "The paper we are about to publish in *Science* will be the top one in my career, historically," he told me with enthusiasm. That may or may not be true, but Venter has to believe it to keep on living.

From an evolutionary perspective, it makes sense to have a subset of the human population programmed this way. For many the outcome will be early death, not greatness. Venter almost got killed over a haircut before he ever entered a science lab. The cold truth is that humanity has a large supply of people to waste, and in the calculus of evolution a bunch of troublemakers who come to no good are a fair price for a Meriwether Lewis or a Craig Venter.

There is another important link between Lewis and Venter, one that is almost uncanny. The two men are related by blood. Though Clinton had no awareness of their genealogy when he compared Venter to the man who discovered the Northwest Passage, Venter is Lewis's descendant, not just metaphorically, but literally (it has now been checked against the extensive genealogical records kept by the Mormon Church). It is, therefore, quite possible that Venter inherited his hypomanic temperament from the explorer himself.

THE FUTURE

What's Next?

Many scientists believe that amazing discoveries are within our grasp now that we have cracked the human genome. For example, HGS, Venter's former sister company, has located a gene that orders the body to manufacture a protein, KGF-2, that stimulates the growth of human skin. When you cut yourself, KGF-2 is triggered and you heal. Clinical trials are finding it effective in its ability to heal a wide variety of skin conditions that affect millions of people. Now the skin regenerates itself because we tell it to. This is a small example of what lies ahead.

The greatest medical problem that has eluded cure has been cancer. The treatments we have now are woefully inadequate, blunt instruments that work at the level of the symptoms, not the cause. Surgery often fails to remove all the cancer cells. Radiation and chemotherapy make patients sick by indiscriminately killing healthy tissue along with cancer cells. The *cure* to cancer exists on the level of the genome. The growth of cells is controlled by a complex series of checks and balances embedded in our genes. Some proteins initiate cell growth; others modulate or inhibit it. In cancer, this system has broken down, and cells reproduce rampantly. The cure may be as simple as finding the protein that toggles the off switch.

If we can manipulate these on and off switches for cellular growth, we may be able to tell the body to grow a new liver or heart. The field of *regenerative medicine* is in its infancy. NIH researcher Ronald McKay believes that "people will routinely be reconstituting liver, regenerating heart, routinely building pancreatic islets, routinely putting cells into the brain that get incorporated into normal circuitry. They will routinely rebuild all tissues." [136]

Such changes will dramatically increase our life expectancy. For most of human history, the average person lived to age twenty-five, basically long enough to reproduce. Our average life span has been steadily on the rise, with improvements in nutrition, sanitation, and medicine, particularly the discovery of antibiotics. In 1900, the average life expectancy was fifty. Now it is in the mid-eighties in industrialized nations. Clearly, the elimination of cancer and advances in regenerative medicine will push that average higher. But genetic research on aging itself promises to make even more dramatic improvements in longevity. Since the roundworm genome was decoded in 1998, scientists have found several genes they could alter to increase the worm's life span sixfold. "I believe that our generation is the first to be able to map a possible route to individual immortality," said William Haseltine.[137] That may be an exaggeration, but "for the first time in history, biologists have a rational ground for thinking it may be possible to extend the human life span," not simply by curing diseases that kill us but by turning on genes that activate regeneration and turning off others that activate aging.[138] Stopping the aging process might be as simple as taking a pill. How far can we go? No one knows. Today's scientists would not be surprised if our grandchildren lived to 120. But ultimately, there is no absolute limit that we know of.

The last question I asked Craig Venter was: How is this genome going to change things?

"It's the beginning of the beginning," he answered. "This is the quiet revolution. The digital revolution was in your face. The genome revolution is behind the scenes, slowly transforming how we think about life, how we treat disease, how we organize our lives, how we view our history. It's going to change how we live, from the food we eat to how we manufacture drugs and chemicals. It will change how we think of our species."

The Genesis Project

After Celera fired him, Venter "was looking for something else to do to change the world."[139] "Craig rebounded the only way he knows how," Smith told me, "by tackling a project even more grandiose than the one before." And once again, he dragged his good friend Hamilton Smith into it.

On November 14, 2003, Venter and Smith made a startling announcement. They had built a virus "from scratch," synthesizing the DNA themselves and assembling the nucleotides in the right order, using the genomic sequence as a cookbook. They did not alter an organism's genes or clone them. They *built* them and used

289

their handmade genes to successfully produce a well-known simple virus—phiX, the first organism to ever have its gene sequence decoded.

They *created life*. Venter nicknamed it the "Genesis Project." [140]

A year earlier, a group of researchers at the State University of New York at Stony Brook had synthesized the polio virus. Venter had publicly criticized them at that time for conducting research that could enable bioterrorists. "I think Craig was just jealous that they beat us," Smith confessed. In contrast, Venter claimed that the virus he had synthesized was safe because it was not a human pathogen. PhiX infects only bacteria. "But that doesn't really make any difference," Smith admitted. "You could still adapt the same technology easily to make human pathogens." Eckhard Wimmer, one of the Stony Brook scientists Venter had criticized, made the same point to the press: the notion that Venter's work was completely safe was "just baloney," he said. "You could use the same technology to make HIV in two weeks." [141]

They weren't first, but Venter and Smith's work was a breakthrough nonetheless. It took the SUNY researchers three years to manufacture their virus. Venter's group produced a perfect specimen in just *fourteen days*. They were hypomanic days, of course— "exhilarating hours in the lab, pulling all-nighters and ordering pizza." [142] Hamilton Smith, a man in his mid-seventies, worked round the clock. Even Wimmer, their Stony Brook rival, had to admit that Venter and Smith's work was "most impressive." [143] Once again, Venter was speeding things up. "The new process is so easy, I could give this to undergraduates and they could do it," said Peter Sorger, professor of biology and bioengineering at MIT. [144]

Spencer Abraham, head of the Department of Energy (DOE), stood next to Venter and Smith on the podium on November 14, 2003. He declared them "prophets of a new age of research." [145] The DOE had funded their work, hoping it would yield designer microorganisms capable of producing hydrogen fuel, devouring oil spills, and gobbling up greenhouse gases. Abraham predicted, "With this advance, it is easier to imagine, in the not-too-distant future, a colony of specially designed microbes living within the emission-control system of a coal-fired plant, consuming its pollution and its carbon dioxide, or employing microbes to radically reduce water pollution, or to reduce the toxic effects of radioactive waste."[146]

At the beginning of 2003, the Energy Department announced a $3 million grant to Venter's new nonprofit company, the Institute for Biological Energy Alternatives (IBEA). In April 2003, the DOE gave it $9 million more. Abraham drove to the institute to personally hand Venter the $9 million check, cut only a few weeks after Venter submitted a proposal "about a paragraph long," according to one IBEA employee I spoke with. "He's a god to the people at the Department of Energy. If Craig says it, they'll fund it." On November 14, 2003, Abraham announced that the department "was forming a new committee to accelerate this research.

Some people have pointed out that there are safe, reliably tested technologies for reducing pollution already on the shelf. It seemed silly to propose solving the global energy crisis by releasing imaginary new life-forms (about which we can know little and whose environmental impact no one can predict). Both partisan and nonpartisan critics have charged the DOE with using futuristic promises as political cover for increasing current pollution. Hamilton Smith agreed: "Craig hyped the hell out of the thing, as usual. I was embarrassed. We're not going to solve the world's energy and environmental problems anytime soon with this research. There are probably better ways to do that. . . . But I shouldn't say any more." Smith stopped there, realizing perhaps that it might be unwise to criticize the government agency that was funding his research, precisely because it had bought Craig's hype.

Nonetheless, the discovery marked an early step in the burgeoning new field of "synthetic biology." Scientists hope to learn "how

291

to design and build biological systems the way they can now build machines . . . custom building entirely new kinds of life with new abilities." [147] And Venter was bragging that his technique would get us there: "It's fast, it's cheap and it's accurate. That's what we'll need to build larger things." [148] The hoopla may be a bit premature, but it is not unwarranted. "Craig will tell you we can do it this year. We can't. But *someday* we will be able to design and build any organism you want," Smith told me. Their results were published in the December 2003 issue of *Proceedings of the National Academy of Sciences,* where they described the potential applications of this technology as "limitless." [149] That's not hype.

As the word "limitless" suggests, it is impossible to imagine this technology's full potential—for good or evil. We can never entirely predict the behavior of living things. *The Times* of London, among many others, expressed alarm about "Frankenforms escaping Petri dishes." [150] Venter breezily dismissed such concerns as "hysterical." [151] He pointed out that his work had been cleared "at the highest levels of the US government," as if that were a guarantee that nothing could go wrong. [152]

We have breached a barrier, for good or ill, and can no more predict what lies ahead than Columbus could have imagined the modern United States. Up until 2003, only God could claim to have created life. The Almighty must now share that honor with a hypomanic American.

Conclusion

Hypomania's Past and Future

HYPOMANIA PAST: AN EVOLUTIONARY THEORY

Does hypomania predate humanity? On a sheer statistical basis, the odds are that it does. We differ in only 1 percent of our DNA from our closest relative, the chimpanzee. What makes the question more compelling are startling new behavioral observations made by primatologists. Charismatic leadership didn't begin with man.

Primatologists have always presented a very benign view of chimpanzee social organization. They live in cooperative groups where prosocial behaviors such as food sharing, grooming, and mutuality predominate. There is fierce competition among males for dominance, but these dueling aggressive performances, appropriately enough called "displays," fall short of mortal combat. Males growl, beat their chests, stomp the ground, and charge at each another, but rarely hurt each other. When I interviewed Frans de Waal, author of *Chimpanzee Politics,* he likened a chimp community to a corporation. "Of course, the people within the company are competing with each other all the time, but there must be a

293

limit if they are to function as a group," he told me.[1] They have to get along because they have to live together.

As it turns out, this benign view is wrong, or at the very least, incomplete. Mankind has long been considered the only species capable of murder. No longer. Richard Wrangham is a Harvard anthropologist who has spent many years observing chimpanzees in the Gombe National Park in Tanzania—the famous colony founded by Jane Goodall in the 1960s. Until very recently, primatologists had been limited to observing only *single* communities of chimps, either in captivity or in the wild. Thus, everything we knew about their relationships was based on *within*-group behavior. Wrangham, however, studied a group that had split into two communities. He was able to witness *between*-group behavior. It seems that chimpanzee groups do what human groups do: they have wars. In his book *Demonic Males,* Wrangham described a systematic string of raids by a band of male chimpanzees against their neighbors. How do these raids start? A charismatic leader appears to initiate them:

> The most dominant male—the alpha male—charged between the small parties, dragging branches, clearly excited. Others would watch and soon *catch his mood.* After a few minutes they would join him. The alpha male would only have to check back over his shoulder a few times. The group would move briskly [emphasis added].[2]

The alpha male's extreme excitement would catch fire with the other dominant males in the Kasekela region and propel them toward collective action. In one instance, they traveled to the boundary of their territory, climbed to the top of a ridge, and sat surreptitiously for hours staring down into the Kahama Valley—until they saw Goliath, an elderly male in his fifties who wandered into the wrong place at the wrong time. "He was well past his prime, with a bald head, and worn teeth. He was little threat to anyone." Furthermore, he was an individual well known to the raiders. He had been part of their group before the community split into two. That earned him no mercy:

> The raiders rushed madly down the slope to their target. While Goliath screamed and the patrol hooted and displayed, he was held and beaten and kicked and lifted and dropped and bitten and jumped on. At first he tried to protect his head, but soon he gave up and lay stretched out and still. His aggressors showed their excitement in a continuous barrage of hooting and drumming and charging and branch waving and screaming. They kept up the attack for eighteen minutes, then turned for home, still energized, running and screaming and banging on tree root buttresses.[3]

"It's clear that they just love it," Wrangham told me with a cheerful British accent, describing this grisly murder.[4]

Through repeated raids of this sort, the Kasekela males destroyed the Kahama community, absorbing both its land and its females. The victorious Kasekelas celebrated with a population explosion. With more females to impregnate, their birthrate went up, and, mysteriously, infant mortality went down. They were fruitful and multiplied. The group with a charismatic leader expanded its territory and population. The other group perished. "Kahama was no more."

This phenomenon has also been witnessed by Dr. John Mitani, who observes the largest chimp community in the world, on the opposite end of the same East African national park. Wrangham, who put me in touch with Mitani, told me, "Ask him about Ellington." Ellington does not theatrically hoot and drag tree limbs to whip up the crowd. He doesn't have to. He merely appears in public, sits down—and excitement begins to swirl around him. The other males hoot and jump with pleasure in anticipation of what is to come. The males begin a wild dance, throwing dirt and stones, dragging tree limbs, charging madly back and forth. They playfully slap one another with increasing force and excitement. "They look like they're drunk or a little high," said Mitani.[5] After the raucous celebration, the chimpanzees are almost postorgasmic. Sweating and panting, they lie down, and many nap.

If they don't wake up fast enough, Ellington will rouse them. They have miles to go before they sleep. Ellington initiates what will be an all-day march. When his troops seem to tire, Ellington literally pushes them forward. "It's as if he's dragging the group," Mitani said. In the field, his energy is relentless. Like the Kasekelas, the raiding party will wait in ambush, picking off their neighbors one at a time. These chimps also seem to enter a frenzied state of excitement when they are killing. Mitani had noted that in this mental state they become uncharacteristically brave. Under normal circumstances a chimp will easily become frightened and run away from a human. "Chimps are crybabies. They're pathetic. But when they are in one of these killing frenzies, you can come right up behind them and they won't seem to care or even notice. They're not looking scared. They're looking excited," said Mitani. All thought of risk has fled their minds.

The march of human civilization has not been pretty. From the beginning of recorded history till the present, wars over attempted territorial expansion have continued without end. And they are virtually all led by charismatic alphalike males. Maybe that's why we find bipolars in every society on Earth we've studied.[6] Any group of *Homo sapiens* without bipolar genes in its gene pool long ago went the way of the Kahama.

At his core, was Christopher Columbus that different from Ellington? He led Europeans on an aggressive expansion into new territory, also wiping out the native population. Craig Venter was an explorer, too, like his ancestor Meriwether Lewis, but in the domain of science. Even in this field, he employed the tried-and-true Ellington method: he used his charisma to rally a band of scientists to invade NIH's territory. The impulse to conquer has been directed toward more abstract, sublimated, and civilized goals but has remained, in its basic structure, unchanged for millions of years.

Capitalism is another example of how the drive to compete can be sublimated in the competition for market share, a form of territory. An evolutionary theory is always a theory, since we cannot observe what happened millions of years ago. But it is possible that American entrepreneurs may be the biological descendants of prehistoric Ellingtons. During the 1990s, boasting American entrepreneurs figuratively beat their chests, made impressive displays, and got investors excited in response. When I checked my portfolio online and discovered I had "earned" more in a day than I normally saw in the better part of a year, I must admit that I hooted like an elated primate. If I could have danced around a fire slapping five with my fellow investors, I would have. Like Ellington's followers, I was uncharacteristically unafraid, giddy to risk my life savings.

The paradox is that the traits that push mankind toward continuous *advancement* are really quite *primitive*.

HYPOMANIA FUTURE: THREE PREDICTIONS

Americans Are from Mars, Other Earthlings Are from Venus

In 1904, Max Weber wrote that religious zealots, such as the Puritans who founded New England, are a "distinct species of men." And in a way you could say that the zealous American is, if not a different species, at least a unique variety of *Homo sapiens*. The rest of the world, particularly our European friends, have a host of conflicting feelings about America and Americans. They like our cheerful optimism, even if it seems naive. They appreciate our confidence, but not when it veers toward arrogance. They admire our inventiveness and creativity, even as they laugh at the wacky trends we follow. They envy our wealth, even as they decry our shallow materialism. They admire our can-do energy, but don't understand why we can't stop our engines and take long vacations as they do. How an advanced nation can be so ripe with religious zealots mystifies them. And our messianic streak scares the hell out of them, especially since the Iraq war. Everything the world loves and hates about America is a manifestation of our hypomanic temperament. We are an enigma to the world, but really we're not that hard to understand.

We're a hypomanic nation.

Therefore, I predict we will continue to act like one, sometimes wisely, sometimes not.

Ellis Island Blues

America's hypomanic immigrant genes have made us what we are. But after the attacks of September 11, America may be tempted to abandon the pro-immigrant ethos that made her great. Such a reaction would be understandable, but it would be a terrible mistake. Since the attacks, the government has cracked down on "illegal immigrants." But this term covers a wide range of people. Most of the people who came here without official sanction overcame many obstacles, proving they are people of drive, initiative, and courage. It has distressed me to read about the Department of Homeland Security busting Hispanic cleaning crews at Wal-Mart. Technically, these workers who are grasping the first rung of the American ladder are here illegally. But they are hard-working Americans in my book and certainly pose no risk to national security. The world has changed, and we must adapt. We must find new ways to practice *safe immigration*. But we must not turn inward. "If we close our borders to new immigration, you can kiss good-bye the new energy, new tastes, new strivers who want to lunge into the future. That's the real threat to the American creed," wrote David Brooks of

The New York Times.[7] It has been too often said that if we alter any aspect of our lifestyle to enhance national security, "the terrorists have won." But if America stops being a nation of immigrants, the terrorists really *will* have won.

Andrew Carnegie said that immigration was America's "golden stream." I predict that when that stream dries up, it will mark the beginning of the decline of the American Empire.

An Endangered Species?

In the near future, genetic testing may allow a couple to decide to abort a manic-depressive fetus, as they can a Down syndrome child.* Or, in a slightly more distant future, a genetic counselor will read a couple's genograms and offer them the option of having "diseased" genes fixed before conception through a simple procedure covered by health insurance. The decision may feel like a no-brainer. What couple would knowingly choose to have a mentally ill child? Yet, what would be the collective result of these individual rational decisions? It would be sadly ironic if Craig Venter's genetic technology led to the extinction of *Homo sapiens var. Venter.* Genes that have survived millions of years of brutal competition could slip away in a generation without a fight.

Hypomanics are on this earth for good reason. And I predict that if we take them out of the gene pool, tomorrow's Christopher Columbuses will never be born, and our descendants won't find their new worlds.

I began this book with a discussion of entrepreneurs. Economist Joseph Nye argued that successful entrepreneurs are "lucky fools." To believe with utter certainty that your new company will be a smash hit, when the realistic odds are remote, is irrational and hence foolish. But once in a while, a fool gets lucky and strikes oil.

* Dr. Kay Jamison first brought this concern to my attention during a conversation in 1994.

Columbus was a lucky fool. He stumbled across America, claiming to have found China, King Solomon's Mines, and the Garden of Eden—all part of his master plan to usher in the Apocalypse. You can't get much more foolish than that. But it's precisely this type of person who goes where no man has gone before. If we want to keep human genius alive, we'll have to suffer fools gladly.

Appendix

BIOGRAPHER RATINGS FOR ALEXANDER HAMILTON ON HYPOMANIC DIAGNOSTIC CRITERIA

Diagnostic Criterion	BIOGRAPHER					Average
	1	2	3	4	5	
Overall	5	4	5	5	4	4.6
Energy	5	4	5	5	5	4.8
Restless	5	4	5	4	4	4.4
Active	5	4	5	5	5	4.8
Quick-thinking	5	5	5	5	5	5
Jumps from idea to idea	3	5	3	1	3	3
Distractible	Don't know	2	3	1	1	1.75
Fast-talking	Don't know	Don't know	Don't know	4	5	4.5
Talks a lot	5	Don't know	Don't know	5	5	5
Dominates conversation	5	4	4	5	4	4.4
Grandiose	5	4	5	5	3	4.4
Feels destined	5	4	5	5	5	4.8
Elated	5	3	5	5	5	4.6
Charismatic	4	4	5	5	5	4.6
Charming	5	4	5	5	5	4.8
Attractive	5	4	5	5	5	4.8

(continued)

Diagnostic Criterion	BIOGRAPHER					Average
	1	2	3	4	5	
Irritable	5	3	5	4	2	3.8
Explosive	5	5	4	4	1	3.6
Suspicious	5	5	4	4	2	4
Impulsive	5	3	4	4	2	3.6
Acts on ideas immediately	5	2	5	1	1	2.8
Risk taker (general)	5	5	5	5	4	4.8
Risk taker (financial)	5	5	2	5	4	4.2
Overspends	5	4	2	3	4	3.6
Risk taker (physical)	4	2	5	5	4	4
Risk taker (sexual)	5	5	5	5	5	5
Sex drive	5	5	5	5	4	4.8
Needs little sleep	Don't know	4	Don't know	5	Don't know	4.5
Dresses for attention	5	5	4	3	4	4.2

Notes

Introduction: The Hypomanic American

1. Michael Lewis, *The New New Thing* (New York: Norton, 2003), p. 180.

2. Ibid., p. 103.

3. Ibid., p. 100.

4. Ibid., p. 124.

5. Joseph Nocera, "I Lost $800 Million in Eight Months. Why Am I Still Smiling?," *Fortune,* March 5, 2001, p. 72.

6. Sylvia Simpson, Susan Folstein, Deborah Meyers, Francis McMahon, Diane Brusco, and Raymond DePaulo, "Bipolar II: The Most Common Bipolar Phenotype?," *American Journal of Psychiatry* 150, vol. 6 (1993), pp. 901–903.

7. Frederick K. Goodwin and Kay Redfield Jamison, *Manic-Depressive Illness* (New York: Oxford University Press, 1990), p. 23.

8. American Psychiatric Association, *Diagnostic and Statistical Manual,* 4th ed. (Washington, D.C.: American Psychiatric Association, 1994), p. 332.

9. Ibid., p. 337.

10. For a review, see Goodwin and Jamison, *Manic-Depressive Illness,* pp. 157–184.

11. Hagop Aksikal, Marc Bourgeois, Jules Angst, Robert Post, Hans-Jurgen Moller, and Robert Hirshfield, "Re-evaluating the Prevalence of and Diagnostic Composition Within the Broad Clinical Spectrum of Bipolar Disorders," *Journal of Affective Disorders* 59 (2000), pp. s5–s30; Jules Angst, "The Emerging Epidemiology of Hypomania and Bipolar II Disorder," *Journal of Affective Disorders* 50 (1998), pp. 143–151.

12. Ruth Richards and Dennis Kinney, "Mood Swings and Creativity," *Creativity Research Journal* 3 (1990), pp. 202–217.

13. Erica Goode, "Most Ills Are a Matter of More Than One Gene," *The New York Times,* June 27, 2000, p. D1; James Potash and J. Raymond De-Paulo, Jr., "Searching High and Low: A Review of the Genetics of Bipolar Disorder," *Bipolar Disorders* 2 (2000), pp. 8–26.

14. James Potash, Virginia Willour, Yen-Feng Chiu, Sylvia Simpson, Dean MacKinnon, Godfrey Pearlson, J. Raymond DePaulo, Jr., and Melvin McInnis, "The Familial Aggregation of Psychotic Symptoms in Bipolar Pedigree," *American Journal of Psychiatry* 158 (2001), pp. 1258–1264.

15. William Coryell, Jean Endicott, Martin Keller, Nancy Andreasen, William Grove, Robert Hirschfield, and William Scheftner, "Bipolar Affective Disorder and High Achievement: A Familial Association," *Psychiatry* 146, no. 8 (August 1989), pp. 983–988; M. Eisemann, "Social Class and Social Mobility in Depressed Patients," *Acta Psychiatrica Scandinavica* 73 (1986), pp. 399–402; Helene Verdoux and Marc Bourgeois, "Social Class in Unipolar and Bipolar Probands and Relatives," *Journal of Affective Disorders* 33 (1995), pp. 181–187.

16. James Jaspers, *Restless Nation: Starting Over in America* (Chicago: University of Chicago Press, 2000), p. 11.

17. Goodwin and Jamison, *Manic-Depressive Illness,* p. 182.

18. F. Rouillon, "Epidémiologie du trouble bipolaire," *L'Encéphale* 23 (1997), pp. 7–11; Myrna Weissman, Roger Bland, Glorisa Canino, Carlo Faravelli, Steven Greenwald, Hai-Gwo Hwu, Peter Joyce, Elie Karam, Chung-Kyoon Lee, Joseph Lellouch, Jean Pierre Lepine, Stephen Newman, Maritza Rubio-Stipec, Elisabeth Wells, Priya Wickramaratne, Hans-Ulrich Wittchen, and Eng-Kung Teh, "Cross-National Epidemiology of Major Depression and Bipolar Disorder," *The Journal of the American Medical Association* 276 (July 24–31, 1996), pp. 293–299.

19. David Brooks, *On Paradise Drive: How We Live Now (and Always Have) in the Future Tense* (New York: Simon and Schuster, 2004), p. 76.

20. Michael A. Ledeen, *Tocqueville on American Character* (New York: Truman Talley, 2000), p. 13.

21. Alexis de Tocqueville, *Democracy in America,* vol. 2, ed. Phillips Bradley (New York: Alfred A. Knopf, 1972), p. 247.

22. Tocqueville, *Democracy in America,* vol. 1, p. 295.

23. Steven Greenhouse, "Ideas and Trends: Running on Empty: So Much Work, So Little Time," *The New York Times,* September 5, 1999; Juliet B.

Schor, *The Overworked American: The Unexpected Decline of Leisure* (New York: Basic Books, 1992).

24. Tocqueville, *Democracy in America,* vol. 2, pp. 248–249.

25. Bernard Wysocki, Jr., "Where We Stand," *The Wall Street Journal,* September 27, 1999, p. R5.

26. John Leland, "Why America Sees the Silver Lining," *The New York Times,* June 13, 2004, sec. 4, p. 1.

27. Rupert Wilkinson, *The Pursuit of American Character* (New York: Harper and Row, 1988), p. 25.

28. David Aronson, ed., "Immigrant Entrepreneurs," in *Research Perspectives on Migration,* vol. 1, no. 2, published as a joint program of the International Migration Policy Program and the Carnegie Endowment for International Peace and the Urban Institute, Washington, D.C., January–February 1997.

29. Andrew Zacharakis, Paul D. Reynolds, and William D. Bygrave, *Global Entrepreneurship Monitor: 1999 Executive Report* (Kansas City, Mo.: Kauffman Center for Entrepreneurial Leadership, 1999).

30. "Culture and the Entrepreneurial Climate: A New 10-Country Study Attempts to Pinpoint Factors That Make Start-ups Thrive or Starve," *Business Week Online,* June 22, 1999.

31. Brooks, *On Paradise Drive,* p. 79.

32. Edward Chancellor, *Devil Take the Hindmost: A History of Financial Speculation* (New York: Plume, 2000), p. 154.

I: Christopher Columbus: Messianic Entrepreneur

1. Marianne Mahn-Lot, *Columbus* (New York: Grove, 1961), p. 62.

2. Delno C. West and August Kling (trans. and commentary), *The* Libro de las profecias *of Christopher Columbus* (Gainesville: University of Florida Press, 1992), p. 105.

3. Ibid.

4. Felipe Fernández-Armesto, *Columbus* (New York: Oxford University Press, 1991), p. vii.

5. West and Kling, *The* Libro de las profecias, p. 107.

6. Frederick K. Goodwin and Kay Redfield Jamison, *Manic-Depressive Illness* (New York: Oxford University Press, 1990), p. 37.

7. Ibid., p. 26.

8. Ibid.

9. Ibid.

10. Pauline Moffitt Watts, "Prophecy and Discovery: On the Spiritual Origins of Christopher Columbus' Enterprise of the Indies," *American Historical Review* 90 (1985), p. 74.

11. Ibid., p. 73.

12. West, "Christopher Columbus," p. 521.

13. John Leddy Phelan, *The Millennial Kingdom of the Franciscans in the New World* (Berkeley: University of California Press, 1970), p. 22.

14. Gianni Granzotto, *Christopher Columbus: The Dream and the Obsession* (London: Graffon, 1988), p. 58.

15. Ibid., p. 59.

16. Ibid.

17. John Larner, "The Certainty of Columbus: Some Recent Studies" *History* 73 (1988), pp. 3–23.

18. Granzotto, *Christopher Columbus,* p. 55.

19. Mahn-Lot, *Columbus,* p. 48.

20. Ibid., p. 50.

21. John Stewart Collis, *Christopher Columbus* (New York: Stein and Day, 1977), p. 50.

22. Ibid.

23. Granzatto, *Christopher Columbus,* p. 74.

24. Collis, *Christopher Columbus,* p. 50.

25. Samuel Eliot Morison, *Admiral of the Ocean Sea: A Life of Christopher Columbus* (Boston: Little, Brown, 1942), p. 114.

26. Collis, *Christopher Columbus,* p. 50.

27. Granzotto, *Christopher Columbus,* p. 84.

28. Ibid., p. 78.

29. Ibid., p. 83.

30. Ibid.

31. Ibid., p. 84.

32. Ibid., p. 83.

33. Ibid., p. 90.

34. Ibid., p. 91.

35. Salvador de Madariaga, *Christopher Columbus: Being the Life of the Very Magnificent Lord, Don Cristóbal Colón* (New York: Macmillan, 1940), p. 176.

36. Helen Nader (trans. and ed.), *The Book of Privileges to Christopher Columbus by King Ferdinand and Queen Isabella* (Berkeley: University of California Press, 1996), p. 25.

37. Paolo Emilio Taviani, *Columbus: The Great Adventure* (New York: Orion, 1991), p. 75.

38. Mahn-Lot, *Columbus,* p. 62.

39. Granzotto, *Christopher Columbus,* p. 91.

40. Ibid., p. 92.

41. Ibid.

II: Winthrop, Williams, and Penn:
Prophets Prosper in the Land of Promised Lands

1. William James, *The Varieties of Religious Experience: A Study in Human Nature* (New York: Mentor, 1958), pp. 208–212.

2. Ibid., p. 221.

3. Lee Schweninger, *John Winthrop* (Boston: Twayne, 1990), p. 23.

4. Francis J. Bremer, *John Winthrop: America's Forgotten Founding Father* (New York: Oxford University Press, 2003), p. 97.

5. Schweninger, *John Winthrop,* p. 23.

6. Ibid., p. 27.

7. Ibid., p. 28.

8. Peter N. Carroll, *Puritanism and the Wilderness* (New York: Columbia University Press, 1969), p. 21.

9. Alan Heimert and Andrew Delbanco, eds., *The Puritans in America: A Narrative Anthology* (Cambridge, Mass.: Harvard University Press, 1985), p. 69.

10. Carroll, *Puritanism,* p. 23.

11. Robert Winthrop, *The Life and Letters of John Winthrop* (Boston: Ticknor and Fields, 1864, reprinted by Higginson Book Company), p. 309.

12. Allan Kulikoff, *From British Peasants to Colonial American Farmers* (Chapel Hill: University of North Carolina Press, 2000), p. 41.

13. Winthrop, *Life and Letters,* p. 310.

14. Kulikoff, *From British Peasants,* p. 2.

15. John Frederick Martin, *Profits in the Promised Land: Entrepreneurship and the Founding of New England Towns in the Seventeenth Century* (Chapel Hill: University of North Carolina Press, 1991), p. 123.

16. Max Weber, *The Protestant Ethic and the Spirit of Capitalism* (New York: Charles Scribner's Sons, 1958), p. 65.

17. Loren Baritz, *City on a Hill* (New York: Wiley, 1964), p. 68.

18. David Brooks, "Reagan's Promised Land," *The New York Times,* June 8, 2004, p. A23.

19. Edmund Morgan, *Roger Williams: The Church and the State* (New York: Harcourt and Brace, 1967), p. 114.

20. David Brooks, *On Paradise Drive: How We Live Now (and Always Have) in the Future Tense* (New York: Simon and Schuster, 2004), p. 76.

21. Jon Krakauer, *Under the Banner of Heaven: A Story of Violent Faith* (New York: Anchor Books, 2003), p. 136.

22. John Winthrop, "Winthrop's Journal," in *Roger Williams and the Massachusetts Magistrates,* ed. Theodore P. Greene (Boston: Heath, 1964), p. 1.

23. Perry Miller, *Roger Williams: His Contribution to the American Tradition* (New York: Bobbs-Merrill, 1953), p. 30.

24. Ibid., p. 31.

25. Glenn W. LaFantasie, ed., *The Correspondence of Roger Williams,* vol. 1 (Providence, R.I.: Brown University Press, 1988), p. 12.

26. Edmund Morgan, *The Puritan Dilemma: The Story of John Winthrop* (New York: Little, Brown, 1958), p. 117.

27. Ibid., p. 121.

28. Paul Johnson, *A History of the American People* (New York: HarperCollins, 1997), p. 49.

29. Morgan, *Puritan Dilemma,* p. 119.

30. LaFantasie, *Correspondence of Roger Williams,* p. 13.

31. Ibid.

32. Winthrop, *Life and Letters,* p. 2.

33. LaFantasie, *Correspondence of Roger Williams,* p. 19.

34. Morgan, *Puritan Dilemma,* p. 123.

35. Ibid., p. 124.

36. LaFantasie, *Correspondence of Roger Williams,* p. 19.

37. Ibid., p. 20.

38. Ibid., p. 21.

39. Morgan, *Puritan Dilemma,* p. 128.

40. Ibid., p. 129.

41. Miller, *Roger Williams,* p. 94.

42. Morgan, *Puritan Dilemma,* p. 128.

43. Ibid., p. 131.

44. Ibid., p. 132.

45. Morgan, *Roger Williams,* p. 109.

46. Perry Miller, *Orthodoxy in Massachusetts, 1630–1650* (Gloucester, Mass.: Peter Smith, 1933), p. 167.

47. Johnson, *A History of the American People,* p. 49.

48. Ola Elizabeth Winslow, *Master Roger Williams* (New York: Macmillan, 1957), p. 259.

49. Johnson, *A History of the American People,* p. 50.

50. Morgan, *Roger Williams,* p. 99.

51. Jonathan Hughes, *The Vital Few* (London: Oxford University Press, 1965), p. 50.

52. H. Larry Ingle, *First Among Friends: George Fox and the Creation of Quakerism* (New York: Oxford University Press, 1994), p. 48.

53. Ibid., p. 32.

54. Ibid., p. 34.

55. James, *Varieties of Religious Experience,* p. 25.

56. Ingle, *First Among Friends,* p. 44.

57. Ibid.

58. Winslow, *Master Roger Williams,* p. 278.

59. Ibid., p. 273.

60. Ibid., p. 311, n. 12.

61. Vernon Noble, *The Man in Leather Breeches: The Life and Times of George Fox* (New York: Philosophical Library, 1953), p. 222.

62. H. W. Brands, *The First American: The Life and Times of Benjamin Franklin* (New York: Anchor, 2000), p. 26.

63. Hughes, *The Vital Few,* p. 51.

64. Ibid., p. 24.

65. Johnson, *A History of the American People,* p. 66.

66. Ibid.

67. Brands, *First American,* p. 37.

III: Alexander Hamilton: Father of Our Economy

1. James Thomas Flexner, *The Young Hamilton: A Biography* (New York: Fordham University Press, 1997), pp. 4–5.

2. Richard Brookhiser, *Alexander Hamilton, American* (New York: Free Press, 1999), p. 8.

3. Ron Chernow, *Alexander Hamilton* (New York: Penguin, 2004), pp. 5, 53.

4. Arnold Rogow, *A Fatal Friendship: Alexander Hamilton and Aaron Burr* (New York: Hill and Wang, 1998), pp. 207–208.

5. Ibid., p. 206.

6. Robert Irving Warshow, *Alexander Hamilton: First American Business-man* (Garden City, N.Y.: Garden City Publishing, 1931), p. 3.

7. Ibid.

8. Adam Bellow, personal communication.

9. Flexner, *The Young Hamilton,* p. 21.

10. Ibid., p. 11.

11. Ibid., p. 21.

12. Forrest McDonald, *Alexander Hamilton: A Biography* (New York: Norton, 1979), p. 7.

13. Flexner, *The Young Hamilton,* p. 33.

14. Ibid., p. 34.

15. Ibid., p. 41.

16. Ibid., p. 34.

17. David Loth, *Alexander Hamilton: Portrait of a Prodigy* (New York: Carrick and Evans, 1939), p. 27.

18. Noemie Emery, *Alexander Hamilton: An Intimate Portrait* (New York: G. P. Putnam's Sons, 1982), p. 36.

19. Author's interview with Roger Kennedy, June 25, 2002.

20. Flexner, *The Young Hamilton,* p. 48.

21. Ibid.

22. McDonald, *Alexander Hamilton,* p. 10.

23. Flexner, *The Young Hamilton,* p. 56.

24. McDonald, *Alexander Hamilton,* p. 12.

25. Broadus Mitchell, *Alexander Hamilton,* vol. 1: *Youth to Maturity, 1755–1788* (New York: Macmillan, 1957), p. 31.

26. Brookhiser, *Alexander Hamilton,* p. 9.

27. Flexner, *The Young Hamilton,* p. 63.

28. Loth, *Alexander Hamilton,* p. 51.

29. Author's interview with Roger Kennedy, June 25, 2002.

30. Chernow, *Alexander Hamilton,* p. 5.

31. Frederick K. Goodwin and Kay Redfield Jamison, *Manic-Depressive Illness* (New York: Oxford University Press, 1990), pp. 352–356.

32. Flexner, *The Young Hamilton,* p. 72.

33. Ibid., p. 76.

34. Ibid., p. 78.

35. Chernow, *Alexander Hamilton,* p. 64.

36. Flexner, *The Young Hamilton,* p. 83.

37. Ibid.

38. Ibid., p. 90.

39. Ibid., p. 91.

40. Ibid., p. 132.

41. Ibid., p. 164.

42. Ibid., p. 133.

43. Author's interview with Roger Kennedy, June 25, 2002.

44. Emery, *Alexander Hamilton,* p. 42.

45. Ibid.

46. Adam Bellow, *In Praise of Nepotism* (New York: Doubleday, 2003), p. 286.

47. John Miller, *Alexander Hamilton: Portrait in Paradox* (New York: Harper & Brothers, 1959), p. 22.

48. Emery, *Alexander Hamilton,* p. 40.

49. Ibid., p. 39.

50. Ibid., p. 40.

51. Flexner, *The Young Hamilton,* p. 334.

52. Thomas Fleming, *Duel: Alexander Hamilton, Aaron Burr and the Future of America* (New York: Basic Books, 1999), p. 70.

53. Brookhiser, *Alexander Hamilton,* p. 187.

54. Flexner, *The Young Hamilton,* p. 226.

55. Ibid.

56. Ibid., p. 227.

57. Ibid.

58. Ibid., p. 231.

59. Ibid., p. 233.

60. Author's interview with Roger Kennedy, June 25, 2002.

61. Emery, *Alexander Hamilton*, p. 35.

62. Mitchell, *Alexander Hamilton*, vol. 1, p. 226.

63. Chernow, *Alexander Hamilton*, p. 5.

64. Flexner, *The Young Hamilton*, p. 335.

65. Emery, *Alexander Hamilton*, p. 50.

66. Warshow, *Alexander Hamilton*, p. 78.

67. Emery, *Alexander Hamilton*, p. 51.

68. Chernow, *Alexander Hamilton*, p. 128.

69. Warshow, *Alexander Hamilton*, pp. 85–86.

70. Peter McNamara, *Political Economy and Statesmanship: Smith, Hamilton, and the Foundation of the Commercial Republic* (Dekalb: Northern Illinois University Press, 1998), p. 97.

71. Warshow, *Alexander Hamilton*, p. 79.

72. Ibid., p. 80.

73. Flexner, *The Young Hamilton*, p. 340.

74. Ibid.

75. Ibid., p. 341.

76. Mitchell, *Alexander Hamilton*, vol. 1, p. 243.

77. Flexner, *The Young Hamilton*, p. 346.

78. Ibid., p. 347.

79. Ibid., p. 357.

80. Ibid.

81. Ibid., p. 359.

82. Mitchell, *Alexander Hamilton*, vol. 1, p. 257.

83. Flexner, *The Young Hamilton*, p. 365.

84. Ibid.

85. Brookhiser, *Alexander Hamilton*, p. 50.

86. Ibid.

87. Richard Morris, *Witness at Creation: Hamilton, Madison, Jay and the Constitution* (New York: Holt, Rinehart and Winston, 1985), p. 125.

88. Miller, *Alexander Hamilton*, p. 149.

89. Morris, *Witness at Creation*, p. 15.

90. McDonald, *Alexander Hamilton*, p. 92.

91. Ibid., p. 93.

92. Morris, *Witness at Creation,* p. 125.

93. Emery, *Alexander Hamilton,* p. 92.

94. Ibid., pp. 94–95.

95. Ibid., p. 94.

96. Ibid.

97. Miller, *Alexander Hamilton,* p. 157.

98. Broadus Mitchell, *Alexander Hamilton,* volume 2: *The National Adventure, 1788–1804* (New York: Macmillan, 1962), p. 390.

99. Emery, *Alexander Hamilton,* p. 95.

100. Ibid., p. 98.

101. Morris, *Witness at Creation,* p. 210.

102. Mitchell, *Alexander Hamilton,* vol. 2, p. 170.

103. Ibid.

104. Author's interview with Noemie Emery, June 28, 2002.

105. Emery, *Alexander Hamilton,* p. 101.

106. Miller, *Alexander Hamilton,* p. 177.

107. Ibid., p. 179.

108. Emery, *Alexander Hamilton,* p. 104.

109. Ibid., p. 103.

110. McDonald, *Alexander Hamilton,* p. 107.

111. Emery, *Alexander Hamilton,* p. 104.

112. Miller, *Alexander Hamilton,* p. 192.

113. Mitchell, *Alexander Hamilton,* vol. 2, p. 457.

114. Bellow, *In Praise of Nepotism,* p. 288.

115. Alexander Hamilton, *Writings,* ed. Joanne B. Freeman (New York: Columbia University Press, 1979), "The Federalist, No. 1," p. 173.

116. Alexander Hamilton, "Speech in the New York Ratifying Convention on Interests and Corruption," in *Writings,* ed. Joanne B. Freeman (New York: Columbia University Press, 1979), p. 497.

117. Emery, *Alexander Hamilton,* p. 119.

118. Miller, *Alexander Hamilton,* p. 213.

119. Warshow, *Alexander Hamilton,* p. 106.

120. Ibid., pp. 106–107.

121. John Steele Gordon, *Hamilton's Blessing: The Extraordinary Life and Times of Our National Debt* (New York: Walker and Company, 1997), p. 12.

122. Joseph Ellis, *Founding Brothers: The Revolutionary Generation* (New York: Alfred A. Knopf, 2001), p. 61.

123. David McCullough, *John Adams* (New York: Simon and Schuster, 2001), p. 424.

124. Robert Sobel, *Panic on Wall Street: A Classic History of America's Financial Disasters* (New York: Dutton, 1988), p. 10.

125. Ellis, *Founding Brothers,* p. 65.

126. Sobel, *Panic on Wall Street,* p. 18.

127. Richard K. Matthews, *The Radical Politics of Thomas Jefferson: A Revisionist View* (Lawrence: University of Kansas Press), p. 37.

128. McDonald, *Alexander Hamilton,* p. 175.

129. Chernow, *Alexander Hamilton,* p. 5.

130. Emery, *Alexander Hamilton,* p. 133.

131. Miller, *Alexander Hamilton,* p. 265.

132. Ibid., p. 270.

133. Sobel, *Panic,* p. 19.

134. Ibid.

135. Ibid., p. 28.

136. Ibid., p. 19.

137. Warshow, *Alexander Hamilton,* p. 139.

138. Matthews, *The Radical Politics of Thomas Jefferson,* p. 116.

139. Ibid., p. 110.

140. Ibid., p. 49.

141. Miller, *Alexander Hamilton,* p. 279.

142. James F. Simon, *What Kind of Nation: Thomas Jefferson, John Marshall and the Epic Struggle to Create a United States* (New York: Simon and Schuster, 2002), p. 29.

143. Fleming, *Duel,* p. 26.

144. Brookhiser, *Alexander Hamilton,* p. 141.

145. Author's interview with Thomas Fleming, June 28, 2002.

146. McDonald, *Alexander Hamilton,* p. 356.

147. Allan McLane Hamilton, *The Intimate Life of Alexander Hamilton* (New York: Scribner's and Sons, 1911), p. 210.

148. Emery, *Alexander Hamilton,* p. 212.

149. Miller, *Alexander Hamilton,* p. 549.

150. Hamilton, *Intimate Life,* p. 219.

151. Chernow, *Alexander Hamilton,* pp. 655, 690.

152. Fleming, *Duel,* p. 80.

153. Ibid., p. 81.

154. Roger Kennedy, *Burr, Hamilton and Jefferson: A Study in Character* (New York: Oxford University Press, 2000), p. 261.

155. Ibid., p. 381.

156. Ibid., p. 262.

157. Ibid., p. 395.

158. Ibid., p. 393.

159. Ibid., p. 230.

160. Miller, *Alexander Hamilton*, p. 569.

161. Fleming, *Duel*, p. 293.

162. Ellis, *Founding Brothers*, p. 32.

163. Ibid., p. 33.

164. Ibid.

165. Kennedy, *Burr, Hamilton and Jefferson*, p. 84.

166. Author's interview with Thomas Fleming, June 28, 2002.

167. Ibid.

168. Fleming, *Duel*, p. 315.

169. Ibid.

170. Ibid., p. 310.

171. Ibid.

172. Ibid.

173. Ellis, *Founding Brothers*, p. 23.

174. Ibid.

IV: Andrew Carnegie: Industrial Revolutionary

1. Joseph Frazier Wall, *Andrew Carnegie* (New York: Oxford University Press, 1970), p. 26.

2. Ibid., p. 32.

3. Ibid., p. 56.

4. Ibid.

5. Peter Krass, *Carnegie* (New York: Wiley, 2002), p. 10.

6. Ibid.

7. Andrew Carnegie, *Autobiography of Andrew Carnegie* (Boston: Houghton Mifflin, 1920), pp. 8–9.

8. Wall, *Andrew Carnegie*, p. 20.

9. Ibid., pp. 17–18.

10. Carnegie, *Autobiography*, p. 3.

11. Richard S. Tedlow, *Giants of Enterprise: Seven Business Innovators and the Empires They Built* (New York: HarperBusiness, 2001), p. 27.

12. Burton J. Hendrick, *The Life of Andrew Carnegie* (Garden City, N.Y.: Doubleday, Doran & Company, 1932), p. 89.

13. Wall, *Andrew Carnegie,* p. 32.

14. Krass, *Carnegie,* p. 70.

15. Carnegie, *Autobiography,* p. 16.

16. Ibid., p. 18.

17. Ibid., pp. 36–37.

18. Ibid., p. 12.

19. Ibid., p. 13.

20. Wall, *Andrew Carnegie,* p. 65.

21. Carnegie, *Autobiography,* p. 13.

22. Ibid., p. 25.

23. Wall, *Andrew Carnegie,* p. 71.

24. Ibid.

25. Ibid., p. 73.

26. Ibid., p. 74.

27. Carnegie, *Autobiography,* p. 30.

28. Harold C. Livesay, *Andrew Carnegie and the Rise of Big Business* (New York: HarperCollins, 1975), p. 18.

29. Carnegie, *Autobiography,* p. 34.

30. Ibid., p. 33.

31. Ibid., p. 34.

32. Ibid., p. 46.

33. Ibid., p. 39.

34. Krass, *Carnegie,* p. 35.

35. Carnegie, *Autobiography,* p. 55.

36. Krass, *Carnegie,* p. 36.

37. Carnegie, *Autobiography,* p. 56.

38. Ibid., pp. 56–57.

39. Ibid., pp. 62–63.

40. See Tedlow, *Giants of Enterprise,* pp. 29–32, for a further discussion of Carnegie as Oedipal victor.

41. Carnegie, *Autobiography,* p. 16.

42. Sigmund Freud, "A Childhood Recollection, Dichtung and Wahr-

heit" (1917), in *Complete Works of Sigmund Freud, Standard Edition,* vol. 17, ed. James Strachey and Anna Freud (London: Hogarth Press, 1964), p. 145.

43. Tedlow, *Giants of Enterprise,* p. 35.

44. Carnegie, *Autobiography,* p. 48.

45. Krass, *Carnegie,* p. 36.

46. Ibid.

47. Carnegie, *Autobiography,* p. 58.

48. Ibid., p. 59, n. 1.

49. Ibid., p. 61.

50. Wall, *Andrew Carnegie,* pp. 101–102.

51. Krass, *Carnegie,* p. 47.

52. Wall, *Andrew Carnegie,* p. 99.

53. Krass, *Carnegie,* p. 47.

54. Wall, *Andrew Carnegie,* p. 99.

55. Krass, *Carnegie,* p. 46.

56. Wall, *Andrew Carnegie,* p. 100.

57. Krass, *Carnegie,* p. 41.

58. H. W. Brands, *Masters of Enterprise* (New York: Free Press, 1999), p. 67.

59. Krass, *Carnegie,* p. 48.

60. Carnegie, *Autobiography,* p. 71.

61. Livesay, *Andrew Carnegie,* p. 37.

62. Carnegie, *Autobiography,* p. 70.

63. Ibid., p. 79.

64. Ibid.

65. Ibid., p. 80.

66. Krass, *Carnegie,* p. 52.

67. Andrew Carnegie, *Triumphant Democracy,* vol. 1 (Port Washington, N.Y.: Kennikat Press, 1886), pp. 297–298.

68. Krass, *Carnegie,* p. 205.

69. Tedlow, *Giants of Enterprise,* p. 36.

70. Krass, *Carnegie,* p. 60.

71. Livesay, *Andrew Carnegie,* p. 40.

72. Carnegie, *Autobiography,* p. 93.

73. Ibid., p. 99.

74. Ibid., p. 100.

75. Krass, *Carnegie,* p. 62.

76. Carnegie, *Autobiography,* p. 100.

77. Ibid., p. 82.

78. Krass, *Carnegie,* p. 64.

79. Ibid., p. 63.

80. Carnegie, *Autobiography,* pp. 101–102.

81. Krass, *Carnegie,* pp. 68–69.

82. Carnegie, *Autobiography,* p. 110.

83. Ibid., pp. 110–111.

84. Ibid., p. 112.

85. Livesay, *Andrew Carnegie,* p. 54.

86. Ibid., p. 46.

87. Krass, *Carnegie,* p. 111.

88. Ibid., p. 97.

89. Ibid., pp. 97–98.

90. Carnegie, *Autobiography,* p. 176.

91. Ibid., p. 170.

92. Krass, *Carnegie,* p. 116.

93. Ibid., p. 124.

94. Ibid., pp. 116–117.

95. Ibid., p. 168.

96. Krass, *Carnegie,* p. 157.

97. Wall, *Andrew Carnegie,* p. 297.

98. Ibid., p. 303.

99. Ibid., p. 318.

100. Carnegie, *Autobiography,* p. 173.

101. Livesay, *Andrew Carnegie,* p. 105.

102. Wall, *Andrew Carnegie,* p. 332.

103. Livesay, *Andrew Carnegie,* p. 105.

104. Krass, *Carnegie,* p. 383.

105. Carnegie, *Autobiography,* p. 187.

106. Krass, *Carnegie,* p. 178.

107. Carnegie, *Autobiography,* p. 135.

108. Ibid.

109. Ibid., pp. 182–183.

110. Livesay, *Andrew Carnegie,* p. 89.

111. Ibid.

112. Ibid., p. 116.

113. Jonathan Hughes, *The Vital Few* (London: Oxford University Press, 1965), p. 239.

114. Krass, *Carnegie,* p. 139.

115. Ibid., p. 142.

116. Livesay, *Andrew Carnegie,* p. 118.

117. Krass, *Carnegie,* p. 143.

118. Ibid., pp. 125–126.

119. Hughes, *The Vital Few,* p. 242.

120. Krass, *Carnegie,* p. 168.

121. Hughes, *The Vital Few,* p. 241.

122. Ibid.

123. Ibid.

124. Krass, *Carnegie,* p. 321.

125. Ibid.

126. Ibid.

127. Ibid., p. 243.

128. Ibid., p. 154.

129. Carnegie, *Autobiography,* p. 206.

130. Krass, *Carnegie,* p. 219.

131. Hughes, *The Vital Few,* p. 222.

132. Krass, *Carnegie,* p. 346.

133. Ibid., p. 174.

134. Carnegie, *Autobiography,* p. 230.

135. Krass, *Carnegie,* p. 283.

136. Ibid., pp. 285–286.

137. Carnegie, *Autobiography,* p. 232.

138. Ibid.

139. Krass, *Carnegie,* p. 292.

140. Tedlow, *Giants of Enterprise,* p. 14.

141. Krass, *Carnegie,* p. 411.

142. Ibid.

143. Tedlow, *Giants of Enterprise,* p. 64.

144. Hughes, *The Vital Few,* p. 226.

145. Krass, *Carnegie,* p. 161.

146. Ibid.

147. Ibid., p. 455.

148. Hughes, *The Vital Few,* p. 220.

149. Ibid.

150. Krass, *Carnegie*, p. 418.

151. Ibid.

152. Carnegie, *Autobiography*, p. 295.

153. Krass, *Carnegie*, p. 162.

154. Ibid., p. 251.

155. Ibid., p. 242.

156. Carnegie, *Autobiography*, p. 287.

157. Krass, *Carnegie*, p. 464.

158. Ibid., p. 432.

159. Ibid., p. 415.

160. Ibid., p. 186.

161. Ibid.

162. Wall, *Andrew Carnegie*, p. 386.

163. Ibid.

164. Krass, *Carnegie*, p. 194.

165. Ibid., p. 187.

166. Ibid., pp. 186–187.

167. Ibid., p. 194.

168. Ibid., p. 188.

169. Ibid., p. 199.

170. Hendrick, *The Life of Andrew Carnegie*, p. 259.

171. Krass, *Carnegie*, p. 200.

172. Hendrick, *The Life of Andrew Carnegie*, p. 259.

173. Carnegie, *Triumphant Democracy*, vol. 1, p. v.

174. Ibid., p. iii.

175. Ibid., p. vi.

176. Ibid., p. 1.

177. Carnegie, *Triumphant Democracy*, vol. 2, p. 283.

178. Carnegie, *Triumphant Democracy*, vol. 1, p. 40.

179. Hughes, *The Vital Few*, p. 220.

180. Carnegie, *Triumphant Democracy*, vol. 1, pp. 35–37.

181. Ibid., pp. 35–36.

182. Carnegie, *Triumphant Democracy*, vol. 2, p. 315.

183. Carnegie, *Triumphant Democracy*, vol. 1, p. 125.

184. Krass, *Carnegie*, p. 202.

185. Hendrick, *The Life of Andrew Carnegie*, p. 278.

186. Ibid., p. 277.

187. Ibid., pp. 277–278.

188. Krass, *Carnegie*, p. 329.

189. Hendrick, *The Life of Andrew Carnegie*, p. 422.

190. Krass, *Carnegie*, p. 371.

191. Ibid., p. 369.

192. Ibid.

193. Ibid.

194. Ibid., p. 270.

195. Ibid.

196. Ibid., p. 372.

197. Ibid., p. 272.

198. Ibid., pp. 459–460.

199. Ibid., p. 467.

200. Ibid., p. 489.

201. Ibid., p. 488.

202. Carnegie, *Autobiography*, p. 370.

203. Tedlow, *Giants of Enterprise*, p. 67.

204. Ibid., p. 68.

205. Carnegie, *Autobiography*, pp. 370–371.

206. Krass, *Carnegie*, p. 486.

207. Ibid., p. 488.

208. Ibid., p. 486.

209. Ibid., p. 489.

210. Ibid., pp. 492–494.

211. Ibid., p. 490.

212. Ibid., p. 496.

213. Ibid., p. 503.

214. Ibid., p. 469.

215. Ibid., p. 518.

216. Hughes, *The Vital Few*, p. 222.

217. Carnegie, *Autobiography*, p. v.

218. Ibid., p. 372.

219. Krass, *Carnegie*, p. 519.

220. Wall, *Andrew Carnegie*, p. 1030.

221. Ibid.

222. Krass, *Carnegie*, p. 531.

V: The Selznicks and the Mayers: A Hollywood Family

1. S. M. Dubnow, *History of the Jews in Russia and Poland from the Earliest Times to the Present Day* (Philadelphia: Jewish Publication Society of America, 1918), p. 278.

2. Ibid., p. 270.

3. Gerald Sorin, *A Time for Building: The Third Migration, 1880–1920* (Baltimore: Johns Hopkins University Press, 1992), p. 31.

4. Ibid., p. 41.

5. Ibid.

6. Michael Freedland, *The Warner Brothers* (London: Harrap, 1983), p. 6.

7. Ibid.

8. Sorin, *A Time for Building*, p. 40.

9. All quotes from Daniel Mayer Selznick are from my interview with him on November 14, 2003, unless otherwise specified.

10. Bob Thomas, *Selznick* (New York: Pocket Books, 1972), p. 11.

11. David Thomson, *Showman: The Life of David O. Selznick* (New York: Knopf, 1992), p. 23.

12. Thomas, *Selznick*, p. 13.

13. Ibid., p. 14.

14. Thomson, *Showman*, p. 22.

15. Thomas, *Selznick*, p. 17.

16. Norman Zierold, *The Moguls* (New York: Coward-McCann, 1969), p. 24.

17. Thomson, *Showman*, p. 24.

18. Thomas, *Selznick*, p. 3.

19. Ibid., p. 49.

20. Irene Mayer Selznick, *A Private View* (New York: Knopf, 1982), p. 96.

21. Ibid.

22. Budd Schulberg, *Moving Pictures: Memoirs of a Hollywood Prince* (New York: Stein and Day, 1981), p. 11.

23. Zierold, *The Moguls*, back cover.

24. Ibid., p. 151.

25. Samuel Marx, *Mayer and Thalberg: The Make-Believe Saints* (New York: Warner Books, 1975), p. 41.

26. Bosley Crowther, *Hollywood Rajah: The Life and Times of Louis B. Mayer* (New York: Holt, Rinehart and Winston, 1960), p. 254.

27. Charles Higham, *Merchant of Dreams: Louis B. Mayer, M.G.M. and the Secret of Hollywood* (New York: Laurel, 1993), p. 45.

28. Crowther, *Hollywood Rajah,* p. 214.

29. Neal Gabler, *An Empire of Their Own: How the Jews Invented Hollywood* (New York: Anchor, 1988), p. 111.

30. Ibid., p. 109.

31. Canadian Broadcast Network, "The Canadians: Louis B. Mayer."

32. Zierold, *The Moguls,* p. 290.

33. CBC, "The Canadians."

34. Ibid.

35. Joel Greenberg, "Casey Robinson: Master Adaptor," in *Backstory: Interviews with Screen Writers of Hollywood's Golden Age,* ed. Pat McGilligan (Berkeley: University of California Press, 1986), p. 296.

36. Schulberg, *Moving Pictures,* p. 122.

37. Ibid.

38. Marx, *Mayer and Thalberg,* p. 51.

39. Gabler, *An Empire of Their Own,* p. 80.

40. Selznick, *A Private View,* p. 8.

41. Gabler, *An Empire of Their Own,* pp. 88–89.

42. Ibid., p. 89.

43. Zierold, *The Moguls,* p. 318.

44. Higham, *Merchant of Dreams,* p. 120.

45. Zierold, *The Moguls,* p. 318.

46. Ibid.

47. Selznick, *A Private View,* p. 27.

48. CBC, "The Canadians."

49. Selznick, *A Private View,* p. 27.

50. Robert Sklar, *Movie-Made America: A Cultural History of American Movies* (New York: Vintage, 1994), p. 215.

51. Ibid., p. 219.

52. Ibid., p. 227.

53. Ibid., p. 215.

54. Thomson, *Showman,* p. 10.

55. Ibid., p. 60.

56. Ibid., p. 10.

57. Thomas, *Selznick,* p. 36.

58. Ibid.

59. Ibid., p. 41.

60. Zierold, *The Moguls,* p. 35.

61. Ibid., p. 40.

62. Thomas, *Selznick,* p. 205.

63. Thomson, *Showman,* p. 163.

64. Ibid., p. 274.

65. Ibid., p. 275.

66. Thomas, *Selznick,* p. 204.

67. Thomson, *Showman,* p. 8.

68. Ibid., p. 30.

69. Thomas, *Selznick,* p. 34.

70. Zierold, *The Moguls,* p. 42.

71. Selznick, *A Private View,* p. 106.

72. Thomas, *Selznick,* p. 35.

73. Selznick, *A Private View,* p. 21.

74. Ibid., p. 20.

75. Ibid., p. 96.

76. Ibid., p. 97.

77. Ibid., pp. 98–99.

78. Ibid., p. 109.

79. Thomson, *Showman,* p. 84.

80. Thomas, *Selznick,* pp. 41–42.

81. Selznick, *A Private View,* pp. 113–114.

82. Ibid., p. 120.

83. Ibid., p. 121.

84. Ibid., p. 135.

85. Thomas, *Selznick,* p. 48.

86. Selznick, *A Private View,* p. 149.

87. Ibid., p. 150.

88. Thomson, *Showman,* p. 120.

89. Selznick, *A Private View,* p. 150.

90. Ibid., p. 152.

91. Ibid., p. 154.

92. Ibid., p. 155.

93. Ibid., p. 156.

94. Thomson, *Showman,* p. 131.

95. Ibid., p. 129.

96. Selznick, *A Private View,* p. 147.

97. Ibid., p. 165.

98. Ibid.

99. Ibid., p. 148.

100. Zierold, *The Moguls,* p. 66.

101. Selznick, *A Private View,* pp. 165, 167.

102. Thomson, *Showman,* p. 162.

103. Selznick, *A Private View,* p. 167.

104. Ibid., p. 174.

105. Ibid.

106. Thomson, *Showman,* p. 142.

107. Ibid., pp. 148–149.

108. Ibid., p. 149.

109. Selznick, *A Private View,* p. 187.

110. Thomson, *Showman,* p. 156.

111. Selznick, *A Private View,* p. 201.

112. Thomson, *Showman,* p. 146.

113. Author's interview with Robert Post, July 9, 2003; Robert Post, Susan R. B. Weiss, and Agu Pert, "Animal Models of Mania," in *The Mesolimbic Dopamine System: From Motivation to Action,* ed. Paul Wilner and J. Scheel-Kruger (New York: Wiley, 1991), pp. 443–472. Also see Frank H. Gawin and Everett H. Ellinwood, "Consequences and Correlates of Cocaine Abuse: Clinical Phenomenology," in *Cocaine in the Brain,* ed. Nora D. Volkow and Alan Swan (New Brunswick, N.J.: Rutgers University Press, 1990).

114. Selznick, *A Private View,* p. 217.

115. Thomas, *Selznick,* pp. 146–147.

116. Thomson, *Showman,* p. 292.

117. Ibid., pp. 293–294.

118. Ibid., p. 294.

119. Aljean Harmetz, *On the Road to Tara: The Making of* Gone With the Wind (New York: Harry N. Abrams, 1996), p. 52.

120. Thomson, *Showman,* p. 296.

121. Ibid., p. 298.

122. Harmetz, *On the Road to Tara,* p. 30.

123. Thomson, *Showman,* p. 299.

124. Ibid., p. 298.

125. Thomas, *Selznick,* p. 160.

126. Selznick, *A Private View*, p. 227.

127. Ibid., pp. 227–228.

128. Judy Cameron and Paul J. Christman, *The Art of* Gone With the Wind (New York: Prentice Hall, 1989), p. 16.

129. Selznick, *A Private View*, p. 235.

130. Thomson, *Showman*, pp. 375–376.

131. Selznick, *A Private View*, p. 235.

132. Ibid.

133. Ibid., p. 236.

134. Ibid.

135. Thomson, *Showman*, p. 465.

136. Ibid., p. 482.

137. CBC, "The Canadians."

138. David Brooks, *On Paradise Drive: How We Live Now (and Always Have) in the Future Tense* (New York: Simon and Schuster, 2004), p. 80.

VI: Craig Venter: Playing God

1. Richard Preston, "The Genome Warrior: Craig Venter Has Grabbed the Lead in the Quest for Biology's Holy Grail," *The New Yorker,* June 12, 2000, p. 66.

2. James Shreeve, *The Genome War: How Craig Venter Tried to Capture the Code of Life and Save the World* (New York: Alfred A. Knopf, 2004), p. 217.

3. All quotes from Craig Venter are from my interview with him on February 25, 2004, unless otherwise specified.

4. John Carey, "We Are Now Starting the Century of Biology," *Business Week,* August 31, 1998, p. 86.

5. Shreeve, *The Genome War,* p. 69.

6. Ibid., p. 129.

7. Ibid., p. 71.

8. Ingrid Wickelgren, *The Gene Masters: How a Breed of Scientific Entrepreneurs Raced for the Biggest Prize in Biology* (New York: Times Books, 2002), p. 20.

9. Shreeve, *The Genome War,* p. 359.

10. Ibid., p. 74.

11. Ibid., p. 75.

12. Ibid.

13. Ibid.

14. Ibid., p. 77.

15. Author's interview with Hamilton Smith, February 5, 2004.

16. Shreeve, *The Genome War,* p. 92.

17. Ibid., p. 79.

18. Wickelgren, *The Gene Masters,* p. 27.

19. Author's interview with Nicholas Wade, January 28, 2004.

20. John Sulston and Georgina Ferry, *The Common Thread: A Story of Science, Politics, Ethics and the Human Genome* (Washington, D.C.: Joseph Henry Press, 1992), p. 106.

21. Victor K. McElheny, *Watson and DNA: Making a Scientific Revolution* (Cambridge, Mass.: Perseus Books, 2003), p. 267.

22. Ibid., p. 265.

23. Preston, "The Genome Warrior," p. 72.

24. Shreeve, *The Genome War,* p. 134.

25. Sulston and Ferry, *The Common Thread,* p. 105.

26. Preston, "The Genome Warrior," p. 72.

27. Wickelgren, *The Gene Masters,* p. 87.

28. Shreeve, *The Genome War,* p. 67.

29. Author's interview with James Shreeve, February 5, 2004.

30. Wickelgren, *The Gene Masters,* p. 89.

31. Shreeve, *The Genome War,* p. 79.

32. Preston, "The Genome Warrior," p. 73.

33. Wickelgren, *The Gene Masters,* p. 91.

34. Shreeve, *The Genome War,* p. 14.

35. Nicholas Wade, "Scientist's Plan: Map All the DNA Within Three Years," *The New York Times,* May 10, 1998, p. A1.

36. Ed Regis, "Other People's Molecules," *The New York Times,* March 16, 2003, pp. 7–27.

37. Shreeve, *The Genome War,* p. 51.

38. Preston, "The Genome Warrior," p. 74.

39. Sulston and Ferry, *The Common Thread,* p. 154.

40. Ibid., pp. 154–155.

41. Ibid., p. 149.

42. Shreeve, *The Genome War,* p. 53.

43. Sulston and Ferry, *The Common Thread,* p. 160.

44. Ibid., p. 167.

45. Ibid., p. 151.

46. Ibid., p. 166.

47. Ibid., p. 167.

48. Ibid.

49. Ibid.

50. Ibid.

51. Shreeve, *The Genome War*, p. 19.

52. Ibid., p. 189.

53. Ibid., p. 44.

54. Wickelgren, *The Gene Masters*, p. 41.

55. Sulston and Ferry, *The Common Thread*, p. 164.

56. Ibid., p. 170.

57. Nicholas Wade, "One of 2 Teams in Genome-Map Race Sets an Earlier Deadline," *The New York Times*, March 16, 1999, p. A21.

58. Nicholas Wade, *Life Script: How the Human Genome Discoveries Will Transform Medicine and Enhance Your Health* (New York: Touchstone, 2001), p. 49.

59. Preston, "The Genome Warrior," p. 67.

60. Wade, *Life Script*, p. 33.

61. Shreeve, *The Genome War*, p. 236.

62. Ibid., pp. 236–237.

63. Ibid., p. 237.

64. Ibid., p. 139.

65. Author's interview with Heather Kowalski, February 25, 2004.

66. R. House and J. M. Howell, "Personality and Charismatic Leadership," *Leadership Quarterly* 3 (1992), pp. 81–108.

67. Jay Conger, *The Charismatic Leader* (San Francisco: Jossey-Bass, 1989).

68. Author's interview with Jay Conger, May 3, 2002.

69. See also Michael Maccoby, "Narcissistic Leaders: The Incredible Pros, the Inevitable Cons," *Harvard Business Review*, January–February 2000, p. 68.

70. Frederick K. Goodwin and Kay Redfield Jamison, *Manic-Depressive Illness* (New York: Oxford University Press, 1990), pp. 332–368.

71. Ronald R. Fieve, *Moodswing* (New York: Bantam, 1997), p. 171.

72. Justin Gillis, "A Gene Dream: Using One of the World's Most Powerful Computer Clusters, Celera Genomics Plans to Write 'The Book of Life'— and Make It a Bestseller," *The Washington Post*, September 27, 1999, p. F18.

73. Preston, "The Genome Warrior," p. 69.

74. Wade, *Life Script*, p. 59.

75. Nicholas Wade, "On the Road to the Genome, a Milestone in the Fruitfly," *The New York Times,* March 24, 2000, p. A1.

76. Shreeve, *The Genome War,* p. 285.

77. Wade, *Life Script,* p. 51.

78. Shreeve, *The Genome War,* p. 327.

79. Wade, *Life Script,* pp. 13–14.

80. Ibid., p. 16.

81. Ibid., pp. 15–16.

82. Shreeve, *The Genome War,* p. 4.

83. Sulston and Ferry, *The Common Thread,* p. 223.

84. "The Genetic Starting Line," editorial, *The Economist,* July 1, 2000, p. 42.

85. Wade, *Life Script,* p. 62.

86. Ibid., p. 14.

87. Justin Gillis, "The Gene Map and Celera's Detour: Success of Md. Firm's Strategy Shift Debated," *The Washington Post,* February 12, 2001, p. E01.

88. Shreeve, *The Genome War,* p. 292.

89. Wade, *Life Script,* p. 56.

90. Ibid., p. 57.

91. Sulston and Ferry, *The Common Thread,* p. 219.

92. Nicholas Wade, "Genome Feud Heats Up as Academic Team Accuses Commercial Rival of Faulty Work," *The New York Times,* May 2, 2001, p. A15.

93. Gillis, "The Gene Map and Celera's Detour."

94. Nicholas Wade, "Race Is On to Decode the Genome of the Mouse," *The New York Times,* October 6, 2000, p. A22.

95. Ibid.

96. Wade, *Life Script,* p. 54.

97. Nicholas Wade, "Genetic Sequence of Mouse Is Decoded," *The New York Times,* February 13, 2001, p. F5.

98. Shreeve, *The Genome War,* p. 6.

99. Ibid., p. 266.

100. Nicholas Wade, "Mouse Genome Is New Battleground for Project Rivals," *The New York Times,* May 7, 2002, p. F2.

101. Nicholas Wade, "Superior Data on Mice DNA Is Being Cited as Attraction," *The New York Times,* July 10, 2001, p. A13.

102. Wade, "Mouse Genome Is New Battleground."

103. Ibid.

104. Ibid.

105. Nicholas Wade, "Thrown Aside, Genome Pioneer Plots Rebound," *The New York Times,* April 30, 2002, p. F1.

106. McElheny, *Watson and DNA,* p. 267.

107. Rick Weiss, "Scientist Confirms Use of Own DNA in Project; Celera Effort Included Founder's Genes," *The Washington Post,* April 28, 2002, p. A13.

108. Arthur Caplan, "His Genes, Our Genome," *The New York Times,* May 3, 2002, p. A23.

109. Ibid.

110. Wade, "Thrown Aside."

111. Nicholas Wade, "Scientist Reveals Secret of Genome: It's His," *The New York Times,* April 27, 2002, p. A1.

112. Robin McKie, "Human Genome Is Mine, Says 'Darth Vader' of Genetics," *The Observer,* April 28, 2002, p. 3.

113. Shreeve, *The Genome War,* p. 360.

114. Ibid., p. 85.

115. Ibid., p. 86.

116. Wickelgren, *The Gene Masters,* p. 71.

117. Shreeve, *The Genome War,* p. 87.

118. Ibid.

119. Wickelgren, *The Gene Masters,* p. 71.

120. Ibid., p. 70.

121. Shreeve, *The Genome War,* p. 108.

122. Ibid., p. 107.

123. Ibid.

124. Ibid., p. 90.

125. Ibid., p. 235.

126. Ibid., pp. 252–253.

127. Andrew Pollack, "Finding Gold in Scientific Pay Dirt," *The New York Times,* June 28, 2000, p. C1.

128. Preston, "The Genome Warrior," p. 70.

129. Ibid., p. 70.

130. Shreeve, *The Genome War,* p. 307.

131. Preston, "The Genome Warrior," p. 79.

132. Shreeve, *The Genome War,* p. 324.

133. Ibid., p. 368.

134. Ibid., p. 267.

135. Ibid., p. 360.

136. Wade, *Life Script*, p. 120.

137. Ibid., p. 162.

138. Ibid.

139. Shreeve, *The Genome War*, p. 373.

140. Ibid., p. 374.

141. Rick Weiss, "Researchers Create Virus in Record Time; Organism Not Dangerous to Humans," *The Washington Post*, November 14, 2003, p. A10.

142. Gareth Cook, "Fast Method to Build Genes Found; Complete Biological Systems Envisioned," *The Boston Globe*, November 14, 2003, p. A1.

143. Weiss, "Researchers Create Virus."

144. Cook, "Fast Method."

145. Michael Barbaro, "Md. Energy Project Gets Infusion; U.S. Boosts Funds for Effort to Find Alternative Power Sources," *The Washington Post*, April 25, 2003, p. E5.

146. Cook, "Fast Method."

147. Ibid.

148. Weiss, "Researchers Create Virus."

149. Hamilton O. Smith, Clyde A. Hutchinson, and Cynthia Pfannkoch, "Generating a Synthetic Genome by Shole Genome Assembly: F X174 Bacteriophage from Synthetic Oligonucleotides," *Proceedings of the National Academy of Sciences* 100 (December 23, 2003), pp. 15440–15445.

150. Anjana Ahuja, "Genome Pioneer Craig Venter Has Taken the First Step Towards Creating a Living Organism. While He Sees Benefits, Critics Are Fearful," *The Times* (London), November 20, 2003, pp. 2–12.

151. Keay Davidson, "Geneticists Build Viral Genome in 2 Weeks; Researchers Call It Good News for Energy, Waste," *The San Francisco Chronicle*, November 14, 2003, p. A7.

152. Ahuja, "Genome Pioneer Craig Venter."

Conclusion: Hypomania Past and Future

1. Author's interview with Frans de Waal, September 5, 2002.

2. Richard Wrangham and Dale Peterson, *Demonic Males: Apes and the Origins of Human Violence* (New York: Mariner, 1996), p. 14.

3. Ibid., p. 17.

4. Author's interview with Richard Wrangham, September 3, 2002.

5. Author's interview with John Mitani, September 7, 2002.

6. Roger C. Bland, "Epidemiology of Affective Disorders: A Review," *Canadian Journal of Psychiatry* 42 (1997), pp. 367–377; A. B. Negrao, "Mood Disorders Across the Continents," *Molecular Psychiatry* 2, pp. 439–441; Myrna Weissman, Roger Bland, Glorisa Canino, Carlo Faravelli, Steven Greenwald, Hai-Gwo Hwu, Peter Joyce, Elie Karam, Chung-Kyoon Lee, Joseph Lellouch, Jean Pierre Lepine, Stephen Newman, Maritza Rubio-Stipec, Elisabeth Wells, Priya Wickramaratne, Hans-Ulrich Wittchen, and Eng-Kung Teh, "Cross-National Epidemiology of Major Depression and Bipolar Disorder," *The Journal of the American Medical Association* 276 (July 24–31, 1996), pp. 293–299.

7. David Brooks, "The Americano Dream," *The New York Times*, February 24, 2004, p. A27.

Bibliography

Akiskal, Hagop, Marc Bourgeois, Jules Angst, Robert Post, Hans-Jurgen Moller, and Robert Hirschfeld. "Re-evaluating the Prevalence of and Diagnostic Composition within the Broad Clinical Spectrum of Bipolar Disorders." *Journal of Affective Disorders* 59 (2000): s5–s30.

American Psychiatric Association. *Diagnostic and Statistical Manual,* 4th ed. Washington, D.C.: American Psychiatric Association, 1994.

Angst, Jules. "The Emerging Epidemiology of Hypomania and Bipolar II Disorder." *Journal of Affective Disorders* 50 (1998): 143–151.

Aronson, David, ed. *Research Perspectives on Migration,* vol. 1, no. 2. Washington, D.C.: Published as a joint program of the International Migration Policy Program and the Carnegie Endowment for International Peace and the Urban Institute, 1997.

Ashbrook, Tom. *The Leap: A Memoir of Love and Madness in the Internet Gold Rush.* Boston: Houghton Mifflin, 2000.

Barbour, Hugh, and J. William Frost. *The Quakers.* New York: Greenwood Press, 1988.

Baritz, Loren. *City on a Hill.* New York: Wiley, 1964.

Bellow, Adam. *In Praise of Nepotism.* New York: Doubleday, 2003.

Bland, Roger C. "Epidemiology of Affective Disorders: A Review." *Canadian Journal of Psychiatry* 42 (1997): 367–377.

Brands, H. W. *The First American: The Life and Times of Benjamin Franklin.* New York: Anchor, 2000.

———. *Masters of Enterprise.* New York: Free Press, 1999.

Brookhiser, Richard. *Alexander Hamilton, American.* New York: Free Press, 1999.

Brooks, David. *On Paradise Drive: How We Live Now (and Always Have) in the Future Tense.* New York: Simon and Schuster, 2004.

333

Cameron, Judy, and Paul J. Christman. *The Art of* Gone With the Wind. New York: Prentice Hall, 1989.

Canadian Broadcast Network. "The Canadians: Louis B. Mayer." December 8, 1999.

Carnegie, Andrew. *Autobiography of Andrew Carnegie.* Boston: Houghton Mifflin, 1920.

———. *Triumphant Democracy,* vol. 1. Port Washington, N.Y.: Kennikat Press, 1886.

———. *Triumphant Democracy,* vol. 2. Port Washington, N.Y.: Kennikat Press, 1886.

Carroll, Peter N. *Puritanism and the Wilderness.* New York: Columbia University Press, 1969.

Chancellor, Edward. *Devil Take the Hindmost: A History of Financial Speculation.* New York: Plume, 2000.

Chernow, Ron. *Alexander Hamilton.* New York: Penguin, 2004.

Collis, John Stewart. *Christopher Columbus.* New York: Stein and Day, 1977.

Conger, Jay. *The Charismatic Leader.* San Francisco: Jossey-Bass, 1989.

Coryell, William, Jean Endicott, Martin Keller, Nancy Andreasen, William Grove, Robert Hirschfeld, and William Scheftner. "Bipolar Affective Disorder and High Achievement: A Familial Association." *Psychiatry* 146:8, (1989): 983–988.

Crowther, Bosley. *Hollywood Rajah: The Life and Times of Louis B. Mayer.* New York: Holt, Rinehart and Winston, 1960.

Dubnow, S. M. *History of the Jews in Russia and Poland from the Earliest Times to the Present Day.* Philadelphia: Jewish Publication Society of America, 1918.

Eisemann, M. "Social Class and Social Mobility in Depressed Patients." *Acta Psychiatrica Scandinavica* 73 (1986): 399–402.

Emery, Noemie. *Alexander Hamilton: An Intimate Portrait.* New York: G. P. Putnam's Sons, 1982.

Fernández-Armesto, Felipe. *Columbus.* New York: Oxford University Press, 1991.

Fieve, Ronald R. *Moodswing.* New York: Bantam, 1997.

Fleming, Thomas. *Duel: Alexander Hamilton, Aaron Burr and the Future of America.* New York: Basic Books, 1999.

Flexner, James Thomas. *The Young Hamilton: A Biography.* New York: Fordham University Press, 1997.

Freedland, Michael. *The Warner Brothers.* London: Harrap, 1983.

Freud, Sigmund. "A Childhood Recollection, Dichtung and Wahrheit," in James Strachey and Anna Freud, *Complete Works of Sigmund Freud, Standard Edition,* vol. 17. London: Hogarth Press, 1964.

Gabler, Neal. *An Empire of Their Own: How the Jews Invented Hollywood.* New York: Anchor, 1988.

Gawin, Frank H., and Everett H. Ellinwood. "Consequences and Correlates of Cocaine Abuse: Clinical Phenomenology." In *Cocaine in the Brain,* edited by Nora D. Volkow and Alan Swan. New Brunswick, NJ: Rutgers University Press, 1990.

Goodwin, Frederick K., and Kay Redfield Jamison. *Manic-Depressive Illness.* New York: Oxford University Press, 1990.

Gordon, John Steele. *Hamilton's Blessing: The Extraordinary Life and Times of Our National Debt.* New York: Walker and Company, 1997.

Granzotto, Gianni. *Christopher Columbus: The Dream and the Obsession.* London: Grafton, 1988.

Greene, Theodore P., ed. *Roger Williams and the Massachusetts Magistrates.* Boston: Heath, 1964.

Hamilton, Alexander. *Writings.* Edited by Joanne B. Freeman. New York: Columbia University Press, 1979.

Hamilton, Allan McLane. *The Intimate Life of Alexander Hamilton.* New York: Scribner's and Sons, 1911.

Harmetz, Aljean. *On the Road to Tara: The Making of* Gone With the Wind. New York: Harry N. Abrams, 1996.

Heimert, Alan, and Andrew Delbanco, eds. *The Puritans in America: A Narrative Anthology.* Cambridge, Mass: Harvard University Press, 1985.

Hendrick, Burton J. *The Life of Andrew Carnegie.* Garden City, N.Y.: Doubleday, Doran & Company, 1932.

Higham, Charles. *Merchant of Dreams: Louis B. Mayer, M.G.M. and the Secret of Hollywood.* New York: Laurel, 1993.

Hughes, Jonathan. *The Vital Few.* London: Oxford University Press, 1965.

Ingle, H. Larry. *First Among Friends: George Fox and the Creation of Quakerism.* New York: Oxford University Press, 1994.

James, William. *The Varieties of Religious Experience: A Study in Human Nature.* New York: Mentor, 1958.

Jaspers, James. *Restless Nation: Starting Over in America.* Chicago: University of Chicago Press, 2000.

Kennedy, Roger. *Burr, Hamilton and Jefferson: A Study in Character*. New York: Oxford University Press, 2000.

Krakauer, Jon. *Under the Banner of Heaven: A Story of Violent Faith*. New York: Anchor Books, 2003.

Krass, Peter. *Carnegie*. New York: Wiley, 2002.

Kulikoff, Allan. *From British Peasants to Colonial American Farmers*. Chapel Hill: University of North Carolina Press, 2000.

LaFantasie, Glenn W., ed. *The Correspondence of Roger Williams,* vol. 1. Providence, R.I.: Brown University Press, 1988.

Larner, John. "The Certainty of Columbus: Some Recent Studies." *History* 73 (1988): 3–23.

Ledeen, Michael A. *Tocqueville on American Character*. New York: Truman Talley, 2000.

Lewis, Michael. *The New New Thing*. New York: Norton, 2000.

Livesay, Harold C. *Andrew Carnegie and the Rise of Big Business*. New York: HarperCollins, 1975.

Locke, Edwin A. *The Prime Movers: Traits of Great Wealth Creators*. New York: Amacom, 2000.

Loth, David. *Alexander Hamilton: Portrait of a Prodigy*. New York: Carrick & Evans, 1939.

Salvador de Madariaga, *Christopher Columbus: Being the Life of the Very Magnificent Lord, Don Cristóbal Colón*. New York: Macmillan, 1940.

Maccoby, Michael. "Narcissistic Leaders: The Incredible Pros, the Inevitable Cons." *Harvard Business Review* (January/February 2000): 68–79.

Mahn-Lot, Marianne. *Columbus*. New York: Grove, 1961.

Martin, John Frederick. *Profits in the Promised Land: Entrepreneurship and the Founding of New England Towns in the Seventeenth Century*. Chapel Hill: University of North Carolina Press, 1991.

Marx, Samuel. *Mayer and Thalberg: The Make-Believe Saints*. New York: Warner Books.

Matthews, Richard K. *The Radical Politics of Thomas Jefferson: A Revisionist View*. Lawrence: University of Kansas Press, 1984.

McCullough, David. *John Adams*. New York: Simon and Schuster, 2001.

McDonald, Forrest. *Alexander Hamilton: A Biography*. New York: W. W. Norton, 1979.

McElheny, Victor K. *Watson and DNA: Making a Scientific Revolution*. Cambridge, Mass.: Perseus Books, 2003.

McGilligan, Pat, ed. *Backstory: Interviews with Screen Writers of Hollywood's Golden Age.* Berkeley: University of California Press, 1986.

McNamara, Peter. *Political Economy and Statesmanship: Smith, Hamilton, and the Foundation of the Commercial Republic.* Dekalb: Northern Illinois University Press, 1998.

Miller, John. *Alexander Hamilton: Portrait in Paradox.* New York: Harper & Brothers, 1959.

Miller, Perry. *Orthodoxy in Massachusetts, 1630–1650.* Gloucester, Mass.: Peter Smith, 1933.

———. *Roger Williams: His Contribution to the American Tradition.* New York: Bobbs-Merrill, 1953.

Mitchell, Broadus. *Alexander Hamilton.* Vol. 1: *Youth to Maturity, 1755–1788.* New York: Macmillan, 1957.

———. *Alexander Hamilton.* Vol. 2: *The National Adventure, 1788–1804.* New York: Macmillan, 1962.

Morgan, Edmund. *The Puritan Dilemma: The Story of John Winthrop.* New York: Little, Brown, 1958.

———. *Roger Williams: The Church and the State.* New York: Harcourt and Brace, 1967.

———. *Visible Saints: The History of a Puritan Idea.* New York: New York University Press, 1963.

Morris, Richard. *Witness at Creation: Hamilton, Madison, Jay and the Constitution.* New York: Holt, Rinehart and Winston, 1985.

Morison, Samuel Eliot. *Admiral of the Ocean Sea: A Life of Christopher Columbus.* Boston: Little, Brown, 1942.

Nader, Helen, trans. and ed. *The Book of Privileges to Christopher Columbus by King Ferdinand and Queen Isabella.* Berkeley: University of California Press, 1996.

Negrao, A. B. "Mood Disorders across the Continents." *Molecular Psychiatry* 2: 439–441.

Noble, Vernon. *The Man in Leather Breeches: The Life and Times of George Fox.* New York: Philosophical Library, 1953.

Phelan, John Leddy. *The Millennial Kingdom of the Franciscans in the New World.* Berkeley: University of California Press, 1970.

Post, Robert, Susan R. B. Weiss, and Agu Pert. "Animal Models of Mania." In *The Mesolimbic Dopamine System: From Motivation to Action,* edited by Paul Wilner and J. Scheel-Kruger. New York: Wiley, 1991.

Potash, James, and J. Raymond DePaulo, Jr. "Searching High and Low: A Review of the Genetics of Bipolar Disorder." *Bipolar Disorders* 2 (2000): 8–26.

Potash, James, Virginia Willour, Yen-Feng Chiu, Sylvia Simpson, Dean MacKinnon, Godfrey Pearlson, J. Raymond DePaulo, Jr., and Melvin McInnis. "The Familial Aggregation of Psychotic Symptoms in Bipolar Pedigree." *American Journal of Psychiatry* 158 (2001): 1258–1264.

Preston, Richard. "The Genome Warrior; Craig Venter Has Grabbed the Lead in the Quest for Biology's Holy Grail." *The New Yorker,* June 12, 2000.

Richards, Ruth, and Dennis Kinney. "Mood Swings and Creativity." *Creativity Research Journal* 3 (1990): 202–217.

Rogow, Arnold. *A Fatal Friendship: Alexander Hamilton and Aaron Burr.* New York: Hill and Wang, 1998.

Rouillon. F. "Epidémiologie du Trouble Bipolaire." *L'Encéphale* 23 (1997): 7–11.

Schor, Juliet B. *The Overworked American: The Unexpected Decline of Leisure.* New York: Basic Books, 1992.

Schulberg, Budd. *Moving Pictures: Memoirs of a Hollywood Prince.* New York: Stein and Day, 1981.

Schweninger, Lee. *John Winthrop.* Boston: Twayne, 1990.

Selznick, Irene Mayer. *A Private View.* New York: Knopf, 1982.

Shreeve, James. *The Genome War: How Craig Venter Tried to Capture the Code of Life and Save the World.* New York: Alfred A. Knopf, 2004.

Simpson, Sylvia, Susan Folstein, Deborah Meyers, Francis McMahon, Diane Brusco, and Raymond DePaulo, Jr. "Bipolar II: The Most Common Bipolar Phenotype?" *American Journal of Psychiatry* 150, no. 6 (1993): 901–903.

Sklar, Robert. *Movie-Made America: A Cultural History of American Movies.* New York: Vintage, 1994.

Smith, Hamilton O., Clyde A. Hutchinson, and Cynthia Pfannkoch. "Generating a Synthetic Genome by Shole Genome Assembly: $\Phi\chi 174$ Bacteriophage from Synthetic Oligonucleotides." *Proceedings of the National Academy of Science* 100 (December 23, 2003): 15440–15445.

Sobel, Robert. *Panic on Wall Street: A Classic History of America's Financial Disasters.* New York: Dutton, 1988.

Sorin, Gerald. *A Time for Building: The Third Migration, 1880–1920.* Baltimore: Johns Hopkins University Press, 1992.

Strachey, James, and Anna Freud. *Complete Works of Sigmund Freud, Standard Edition,* vol. 17. London: Hogarth Press, 1964.

Sulston, John, and Georgina Ferry. *The Common Thread: A Story of Science, Politics, Ethics and the Human Genome.* Washington, D.C.: Joseph Henry Press, 1992.

Taviani, Paolo Emilio. *Columbus: The Great Adventure.* New York: Orion, 1991.

Tedlow, Richard. *Giants of Enterprise: Seven Business Innovators and the Empires They Built.* New York: HarperBusiness, 2001.

Thomas, Bob. *Selznick.* New York: Pocket Books, 1972.

Thomson, David. *Showman: The Life of David O. Selznick.* New York: Knopf, 1992.

Tocqueville, Alexis de. *Democracy in America,* vol. 1. Edited by Phillips Bradley. New York: Alfred A. Knopf, 1972.

———. *Democracy in America,* vol. 2. Edited by Phillips Bradley. New York: Alfred A. Knopf, 1972.

Verdoux, Helene, and Marc Bourgeois. "Social Class in Unipolar and Bipolar Probands and Relatives." *Journal of Affective Disorders* 33 (1995): 181–187.

Volkow, Nora D., and Alan Swan, eds. *Cocaine in the Brain.* New Brunswick, N.J.: Rutgers University Press, 1990.

Wade, Nicholas. *Life Script: How the Human Genome Discoveries Will Transform Medicine and Enhance Your Health.* New York: Touchstone, 2001.

Wall, Joseph Frazier. *Andrew Carnegie.* New York: Oxford University Press, 1970.

Warshow, Robert Irving. *Alexander Hamilton: First American Businessman.* Garden City, N.Y.: Garden City Publishing, 1931.

Watts, Pauline Moffitt. "Prophecy and Discovery: On the Spiritual Origins of Christopher Columbus' Enterprise of the Indies." *American Historical Review* 90 (1985): 73–102.

Weissman, Myrna, Roger Bland, Glorisa Canino, Carlo Faravelli, Steven Greenwald, Hai-Gwo Hwu, Peter Joyce, et al. "Cross-National Epidemiology of Major Depression and Bipolar Disorder." *Journal of the American Medical Association* 276 (July 24/31, 1996): 293–299.

Wertenbaker, Thomas Jefferson. *The Puritan Oligarchy.* New York: Charles Scribner's Sons, 1947.

West, Delno. "Christopher Columbus, Lost Biblical Sites and the Last Crusade." *Catholic Historical Review* 78 (1992): 519–541.

West, Delno C., and August Kling, trans. and commentary. *The* Libro de las profecias *of Christopher Columbus*. Gainesville: University of Florida Press, 1992.

Wickelgren, Ingrid. *The Gene Masters: How a Breed of Scientific Entrepreneurs Raced for the Biggest Prize in Biology*. New York: Times Books, 2002.

Wilkinson, Rupert. *The Pursuit of American Character*. New York: Harper and Row, 1988.

Wilner, Paul, and J. Scheel-Kruger, eds. *The Mesolimbic Dopamine System: From Motivation to Action*. New York: Wiley, 1991.

Winthrop, Robert. *The Life and Letters of John Winthrop*. Boston: Ticknor and Fields, 1864.

Wrangham, Richard, and Dale Peterson. *Demonic Males: Apes and the Origins of Human Violence*. New York: Mariner, 1996.

Zacharakis, Andrew, Paul D. Reynolds, and William D. Bygrave. *Global Entrepreneurship Monitor: 1999 Executive Report*. Kansas City, Mo.: Kauffman Center for Entrepreneurial Leadership, 1999.

Zierold, Norman. *The Moguls*. New York: Coward-McCann, 1969.

Ziff, Larner. *Puritanism in America*. New York: Viking, 1973.

Acknowledgments

I have been lucky to have the world's best agent, best friend, and best wife. This book could never have happened without all three. Betsy Lerner saw this book's potential and worked with me till I sold it. My longtime friend, author, and senior editor Adam Bellow nurtured this project for a decade. My wife, Claude Guillemard, took care of our home and family, while I pursued this book like Ahab hunting his whale. She read innumerable drafts, never stopped believing in me, and still loves me. That above all shows I'm *really* lucky.

I am greatly indebted to Alice Mayhew, whose clear, uncompromising vision made this book twice as good and half as long as it would have been. Also many thanks to her associate Emily Takoudes.

A number of people helped me in my research. I must offer special thanks to Kay Redfield Jamison, my supportive colleague at the Department of Psychiatry at Johns Hopkins University Medical School and author of *Touched with Fire,* the groundbreaking work that underlies much of this book. I thank Jim Jackson of Vanderbilt University Medical School, who assisted me with some of the research. I thank the CEOs, whose names I won't reveal, who participated in my pilot study. I am deeply indebted to the Hamilton biographers Richard Brookhiser, Noemie Emery, Thomas Fleming, Roger Kennedy, and Arnold Rogow. I thank Daniel Mayer Selznick, who helped me to understand his family and obtain valuable materials. I thank Craig Venter for his time and assistance. I

341

also thank his assistant Heather Kowalski, brother Keith Venter, and colleague Hamilton Smith as well as Nicholas Wade of *The New York Times* and James Shreeve, author of *The Genome War,* who generously shared their years of reporting on Venter with me. I also thank primatologists Richard Wrangham of Harvard University, John Mitani of the University of Michigan, Frans de Waal of Emory University, and Stephen Suomi, National Institutes of Health, for discussing their research with me.

Within my own field I must thank the following researchers who helped me sort out the empirical literature on bipolar disorder, which I have admittedly synthesized in my own idiosyncratic way. They were all very helpful, even though I quote few of them directly: Lori Altshuler, Department of Psychiatry, UCLA Neuropsychiatric Institute; Jules Angst, Department of Psychiatry, Zurich University; Franco Benazzi, Department of Psychiatry, National Health Service, Italy; Francine Benes, Department of Psychiatry, Harvard University Medical School; Hilary Blumberg, Department of Psychiatry, Yale University Medical School; James Brody, psychologist in private practice, Spring City, Pennsylvania; Raymond DePaulo and James Potash, Department of Psychiatry, Johns Hopkins University Medical School; Wayne Drevets, Husseini Manji, Douglas Meinecke, and Robert Post, National Institute of Mental Health; Russell Gardner, Department of Psychiatry, University of North Dakota School of Medicine; Mark George, Department of Psychiatry, Radiology and Neurology, Medical College of South Carolina; Elie Hantouche, Department of Psychiatry, University of Paris; John Kelsoe, Department of Psychiatry, University of California at San Diego; Terence Ketter, Department of Psychiatry, Stanford University Medical School; Daniel Klein, Department of Psychology, State University of New York, Stony Brook; George Koob, Department of Neuropharmacology, Scripps Research Institute; Mark Lenzenweger, Department of Psychology, State University of New York, Binghamton; Roger Lewin, Sheppard Pratt Hospital; Helen Mayberg, Department of

Psychiatry, University of Toronto Medical School; Geoffrey Miller, Department of Psychology, University of New Mexico; Mike Nader, Department of Physiology, Pharmacology and Radiology, Wake Forest Medical School; Grazyna Rajkowska, Department of Psychiatry, University of Mississippi Medical School; Trevor Robbins, Department of Psychology, University of Cambridge; Jair Soares, Department of Psychiatry and Radiology, University of Texas Medical School; Stephen Strakowski, Department of Psychiatry, University of Cincinnati Medical School.

There are others I interviewed from diverse fields who were also very helpful. I'd like to thank business school professors Jay Conger, McGill University School of Management; Edwin Locke, University of Maryland School of Business; Nigel Nicholson, London Business School; Richard Tedlow, Harvard University Business School. I thank business correspondents Michael Rubin, Brad Spirrison, Philip Chard, and Tom Starnes. Finally, I am grateful to evolutionary scientists William Calvin, Department of Neurophysiology, University of Washington; Richard Klein, Department of Anthropology, Stanford University; Steven Stanley, Department of Earth and Planetary Sciences, Johns Hopkins University; Chris Stringer, Natural History Museum, London.

Special thanks to my good friend Stephanie Susnjara, who suggested the Hollywood chapter, and to the faculty of the Goucher creative nonfiction program, who gave me permission to stop writing like a professor.

I thank my mother, my children, my brothers, and close friends for their support.

Most of all, I wish to acknowledge my late father, the man who inspired this book.

Index

Illustration Credits

1. Courtesy Maryland Commission on Artistic Property, Maryland State Archives
2. Courtesy Massachusetts Historical Society
3. Courtesy Roger Williams University Archives
4. Courtesy Little, Brown and Company
5. Courtesy Library of Congress, Prints and Photographs Division
6. Courtesy Library of Congress, Prints and Photographs Division
7. Courtesy Special Collections, Schaffer Library, Union College
8. Courtesy Carnegie Library of Pittsburgh
9. Courtesy Carnegie Library of Pittsburgh
10. Photograph from Carnegie's *Autobiography*
11. Courtesy David O. Selznick Collection, Harry Ransom Humanities Research Center, University of Texas at Austin
12. Courtesy Daniel Mayer Selznick
13. Courtesy David O. Selznick Collection, Harry Ransom Humanities Research Center, University of Texas at Austin
14. Courtesy David O. Selznick Collection, Harry Ransom Humanities Research Center, University of Texas at Austin
15. Courtesy Daniel Mayer Selznick
16. Courtesy Daniel Mayer Selznick
17. Courtesy J. Craig Venter
18. Photograph by David Peterson
19. AP/Wide World Photos
20. Photograph by Gregory Heisler

ABOUT THE AUTHOR

John D. Gartner graduated from Princeton University and received his Ph.D. in Clinical Psychology from the University of Massachusetts, Amherst. He is widely published in medical journals and books. He is a clinical assistant professor of psychiatry at the Johns Hopkins University Medical School. Gartner is in private practice as a psychotherapist in Baltimore.